THE
EAGLE
RETURNS

THE
EAGLE
RETURNS

The Legal History of the Grand Traverse Band of Ottawa and Chippewa Indians

Matthew L. M. Fletcher

Michigan State University Press | *East Lansing*

⊚ The paper used in this publication meets the minimum requirements of ANSI/NISO
Z39.48-1992 (R 1997) (Permanence of Paper).

 Michigan State University Press
East Lansing, Michigan 48823-5245

Printed and bound in the United States of America.

18 17 16 15 14 13 12   1 2 3 4 5 6 7 8 9 10

LIBRARY OF CONGRESS CATALOGING-IN-PUBLICATION DATA
Fletcher, Matthew L. M.
The eagle returns : the legal history of the Grand Traverse band of Ottawa and Chippewa
indians / Matthew L.M. Fletcher.
p. cm.
Includes bibliographical references and index.
ISBN 978-1-61186-022-1 (cloth : alk. paper) 1. Grand Traverse Band of Ottawa and Chip-
pewa Indians, Michigan—History. 2. Ottawa Indians—Michigan—Grand Traverse Bay
Region—History. 3. Ottawa Indians—Legal status, laws, etc.—Michigan—Grand Traverse
Bay Region. 4. Ottawa Indians—Michigan—Grand Traverse Bay Region—Government
relations. 5. Ojibwa Indians—Michigan—Grand Traverse Bay Region—History. 6. Ojibwa
Indians—Legal status, laws, etc.—Michigan—Grand Traverse Bay Region. 7. Ojibwa
Indians—Michigan—Grand Traverse Bay Region—Goverment relations. 8. Grand Traverse
Bay Region (Mich.)—History. I. Title.
E78.M6F57 2010
977.4'64—dc22
2011008829

Cover and book design by Charlie Sharp, Sharp Des!gns, Lansing, Michigan

g green
press
INITIATIVE
Michigan State University Press is a member of the Green Press Initiative
and is committed to developing and encouraging ecologically responsible
publishing practices. For more information about the Green Press Initiative and the use
of recycled paper in book publishing, please visit *www.greenpressinitiative.org.*

Visit Michigan State University Press on the World Wide Web at *www.msupress.msu.edu*

When the Eagle returns we will again be a great nation.

—Jonas Shawandase, Grand Traverse Band tribal elder, 1930s–1950s

Contents

Introduction

Boozhoo!
This book is a survey of many aspects of the history of the Grand Traverse Band of Ottawa and Chippewa Indians. It is a governmental, legal, and political history, with an emphasis on the status of the tribe both as a treaty tribe and as the very first tribe recognized by the Department of the Interior under its administrative recognition process. It is a story of how a group of Native, indigenous people bound together by kinship, geography, language, and culture changed how they governed themselves over the course of centuries to vest power and authority in a tribal government—a government recognized by the federal government as an Indian tribe. It is the story of survival against the arrival and savage intervention of several European nations—and the United States—in the affairs and property of the Anishinaabek of the Grand Traverse Bay region.

This book is intended to serve as a reference for policymakers, lawyers, and Indian people about how federal Indian law and policy drove an Anishinaabe community to the brink of legal extinction, about how non-Indian economic and political interests conspired to eradicate the community's self-sufficiency, and how Indian people fought back to preserve their culture, laws, traditions, governance, and language. It is not only written as serious legal and political historical scholarship, but is also intended for an educated general audience. Of even more importance, it is written for the people of the Grand Traverse Band, who have not had the benefit of drawing upon one source for the bulk of their legal and political history.

The Grand Traverse Band is located in the Grand Traverse Bay region of northwest lower Michigan. The band, while small and relatively unknown to those unfamiliar to Indian affairs, has long been on the cutting edge of American Indian law and policy. In 1836, the band (and its leaders) were key negotiators in the 1836 Treaty of Washington, agreeing to cede about one-third of the land base for what would become the State of Michigan in 1837. In 1855, the Bureau of Indian Affairs initiated a policy of "allotment" of Indian lands resulting in the near-total dispossession of band land holdings from the 1850s through the 1880s, effectively presaging the national allotment laws enacted by Congress from 1887 on. In the 1870s, the federal government refused to deal with the band any longer, initiating what would become known as "administrative termination," or termination of the federal-tribal relationship by federal bureaucratic fiat. The band and several other Lower Peninsula Ottawa and Potawatomi tribes—all of whom were treaty tribes—suffered from administrative termination. And, perhaps because the band was a treaty signatory, it was the very first Indian tribe to be federally recognized under an administrative process under the Bureau of Indian Affairs. The band also was one of the first "self-governance tribes" authorized to take over control of federal services normally provided to the band and its members by federal agencies. Finally, the band is a leader in creating precedent for the development of off-reservation gaming, one of only a handful of Indian nations that have benefited from certain narrow exceptions to the general bar in the federal Indian gaming statute to off-reservation gaming.

The Grand Traverse Band has become a well-known national leader in advancing Indian treaty rights, gaming, and land-rights federal and state precedent, while at the same time creating and developing its own indigenous tribal justice system that has won national honors from the Harvard Project on American Indian Economic Development.

Contents

Chapters 1 and 2 describe the history of the Grand Traverse Band during treaty times. The band is a signatory and a party to these two key treaties: the Treaty of Washington (1836) and the Treaty of Detroit (1855). In the 1836 Treaty, the band and several other bands of Ottawa and Chippewa communities ceded their claims to one-third of the entire land mass of what is now the State of Michigan. In the 1836 Treaty, the band had reserved 20,000 acres of land for the purpose of creating a reservation. That land eventually included Old Mission Peninsula and parts of the eastern shore of the Grand Traverse Bay. These chapters also provide background information on the political and economic lives of the members of the Grand Traverse Band.

Chapter 3 details the loss of land by the Grand Traverse Band following the

1855 Treaty. The 1855 Treaty set aside several townships in Leelanau County[1] and Antrim County as a reservation in which individual band members could select their own homesteads. Due to incompetence, corruption, and even violence, very little of the land set aside in the 1855 Treaty remained in the hands of tribal members within a few short decades after the execution of the treaty.

Chapter 4 details the story of the administrative termination and then the federal recognition of the Grand Traverse Band. Unlike the vast majority of treaty tribes, the Department of the Interior washed its hands of responsibility toward the band and several other Michigan tribes in the late nineteenth century. The band petitioned for the right to form a tribal constitutional government in the 1930s, but again the Department of the Interior rejected their claim. This chapter details the band's struggle for federal recognition, a struggle that finally succeeded in 1980.

Chapter 5 describes the story of the Grand Traverse Band's treaty-rights fight, and details the experiences of several band members who literally fought that fight against hostile non-Indians, the State of Michigan's Department of Natural Resources, and even other tribes. The treaty-rights fight helped the band develop its independent political and governmental structure. The chapter discusses the band's involvement in *United States v. Michigan*[2] and the 1985 Consent Decree, as well as the 2000 and 2007 Consent Decrees.

Chapter 6 illustrates the development of the Grand Traverse Band's governmental, political, and economic structure since federal recognition in 1980. The band literally started penniless, but in a few short years became a leader nationwide as a self-governance Indian tribe. This chapter also describes much of the modern legal and governmental structure of the band, including its constitution, tribal council authority, tribal judiciary, and federally chartered economic-development corporation and enterprises.

Chapter 7 is the story of the gaming operations and other related business enterprises. The Grand Traverse Band was a leader not only in the State of Michigan but also nationally in litigating critical aspects of the Indian Gaming Regulatory Act, creating important positive precedent for several Michigan tribes, and other tribes nationally. This chapter details *Grand Traverse Band v. United States Attorney*,[3] also known as the Turtle Creek Casino case, and other gaming cases involving the band.

The Afterword is a taste of the future of the Grand Traverse Band, starting with the band's participation in the Supreme Court's 2009 decision in *Carcieri v. Salazar*,[4] which threatened the federal government's authority to acquire trust land for tribes like the band. But, as has happened so many times before, the band became a national leader in responding to the decision by being the first Indian tribe to persuade the government to acquire land in trust for the band after the decision.

Acknowledgments

Without John Petoskey, long-time general counsel of the Grand Traverse Band, and Eva Petoskey, former vice-chair and appellate judge for the band, this book would not have been possible. Both John and Eva have been amazing and inspirational *Anishinaabe* people, and have mentored me and my family over many years.

I also must thank my lovely and brilliant partner and colleague Wenona Singel, a member of the Little Traverse Bay Bands of Odawa Indians, who provided the space and the support that allowed me to work on this material. My parents, June Mamagona Fletcher and Rich Fletcher, have always been there with unwavering support.

I also say *chi-miigwetch* to many of the *Anishinaabe* people who have talked me through this project or otherwise inspired me: Derek Bailey, George Bennett, John Borrows, Dodie Chambers, Liz Cook, Frank and Rochelle Ettawageshik, June Mamagona Fletcher, Zeke Fletcher, JoAnne Gasco, Eric Hemenway, Gordon Henry, Dwayne Jarman, Paul and Val Johnson, Bob Kewaygoshkum, Howard Kimewon, John Low, Bryan Newland, Emily Petoskey, Michael Petoskey, Rose Petoskey, Emily Proctor, Joseph C. "Buddy" Raphael, Nick Reo, Mary Shomin, Tom Shomin, Monique Vondall-Rieke, Tanya Wanageshik, and Karrie Wichtman.

Thanks also to Jeannine Bell, Desmond Berry, Ned Blackhawk, Bill Brooks, Bill Brott, Kirsten Carlson, Kristen Carpenter, Cami Fraser, Ashley Harding, Myriam Jaïdi, Alicia Ivory, Pat LeBeau, Meg Noori, Riyaz Kanji, Bill Rastetter, Stuart Rieke, Angela Riley, Nancy Robinett, Jim Sumbler, Holly Thompson, and Brian Upton. And special thanks to Kate Fort, Jim McClurken, and Charles Wilkinson.

Finally, *chi-miigwetch* to Richard White, who wrote the first significant ethnohistory of the Grand Traverse Band way back in his days at Michigan State University.

THE
EAGLE
RETURNS

CHAPTER ONE

The Story of the 1836 Treaty of Washington

Throughout the nineteenth century Anishinaabeg leaders from the Great Lakes, wearing eagle feather headdresses and elegantly beaded bandolier bags, met in treaty councils with U.S. commissioners. Trained for years as astute listeners and eloquent speakers, these diplomats put their skills to the test as they negotiated with their non-Indian counterparts, whose primary responsibility was to serve the interests of the federal government. The stakes were high, for Native territories and lifeways were often at risk.[1]

The Grand Traverse Band of Ottawa and Chippewa Indians is one of several Indian tribes who are signatories to the 1836 Treaty of Washington. These treaties brought together as a formal legal and political body the loose confederation of Indian communities or bands living in the Grand Traverse Bay region.[2] In both treaties, the Grand Traverse Band people, represented by its leaders or *ogemuk*, sought to preserve a permanent tribal land base; reserve lake and inland hunting, fishing, and gathering rights; establish a government-to-government relationship with the United States; and acquire needed funds, materials, and services from the federal government.

The Three Fires Anishinaabek

Anishinaabek had lived in the Great Lakes area for hundreds of years before the arrival of Europeans. The old stories say that the Anishinaabek came from the eastern seaboard, migrating upriver until they reached the massive inland seas.[3] Vine Deloria Jr. recounted scholarship about four major groups of ancient people from the north and east—the Anishinaabek, the Dakota, the Salish, and pale-skinned people—and how they fought over many, many years until the pale-skinned people left the continent, perhaps as a result of an ice age.[4] Andrew Blackbird wrote that spirits (*Manitouwog*) stole an Ottawa woman's baby and terrorized the Ottawas on the eastern seaboard, so that they moved away from the rising sun, toward the setting sun, and settled on Manitoulin Island.[5]

The Three Fires—the Odawa (or Ottawa), the Ojibwe (or Chippewa or Ojibway), and the Bodewadmi (or Potawatomi)—had been linked together for centuries in Michigan and the western Great Lakes. Later, as they settled the Great Lakes area between 600 and 900 years ago, the Anishinaabek split into three major groups—the Odawa, the Ojibwe, and the Bodewadmi.[6] Consistent with the importance of family to the Anishinaabek, the Ojibwe are often referred to as the "Elder Brother" in the confederacy, with the Odawa known as the "Next Elder Brother," and the Bodewadmi as the "Younger Brother."[7] The Ottawa name likely derives from the word for "trader," and the Chippewa name from the kind of moccasins that Chippewa hunters wore; Potawatomi means "Keepers of the Fire."[8] A nineteenth-century *ogema* (Anishinaabe leader or headman), Chamblee, explained their relationship in Michigan: "We Three nations—Chippewas, Pottawatomis, and Odawas—have but one council fire."[9] These three nations are commonly referred to as the Three Fires.[10]

The community now known collectively as the Grand Traverse Band of Ottawa and Chippewa Indians has occupied the Grand Traverse Bay region since as early as 1675,[11] but Anishinaabe people and others have been living and hunting in Michigan for perhaps as long as 11,000 years. Back then, these Indian people appear to have hunted giant mammals, and fished the lakes and river using nets. Rock paintings recently discovered in the Grand Traverse Bay area demonstrate that Indian hunters armed with spears hunted the Michigan mastodon.[12] These people may have been known by later Michigan indigenous peoples as the "Mammoth People."[13] Other peoples included the Adena and Hopewell cultures.[14]

Before the Treaties: Politics and Economics

Indian people in the Great Lakes region in the decades before the 1836 Treaty of Washington had already undergone centuries of change and conflict as a result of the European arrival in North America. Likely the first people that the Europeans encountered in the western Great Lakes region were the Ottawa, then living on and near Manitoulin Island and the Georgian Bay archipelago.[15] Samuel de Champlain wrote the first European journal entry about his encounters with the Manitoulin Island Ottawas, who claimed to be picking blueberries, in 1615 or 1616.[16] By this time, the Ottawas living on and around Manitoulin Island had been hunting seasonally in northern lower Michigan for hundreds of years.[17]

In the seventeenth century, when the center of Ottawa culture was Manitoulin Island between Lake Huron and the Georgian Bay, the Five Nations of the

Haudenosaunee Confederacy based in New York began military excursions into the western Great Lakes region, fighting the Huron Confederacy, Ottawas, Chippewas, Potawatomis, and dozens of other small Indian tribes in the region for a sixty-year period.[18] In 1650, many Anishinaabe bands abandoned their homelands and relocated to the west, often around Green Bay, before they could return safely.[19] In 1653, the Ottawas and Chippewas united to defeat the Haudenosaunees at Iroquois Point in the Upper Peninsula, allowing the Anishinaabek to reestablish their presence in the region.[20] The conflicts with the Haudenosaunees did not conclude until the 1660s or 1670s.[21] The reassertion of Anishinaabek authority in Michigan quickly followed this period.[22] By 1671, the Odawak had formed a major trading center at Michilimackinac.[23]

The end of the wars with the Haudenosaunees brought the arrival of the French fur traders and missionaries, creating major changes in the focus of the Anishinaabe economy. St. Ignace (Michilimackinac) and Sault Ste. Marie formed the major trading centers of the region.[24] Anishinaabek traders also forged trading routes to the east as far as Montreal and other towns.[25] According to Andrew Blackbird, Ottawa traders likely encountered French traders at Montreal, where they exchanged gifts, with the Ottawas bringing back to Mackinac firearms and axes.[26] Since the Ottawas held the strongest remaining trade ties to the French, and since the Ottawas controlled the Straits of Mackinac, the Ottawas retained "a virtual monopoly over the profitable fur trade."[27] In the late seventeenth century and eighteenth century, the French and the Ottawas became even closer trading partners, with many Frenchmen marrying into Ottawa families, learning to speak Anishinaabemowin, and adopting the custom of gift-giving.[28] From 1671 to 1812, the Anishinaabek were wealthy and powerful.[29] However, because the French government desired greater control over the fur trade, and because the population of French traders increased so greatly, the Ottawa monopoly over the fur trade eventually disappeared.[30]

By the first part of the eighteenth century, a major cluster of Ottawa villages had formed near the Straits of Mackinac and, later, L'Arbre Croche and southward.[31] In 1742, approximately 1,500 to 3,000 Ottawas lived there.[32] It was in this period that Ottawa people settled on lands all down the coast of Lake Michigan, including the Grand Traverse Bay region.[33] The French commander at Fort Michilimackinac wrote in 1741 of the "savages" at the Grand Traverse Bay who had made clearings for villages.[34] These villages consisted of parallel rows of longhouses, called *ktiganigamik*, sixteen to twenty feet long and twelve to fourteen feet wide.[35]

The Grand Traverse and Little Traverse communities have always been interconnected: the name in Anishinaabemowin for Little Traverse Bay is Wikwedongsing, and the name for Grand Traverse Bay is Kitchiwikwedongs- ing.[36] Later, as the Christian missionaries entered the region, a split between the Catholic Indians and the traditional Indians formed, which also may have tracked the Catholic-Protestant divide between Little Traverse and Grand Traverse Anishinaabe communities.[37] This split may have contributed to the decision of some families to choose to settle in Grand Traverse as opposed to Little Traverse, and vice versa.

Because of their close relationship with the French, these Odawa communi- ties eventually took greater control of most of the Lower Peninsula, including the Grand River Valley and areas near and south of Detroit.[38] Some Chippewa people moved toward the northeastern coast of the Lower Peninsula, with the Mackinac region acting as the dividing point.[39]

At least two stories account for the presence of the Ojibwe bands in the Grand Traverse Bay area. One story, propounded by Andrew Blackbird, the famed Odawa historian, holds that the Grand Traverse Ottawas granted hunting rights to the Chippewas in compensation for the murder of a young Chippewa by an Ottawa during a fishing dispute at Mackinac.[40] The other dates to an older period, when the Ottawas, with assistance from the Chippewas, drove the Mascouten people from the L'Arbre Croche region prior to settling there—the Ottawas then granting their Chippewa allies the right to live in the region.[41] Regardless, the people of the two tribes (Ottawa and Chippewa) to this day retain their separateness, despite significant intermarriage. Richard White noted that the key element of difference between the two tribes in the region until the mid-nineteenth century was the greater emphasis by the Ottawas on agriculture.[42] White also argued that the intermarriage between Ottawas and Chippewas at Grand Traverse Bay created a smooth assimilation of the Chippewas into the Ottawa community.[43]

The latter half of the eighteenth century brought the arrival of the British and the Americans,[44] with the French and Indian War driving out the French,[45] Pontiac's War,[46] and the American Revolutionary War.[47] Despite these disruptions, the Michigan Anishinaabek economy, led by the northern Michigan Ottawas, diversified and even prospered.[48]

Each European nation in the region—the French, followed by the British and then the Americans—had a different policy of dealing with Indian tribes in Michigan. It is fair to say that each one was progressively worse than the one before it. While the French often treated the Ottawas as equals, the British treated them as conquered peoples, even though the Ottawas had not been defeated in battle during the French and Indian War.[49] After Pontiac's War, which involved a nearly successful confederacy of dozens of Indian military units, the British became more conciliatory toward the Indians.[50] But the Americans, who pushed the British out of Michigan after the War of 1812 and took control of Michilimackinac in 1815, simply wanted all Indian lands.[51] Moreover, any Indians or traders who sided with the British in the War of 1812 suffered the wrath and retribution of the Americans.[52] In 1837, the State of Michigan became the final sovereign entity that entered Indian affairs.[53]

Throughout all of this disruption, the Ottawa people were the most effective traders in the region.[54] Michigan Ottawas engaged in trade over incredibly long distances, perhaps as far as 1,500 miles.[55] For example, Henry Schoolcraft noticed an Indian pouch belonging to an Indian at Sault Ste. Marie that he recognized as originating at the mouth of the Columbia River on the Pacific Ocean.[56] In 1836, Baptist missionary Abel Bingham was surprised to see Michigan Anishinaabek relying upon wheat flour, tea, coffee, and sugar in the middle of winter, all goods imported from overseas.[57]

The canoes built by the Michigan Anishinaabek were said to be "some of the best in America."[58] These were the finest canoes in the northern hemisphere, capable of carrying over a ton of people and equipment for two-year treks, creating an ability to travel over all of the Great Lakes and their major tributaries.[59] According to Gregory Dowd:

> Men and women made them. The lighter, more elegant, and larger birch-bark canoes took two skilled people a full week to make; elm-bark canoes could be fashioned by two people in half a day. They contained in their making not only the birch or elm bark, collected late in the winter, but also white or red cedar or ash for the frame, sewn together with basswood fiber, elm root, spruce root, cedar root, pine root, or tamarack root, and sealed with a pitch of spruce, white pine, or balsam. Ottawas and Chippewas decorated their canoes with paint and dyes. By the nineteenth century, the canoes could be very large and carry more than a ton.[60]

Contemporary European writers were astounded by the engineering of Anishinaabe canoes, and especially their carrying capacities:

Its length is thirty feet, and its breadth across the widest part, about four feet. It is about two and a half feet deep in the centre, but only about two feet near the bow and stern. Its bottom is rounded, and has no keel.

The materials of which this canoe is built, are birch bark, and red cedar, the whole fastened together with wattap and gum, without a nail, or bit of iron of any sort to confine the parts. The entire outside is bark—the bark of the birch tree—and where the edges join at the bottom, or along the sides, they are sewn with this wattap, and then along the line of the seam, it is gummed. Next to the bark are pieces of cedar, shaven thin, not thicker than the blade of a knife—these run horizontally, and are pressed against the bark by means of these ribs of cedar, which fit the shape of the canoe, bottom and sides, and coming up to the edges, are pointed, and let into a rim of cedar of about an inch and a half wide, and an inch thick, that forms the gunwale of the canoe, and to which, by means of the wattap, the bark and the ribs are all sewed; the wattap being wrapped over the gunwale, and passed through the bark and ribs. Across the canoe are bars, some five or six, that keep the canoe in shape. . . .

But so light is it, and so easily damaged, that precautions are necessary to be taken in loading it, and these are attended to by placing round poles along the bottom. These, resting on the ribs, equally, for the whole length, cause the burden to press equally from one end to the other. Upon these the baggage rests, and also the crew and the passengers. . . .

Our baggage and stores, and the provisions for the voyageurs, and our tents, &c., are estimated to weigh at least five hundred weight; and then there will be eleven of us . . . who will not weigh short of fifteen hundred weight—so this canoe of bark is destined to carry not less than two thousand pounds! The paddles are of red cedar, and are very light. The blade is not over three inches wide, except the steersman's, that is, perhaps, five.[61]

Henry Schoolcraft, who had become a powerful proponent of removal by the late 1830s, lamented that the ability of the Anishinaabek to construct canoes would all but guarantee that no federal plan to remove the Indians to the west would succeed.[62]

And there are trails that Ottawa people from the Grand Traverse and Little Traverse Bays walked to trading centers in Saginaw, Detroit, Toledo, and Chicago.[63] The Michigan Ottawas were situated between the Ojibwe communities in Canada and the Upper Peninsula, who had easy access to the Lake Superior fishery, with the Anishinaabe people in the Grand River and St.

Joseph River Valleys, where Indians grew enormous quantities of corn, fruit, and other edibles.[64] Ottawa people used their superior traveling capabilities and geographic advantages to act as the trading go-between for these nations.[65] According to James McClurken, Ottawa families owned their own trade routes, which could be land-based or water-based.[66] Families intermarried, on occasion, for the purposes of joining or expanding trade routes.[67]

The Ottawa people in the northern Lower Peninsula also enjoyed a strong fishery both on the Great Lakes and inland, a plentiful berry harvest, and a significant crop of corn, beans, and squash—the Three Sisters.[68] Andrew Blackbird wrote in the 1870s about his childhood: "Then I never knew my people to want for anything to eat or to wear, as we always had plenty of wild meat and plenty of fish, corn, vegetables, and wild fruits. I thought (and yet I may be mistaken) that my people were very happy in those days."[69] Grand Traverse Bay area Anishinaabek also grew large gardens, sufficient to feed entire villages—even north, in shorter growing seasons than in the Grand River and St. Joseph River Valleys.[70] On the importance of corn and agriculture, James McClurken wrote:

> The Ottawa way of life was based on growing crops, fishing, and, to a lesser extent, gathering wild foods and hunting.... Most years, a successful corn crop yielded a surplus to be stored for leaner times ahead. The pattern of corn growing and method of land use were so central to their lives that when the Ottawa moved to Michigan's lower peninsula in the 1700s, they again sought lakeshore lands, settling in areas where the warmth of Lake Michigan's waters would aid them in the raising of their crops.[71]

According to McClurken, corn was a critical element in the survival of the Michigan Odawak through lean years, but the Odawak relied upon a variety of foods and food sources as a means of avoiding overreliance on a single food—and the concomitant threat of starvation:

> By relying on a variety of foods, Ottawa society would not be threatened as severely if one food source failed. When the corn crop was damaged by bad weather, they could rely on fishing and hunting. When those sources failed, the Ottawa had reserves of corn. It was this stability which the Ottawa sought to preserve and enhance throughout their history.[72]

As more and more non-Indians arrived in the northern Anishinaabe lands, corn and potatoes become more and more important to the Anishinaabe economy.[73] By the late eighteenth century, the Ottawas at Waganikising grew enough corn to sell their surplus at the trading center in Michilimackinac.[74]

The Anishinaabek lived according to the seasons, and moved to different areas depending on the season.[75] Each month (moon) in the Anishinaabe calendar is delineated by the seasonal activities of the Anishinaabek, helping to maintain their understanding of the culture.[76] According to James McClurken:

> The seasonal cycle that had been established in the eighteenth century continued into the opening decades of the American period. Throughout the British regime, the Ottawa continued to maintain large villages on major waterways where the climate was suitable for corn production and where there was seasonal abundance of fish. The year began with the collection and processing of maple sap for sugar which was used for food and exchange. For this activity, a number of extended families left large villages to occupy their regular territories. Fishing and gathering spring plants were predominant activities until the threat of frost ended. At this point, the Ottawa extended families who had left the major village once again rejoined those who had remained behind; planting took place in the late spring. During the summer months, small groups of related males left the large villages for local hunts, visiting and trading in other regions, and for war. Women, children, and those not able to travel remained at the home village to tend crops. Following fall harvest of crops and fishing, small parties—sometimes entire extended families—once again left the larger villages for winter hunts.[77]

In the winters, the Grand Traverse Anishinaabek retired to their hunting and trapping grounds inland and usually southward, often as far as the Grand River Valley and even Illinois.[78] However, many Grand Traverse people remained relatively close to the bay area, with many Anishinaabek retiring for the winters to the Boardman River area near what is now Traverse City.[79]

The swampy regions near the Grand Traverse Bay, especially those closer to Elk Lake and Torch Lake, offered maple sugar in the spring. Maple-sugar season began in mid-March and went through the end of April. Even before sugar became an important trade good in the 1850s, Grand Traverse Anishinaabek always moved from their inland wintering grounds to the sugaring camps in the spring, when food was at its scarcest.[80]

From the sugar camps, the Odawak moved to their larger summer villages.

They lived in longhouses that could comfortably sleep nine families at a time.[81] The children and women populated the villages, gathering food and materials for the winter months and watching over crops, which included corn, pumpkins, beans, potatoes, apples, and many other fruits and vegetables.[82] The Odawak used this period to travel long distances to hunt and trade.[83] Long before the main group of Ottawas moved into Michigan, Ottawa hunters came through the Lower Peninsula on their hunting expeditions.[84]

Many Anishinaabek moved to the lake shores in October to engage in fishing while the trout and other fish were spawning.[85] Charles Cleland wrote that Indians in the Grand Traverse Bay region and at other Great Lakes shores had used gill-net technology to sustain their lakeshore fisheries for over 1,000 years before treaty times.[86] According to Robert Keller, Henry Schoolcraft wrote:

> The fish and game around Saginaw Bay . . . could entirely support the Indians there. At Michilimackinac we found Indians taking trout, black and white bass, herring, sturgeon, pike, perch, catfish, and muskie. At Sault Ste. Marie 40 lodges of Chippewa seemed to eat only whitefish; their method of dipnetting in the rapids allowed them to catch as many as 500 fish in two hours; afterwards they smoked and stored the fish for winter.[87]

Michigan Anishinaabek fishers used spears as long as 40 or 50 feet to fish for sturgeon on the lakes, even during the winter when the surface froze.[88]

The Grand Traverse Anishinaabek also fished inland. Torch Lake and Torch River derive their names from the Anishinaabe practice of fishing at night with torches,[89] called "flambeauing" by some.[90] The river and inland lake fisheries were extensive, producing sturgeon, brook trout, catfish, and many other species of fish.[91] The Anishinaabe tools of fishing were comprehensive, including the use of seines, gill nets, dip nets, hooks, spears and harpoons, and torches.[92] Great Lakes gill-net technology dates at least as far back as the eighth century, and could be as old as 7,000 years.[93] Indian fishing technology changed little after the arrival of the Europeans,[94] perhaps demonstrating their advanced understanding and abilities compared to the newcomers. As to fishing techniques, the Anishinaabe language—Anishinaabemowin—was detailed:

> "I fish," generically is, "Nin gigoike: (literally the word [s]ignifies, "I make fish"); "Nin pagidawa" means: "I catch fish with nets"; "Nin Pagibadi": "I catch fish with a line on which there are many hooks." "Nin akwawa" means: "I fish

with a spear." We could certainly convey this idea in English with one word, "I spear," still it would not be so comprehensive as the Indian word, in which it is explained that fish are speared.

They have also a separate term for spearing fish by torchlight; they call it "wasswewin" (fishing with a spear in the light).

"Nin wewebanabi" signifies: "I fish with a hook"; it is the only term of the whole category which we can render in one English word, "I angle."[95]

By the time of the 1836 treaty negotiations, the tribal economies had changed again and again. The French, who first interacted with the Ottawas in 1615,[96] brought the demand for fur, which contributed to the near-extinction of many forms of fur-bearing animals in the Great Lakes region by the end of the eighteenth century,[97] though the fur trade endured many cycles as the fur-bearing animal population waxed and waned over the decades.[98] The Ottawas from Grand Traverse had been some of the leading middlemen in the fur trade, and continued trapping as part of this market through the 1860s.[99] By 1836, the Anishinaabek economy had fully integrated with the British and American societies.[100] In fact, the Anishinaabek imported much of their clothing and household items.[101] Indians sold and traded maple sugar, berries (and berry flour), wild rice, and other foodstuff to non-Indians and other Indians.[102]

The Michigan Anishinaabek continued to rely on hunting and fishing as the primary source of sustenance in the 1830s. However, after the 1830s, caribou, elk, and moose populations were in steep decline in Michigan.[103] The American Fur Company, owned by magnate John Jacob Astor, penetrated into the fishing market just as it had the fur trade.[104] But the fur trade, as well as the fishery, was cyclical, with overhunting and overfishing leading to the destruction of the commercial hunting and fishing business, followed by resurgences in game and fish populations a few years or decades later.[105] Astor's American Fur Company, which made him his millions, dissolved in 1834 as a result of these cycles.[106] "By the 1850s, Little Traverse Bay's most accessible fishing grounds became so depleted that many Ottawa farmed for their complete subsistence. . . ."[107] In general, over time, the fish and game could not withstand the repeated overharvesting of the resource. By 1900, for example, there was a mass extinction of the fur-bearing species in the Great Lakes region.[108]

Grand Traverse Villages (Eighteenth Century to 1830s)

The villages surrounding the Grand Traverse Bay prior to the nineteenth century were not entirely permanent, with the Indians summering in the bay area, and wintering inland and southward. The Grand Traverse Anishinaabek lived in bark lodges (usually called wigwams) consistent with their lifeways, until the 1830s, when many of them built more permanent log homes and stick houses.[109] Even before this time, many Grand Traverse Anishinaabek maintained year-round residency in the area.[110]

During this time period, there were two Ojibwe villages in the region and at least four Odawa villages.[111] At the area near Eastport, the Ojibwe *ogema* Aishquagonabe kept his village. The Ojibwe *ogema* Aghosa's village was located at the tip of what is now called Old Mission Peninsula in the Grand Traverse Bay, where Peter Dougherty founded his mission in 1839. The leading Ottawa village, at Leland, was called Chemogobing. Shabwasson's band lived at Suttons Bay. This was the oldest village on the Grand Traverse Bay, featuring an Indian orchard and garden dating back to the sixteenth century.[112]

Ruth Craker recounts that the group that would later move to Peshawbestown in 1852 may have been in existence prior to the 1850s. Craker cites Father Frederic Baraga as establishing the first Catholic mission on Old Mission Peninsula in 1832, for the "Peshaba band of Indians."[113]

Indian Treaty Negotiators: The *Ogemuk*

The Grand Traverse Band's people lived in different villages around the bay, organized mostly by family groups and clans since time immemorial. The social organization of the Grand Traverse Bay communities followed the family and clan system.[114] The primary political unit was the family, with a head of household serving to speak for and represent the rest of the family. According to Gregory Dowd:

> Organization was, at the arrival of the first colonists, based on the village or band. Nonetheless, on the eve of contact, Chippewas, and probably Ottawas, each possessed their own clan structures that transcended the bands, uniting different bands under structures of kinship, that is, under the understanding of family, an understanding that reinforced the sense of what it meant to be an Ottawa or a Chippewa.[115]

It would be hard to say that these communities had chiefs, headmen, or other forms of autocratic or hierarchical leadership, but the heads of large households and villages tended to be called *ogema* (singular) or *ogemuk* (plural), commonly defined as "headman" or "headmen."[116] The family itself would have occupied an entire village, more or less, so that the leading family member would be seen to outsiders to be the leader of the village:

> Each family in the village was represented by a leader who was chosen by consent of all of his family members. Responsible for expressing the opinions and protecting the interests of the families, leaders were chosen for their ability to deal with outsiders and for their generosity to family members and friends. When several families lived in a village, the leaders appointed a head speaker to represent them in dealings with other outside groups. . . .
>
> Leaders did not rule the village. They could not command anyone to do their will.[117]

These were families—and the leader of such families was known as an *ogema*, a person who could care for a larger number of people. There may have been separate clan or *dodem* leaders in each village as well, which may account for academics and outsiders assuming that the title of *ogema* was hereditary.[118] Villages in a particular region, such as the Grand Traverse Bay region or Little Traverse Bay region, often cooperated in the form of confederacy, allying for particular purposes such as war or treaty-making.[119] These *ogemuk* had little or no authority over particular villages, except perhaps their own. They could not order a village to take a particular action, but instead they used persuasion, both rhetorical and economic. Individuals and families that chose not to follow the majority had the option simply to leave, and they often would. On rarer occasions, the regional confederations could join with the larger cultural group now referred to as a tribe, as in the Ottawa tribe or Ojibwe tribe, linked by similar customs and language. Again, the regional confederacies could appoint *ogemuk*, or, as in the case of the 1855 treaty negotiations, individuals who were outstanding speakers but did not have the authority or duties of the *ogemuk*.[120]

Benjamin Ramirez-shkwegnaabi, a member of the Saginaw Chippewa Indian Tribe and a professor at Central Michigan University, described in great detail the character and importance of the *ogemuk* during treaty times:

Anishinaabeg *ogimaag* (leaders) were men and women who excelled in areas such as warfare, medicine, hunting, or singing. They did not lead by force or authority (in the European sense), but rather secured their power through service to their communities. War chiefs were typically young warriors, of lower rank than civil chiefs, who had proved their leadership in war. Ideally they supported the civil *ogimaag* and asserted their authority only in times of conflict. Civil leaders (by the nineteenth century this was often a hereditary rank) had a responsibility to provide for the welfare of their people, much as parents had responsibility for their children. "He was a father to his people; they looked on him as children do to a parent; and his lightest wish was immediately performed," said a principal warrior of Curly Head, a Mississippi Ojibwe civil chief whose relationship with his people was based on ensuring their well-being: "His lodge was ever full of meat, to which the hungry and destitute were ever welcome. The traders vied with one another who should treat him best, and the presents which he received at their hands he always distributed to his people without reserve. When he had plenty, his people wanted not."[121]

Professor Ramirez-shkwegnaabi also explained the careful ceremony and protocol of an Anishinaabe Indian treaty council. Treaty councils began with a speech by the party responsible for calling the treaty council, calling on the negotiators to participate in good faith and, perhaps, to explain the purpose of the meeting. Treaty councils could last for weeks at a time. And gift exchange was perhaps the most important element to many treaty councils.[122] The rhetorical strategy of Anishinaabek speakers bears mention:

> During councils, Anishinaabeg diplomats drew on a number of tactics ranging from rhetorical devices of kinship and supplication to demands for more time and invocation of leadership responsibilities. Many of these tactics were highly ritualized, again rising from time-honored procedures. Anishinaabeg had a long-established diplomatic rhetoric based on kinship and fictive kinship terminology.[123]

The lack of authoritarian legal authority possessed by the *ogemuk* was a source of frustration for American treaty negotiators, who desired Indian leaders who were willing to make broad decisions without tribal consensus:

This informal structure of leadership frequently frustrated Americans who sought one or two leaders with whom they could make political and economic deals. The American way of doing business required negotiation with someone who commanded the obedience of the people and could agree to terms without consulting them. Between 1779 and 1855 when Americans made treaties with the Odawa, the *Ogemuk* from all villages had to be present, which slowed negotiations. From the American perspective, the inability of the *Ogemuk* to make decisions contrary to the will of their people sometimes impeded negotiations.[124]

Without the will of the people backing them, *ogemuk* could quickly fall from power and from favor.[125] For example, an *ogema* from the Grand River Ottawa community who signed the 1821 Treaty of Chicago against the wishes of his community lost all his authority (and his life) as soon as he returned home with the news of the treaty.[126] American treaty negotiators did not want to acknowledge this limitation on the *ogemuk*, and so they ignored it.

Regardless, Great Lakes Anishinaabe leaders understood very well the geopolitics of the European and, later, the American imperative—the land meant absolutely everything. As one Ojibwe *ogema* on Mackinac Island stated in the years following the French and Indian War:

> Englishman! Although you have conquered the French you have not yet conquered us! We are not your slaves. These lakes and these woods and mountains were left to us by our ancestors. They are our inheritance, and we will part with them to none. Your nation supposes that we, like the white people, cannot live without bread and pork and beef. But you ought to know that he—the Great Spirit and master of life—has provided food for us in these broad lakes and upon these mountains.[127]

Later, after the British evacuated Michigan following the War of 1812, an Ottawa *ogema* named Ocaita harshly chastised the British for giving up Indian lands in the Treaty of Ghent without Indian consent.[128]

The experiences of other Anishinaabek communities in the 1795 Treaty of Greenville and in the 1833 Treaty of Chicago, for example, influenced the strategy of the Anishinaabe *ogemuk* leading up to the critical treaty negotiations of 1836. The ogemuk knew that the American treaty commissioners were planning to buy lands outright as a means of clearing all claims to Indian title in Michigan's

Lower Peninsula. Leading American treaty commissioners, such as Lewis Cass, secretary of war during the 1836 treaty negotiations and land speculator,[129] spoke of Great Lakes treaty lands entirely in terms of price, repeatedly assuring his superiors that "any price paid [for Indian lands] would be much less than the lands were worth."[130]

Conversely, Indian negotiators came to the table with a different conception of land sales or cessions. According to Helen Tanner, these negotiators were willing to part with many sticks in the bundle of property rights, but not all:

> Land concepts of Indian people differed markedly from the views motivating the British and American officials with whom they were dealing. In the belief system of Indian people, land, like air and water, was available to all on the basis of need. Personal ownership was limited to things individually crafted, crops raised, or proceeds of hunting and fishing activities. Tribal groups exercised stewardship over particular activities under their control.[131]

In other words, Indian people would continue to use the ceded lands and waters as they always had, excepting perhaps some areas set aside for mining or timber cutting,[132] until and if American "settlement" precluded those activities. The notion that the American government could "purchase" lands for exclusive "ownership," even if they were not being used for any valuable purpose, was not one Indians completely understood, and so it never became part of the treaty language. For the Indian negotiators, one expects that the American notion of property ownership prior to actual use was equivalent to pointless hoarding of lands.

The Negotiation of the Treaty of Washington (1836)

It may have been the Ottawa group living on Manitoulin Island in 1835 that started the process leading to the March 28, 1836, Treaty of Washington,[133] though the L'Arbre Croche Ottawas had suggested a land-sale treaty around that time as well.[134] They contacted Henry Schoolcraft at the Mackinac Indian Agency with an offer to sell Drummond Island.[135] Schoolcraft, an ardent land speculator,[136] prone to fits of deep ethnocentrism,[137] had been looking for an opportunity to exploit "the possibility of an extensive land cession and sent out inquiries about lands that regional Indians might be willing to sell."[138] The southern portion of the Michigan territory, as far north as the Grand River

Valley, home of the Grand River Ottawas, had been the subject of intense land speculation during the time leading up to the 1836 Treaty.[139] North of mid-Michigan, however, the growing season was too short to support much large-scale farming,[140] but the Grand Traverse Anishinaabek were still concerned about the influx of non-Indians into southern Michigan, where many of them asserted territorial hunting rights.[141]

Schoolcraft would find that the Michigan Anishinaabek only had willingness, at that time, "to sell the Manitou Islands, off the Leelanau Peninsula in Lake Michigan, and a tract north of the Straits that they claimed by the right of conquest."[142] A delegation of Odawak from L'Arbre Croche, led by Augustin Hamelin Jr., had left for Washington, D.C., to discuss a treaty in September 1835 under these terms,[143] and to head off a likely attempt by Schoolcraft to convince Secretary of War Lewis Cass that Michigan Indians were ready for a major land cession.[144] Hamelin's delegation instead wanted to raise money to be used to purchase lands in and around Indian villages, to create a buffer from the non-Indians that would eventually permeate the region.[145] The L'Arbre Croche community had previously asked Henry Schoolcraft permission to discuss land cessions in 1833 and 1834, but he had denied their request to travel with federal funds on the grounds that the federal government did not yet "require" their lands.[146]

The Grand River Ottawas strongly, even violently, opposed Hamelin's L'Arbre Croche community in these dealings.[147] Father Frederic Baraga described what must have been a tense meeting between the L'Arbre Croche and Grand River Anishinaabek communities in the spring of 1834, when the Grand River *ogemuk* communicated their displeasure with even the limited land cessions proposed by the L'Arbre Croche community.[148] The Grand River Ottawas sent their own delegation in 1835 to stop the Hamelin delegation from agreeing to sell land, and to inform the federal government that the Hamelin delegation did not speak for the rest of the Ottawas.[149] Of all the Indian communities in Michigan, the Grand River Ottawas especially did not want to cede their lands, having suffered from poor treaty terms in 1821.[150] The presence of two Anishinaabek delegations, even though they had neither authority nor willingness to sell much land, helped Schoolcraft persuade Secretary Cass that the Michigan Indian lands were ripe for cession.[151] The commissioner of Indian Affairs formally asked Schoolcraft if the Michigan Indians were willing to enter into a large land-cession treaty, and although he knew it not to be the case, Schoolcraft said yes.[152]

Henry Schoolcraft had been the Michigan Indian agent since 1822, based first at Sault Ste. Marie, and then moving to Mackinac in 1834 after a federal

Indian Office reorganization.[153] According to Helen Tanner, "His wife, Jane, was the daughter of an Irish trader at Sault Ste. Marie [John Johnston] who had married the daughter of an influential Ojibwe leader at La Pointe [Oshawguscodaywaykwe]. Jane's three brothers were among the eight Schoolcraft relatives who held posts on the staff of Schoolcraft's Indian agency."[154] Jane's name was "*Baamewaawaagizhigokwe*, literally, 'a woman who moves, making sound in the heavens.'"[155] One of Jane's brothers, George Johnston, would figure heavily in the histories of the northern Michigan Indians, and especially the Grand Traverse Band.[156]

Schoolcraft left for Washington, D.C., in November 1835, a month after the Hamelin delegation departed.[157] His companions and actions during his trip demonstrated the larger political and economic powers that held sway in the treaty negotiations.[158] He visited the American Fur Company's headquarters in New York. Many Michigan Anishinaabek owed debts to the company's traders, money that likely would not be paid back as the fur trade declined. In fact, American Fur Trading Company representatives Rix Robinson and John Drew escorted Michigan *ogemuk* to Washington, with Robinson bringing the Grand Traverse Band representatives.[159] These traders pressured the Michigan Anishinaabek to appear at the treaty negotiations.[160] Rix Robinson claimed that Indians owed him $48,000, a huge sum at the time.[161] Robinson would later collect almost $23,000 under the 1836 Treaty terms.[162] Their presence, and the money paid directly to them in the 1836 Treaty, demonstrated that Indian debt played a significant role in convincing the *ogemuk* to sign the treaty.[163]

The strategy of encouraging Indian people to sign treaties ceding lands to the United States government as a means of paying off personal and family debts actually originated with President Thomas Jefferson, who hoped for the decline of the fur trade decades earlier.[164] He suggested that American traders extend credit to Indian people with full intention of using debt to extort Indian land cessions, and for other purposes.[165] Because much of the Great Lakes economy, from the point of view of whites, relied so heavily on this extension of credit to Indians and the resulting economic benefits to non-Indians who collected on this debt, it is no surprise that American traders did not press for the removal of the Anishinaabek.[166]

Another factor persuading the Michigan Anishinaabek that it was time for a treaty was the fact that President Andrew Jackson's administration had slashed the federal Indian Office budget, which meant that the blacksmiths at Michilimackinac and Grand Traverse, important for everything from fishing hooks, to maintaining guns for hunting, and farming equipment, would no longer be available.[167] President Jackson had been the famous "Indian fighter" as a military leader and had been urging the removal of all Indians to the west of the Mississippi River.[168] But the Jackson administration stopped short in 1836 and in later periods of pressing for the ultimate removal of the northern Michigan Indians, because the American government worried that the Indians would escape to Canada and become allies of the British.[169] Schoolcraft and others were aware that Michigan Indians continued to travel to Canada, especially Manitoulin Island, to receive gifts from the English.[170] Moreover, the American military was wary of engaging yet another large group of Indian people willing to fight back if required to remove. Ongoing during the 1836 treaty negotiations was the Second Seminole War, in which thousands of Americans and Seminoles fought and died over land that was not needed for American agriculture.[171]

In general, there were numerous factors leading the Americans and the Anishinaabek to enter into a treaty. There was the southern Michigan land rush, the Jackson administration's push to remove Indians, the reduction in the federal Indian Office budget, and heavy Indian debt. Furthermore, the Michigan Anishinaabek complained that American steamers were pirating timber off of Indian-owned islands in the Great Lakes, and that American commercial fishers were destroying the fishing economy.[172]

The *ogemuk* who attended the 1836 treaty council in Washington, D.C., on behalf of the people of the Grand Traverse Bay region included three primary individuals: Aishquagonabe ("Last Feather"),[173] Aghosa ("Flying Hawk"),[174] and Oshawun Epenaysee, or Chawaneeneese. Aishquagonabe came from and represented the people of the eastern shore of the Grand Traverse Bay, near Elk Rapids, Kewadin, and Torch Lake. Aishquagonabe had been well-known for taking scalps on behalf of the British during the War of 1812.[175] Aghosa represented a group living on what is now known as Old Mission Peninsula. Aishquagonabe and Aghosa were both Ojibwe. The third group, represented by Oshawun Epenaysee, lived on Leelanau Peninsula.[176] There were several smaller Ottawa villages on that peninsula, likely all represented at the 1836 treaty council by Oshawun Epenaysee. These three individuals signed the 1836 Treaty of Washington on behalf of their respective communities.[177]

The 1836 Treaty, from the point of view of the Grand Traverse Anishinaabek, was intended to be an Ottawa treaty, involving the Lower Peninsula Anishinaabek.

There was a clear line between the primarily Ottawa Lower Peninsula territories and the Upper Peninsula Chippewa territories. And yet it was Schoolcraft and Cass who envisioned a much larger treaty cession that would involve half of the Upper Peninsula as well. Gregory Dowd reports that the 1836 treaty delegation consisted primarily of Lower Peninsula Ottawas and Chippewas.[178] The Upper Peninsula Chippewas were only sparsely represented, and then only by individuals with dubious authority at best.[179] The Grand River Ottawa delegation, many of whom opposed land cessions, was badly divided.[180] Moreover, the L'Arbre Croche bands rarely agreed on anything with the Grand River bands.[181] Schoolcraft, as the lead American treaty negotiator, used the very presence of the Upper Peninsula Chippewas as leverage against the Lower Peninsula Ottawas and Chippewas. At any moment, all parties knew, if the Ottawas objected to a large land cession or any other treaty term, Schoolcraft could easily acquire the signatures of the Upper Peninsula Chippewa contingent, regardless of their authority to sign away lands that they did not own. From the American point of view, and especially in the Senate, an Indian mark was an Indian mark. No one in Washington would question the signatories' authority.

On March 14, 1836, in what must have been a surreal experience for the Indians, the Anishinaabek met President Andrew Jackson, Indian fighter and supporter of Indian removal to the west.[182] It should be noted that the Great Lakes Anishinaabek people often brought their entire communities to major treaty negotiations, and that it was relatively rare for treaties to be negotiated in the heart of the United States capital.[183] But for this treaty, a mere twenty-four *ogemuk* attended the treaty council, far from their homelands,[184] out of at least one hundred recognized Anishinaabe *ogemuk* in the treaty cession area.[185] One could interpret this factor in different ways. Surely, the American treaty commissioners wanted to limit the presence of people who could influence the Indian negotiators, and to place the Indians in an uncomfortable position, but the presence of so few Anishinaabe leaders demonstrates the lack of consensus—and consent—from the Anishinaabek as a whole to the large land cession. And yet the Michigan Anishinaabek who attended the 1836 treaty councils were cosmopolitan leaders, with some experience in American political and social machinations, some of whom had undergone the experience of treaty-making with the Americans before.[186] The agreement these Indian negotiators made with the Americans was a powerful document that preserved much of what the Indians hoped for, demonstrating their relative comfort and strength as a group.[187] Of course, after the negotiations concluded, the United States Senate unilaterally abrogated many of the key provisions of the treaty, though a large portion of the Michigan *ogemuk* later ratified those changes.

On the first day of the formal treaty council, March 15, 1836, newly appointed treaty commissioner Henry Schoolcraft addressed the Indian treaty negotiators with his expectations for the final treaty product. He expected the *ogemuk* to agree to cede three-eighths of what would become the State of Michigan—the lands between the Grand River in the Lower Peninsula to the eastern half of the Upper Peninsula as far as Marquette. He did note that he was willing to negotiate for permanent Indian reservations for the bands assembled:

> No objection will be made, if you deem it imperative, to your fixing on proper and limited reservations to be held in common; but the President judges it best that no reservations should be made to individuals. . . . The usual privilege of residing and hunting on the lands sold till they are wanted will be granted.[188]

After this speech, the Anishinaabek retreated to private councils to deliberate over the speech from Schoolcraft. After three days of deliberation, the Anishinaabek responded negatively to Schoolcraft's plan. Gregory Dowd writes:

> When the parties reassembled in the Masonic Hall on March 18, the formalities of the calumet ceremony preceded the discussions. Then the "chief speaker" arose to reject Schoolcraft's offer. It is not clear from the record who this is, and after his objections no individual is referred to in [the treaty journal] as the "chief speaker." Probably it was Aishquagonabee, the first name listed on the treaty, a "Chippewa Chief of Grand Traverse." He lodged two specific objections: the first obvious, the second more obscure. It was obvious that the Indians simply did not wish to sell their rights to most of their lands. Less obvious was their objection to the provisions that would prevent their friends and relations from obtaining private reservations. The Ottawas and Chippewas were considering giving their intermarried relatives among the American citizens small reservations to encourage them to remain near at hand, where they could mediate dealings with other American citizens: "We fear that the whites who will not be our friends will come into our country and trouble us, and that we shall not be able to know where our possessions are, if we do sell our lands, it will be our wish that some of our white friends have lands among us and be associated with us."[189]

Schoolcraft, the crafty treaty negotiator, had a ready response. He threatened to execute a treaty with the Upper Peninsula Chippewa communities, leaving the Lower Peninsula Anishinaabek, mostly Ottawa communities, with nothing.[190] Schoolcraft knew the Upper Peninsula representatives well—they had little authority, but they were individuals who would sign anything he offered them—and he knew how to use intertribal politics to divide and conquer. Eventually, over strident opposition from several Lower Peninsula *ogemuk*, Schoolcraft got his concessions and his large land cession.[191] Again, Dowd writes:

Schoolcraft then threatened to treat separately with the Chippewas of the Upper Peninsula unless the Ottawas and Chippewas of the Lower Peninsula changed their minds before the following Tuesday. Since Upper Peninsular peoples had even less to fear from white settlement than did Ottawas, and since the dubiously representative Chippewa delegation from the Sault Ste. Marie region had been practically handpicked by the agent (and was related by marriage to him), it is not surprising that the Chippewas present were more willing to make a deal.

At that point, Augustin Hamelin [spelled Emlin in the treaty journal], Jr., intervened. He declared in English that the Ottawas had spoken, not from their hearts, but after having been, he claimed, manipulated by "white men who wanted [private] reservations." Hamelin reassured the commissioner that "if the Indians were left alone they would sell, with some Reservations for themselves, he was confident it was their wish to dispose of their lands and derive present benefit." Schoolcraft arranged for a private room in which the Indians could counsel among themselves, and that no one else be allowed to "disturb them." [Rix] Robinson, meanwhile, wrote to Crooks that he and Robert Stuart had fought hard "to get such terms respecting our claims," as Crooks had ordered. Although the Grand River Indians were still holding out for Robinson, Crooks, and others who sought private reserves, Robinson was ready to concede defeat on this point and to "fall into their ranks upon the best terms that I can get."

By the eve of the resumption of formal discussions, it was clear that most of the treating Indians would mark the agreement. Mary Holiday wrote that, while the preceding Friday "most of the Ottawas refused to sell," they had since "called on Mr. Schoolcraft, telling him they would sell, if they would be allowed to make large, permanent reservations for themselves." Holiday understood that Indian reservations [these are not private reservations] would be established. This was critical to the Indian acceptance of the treaty: they would have good-sized, permanent reservations in Michigan.[192]

Before the treaty negotiations, Schoolcraft anticipated that two reservations would be created by the treaty, totaling 100,000 acres. Instead, the treaty created five separate reservations on the Lower Peninsula mainland, including a 20,000-acre reservation for the Grand Traverse Band on the "north shore" of the bay, the Beaver Islands, and a dozen reservations on the Upper Peninsula.[193] According to Helen Tanner, the "north shore" placement of the Grand Traverse Reservation "not only reveals the contemporary geographical perceptions of the terrain but also indicates that Schoolcraft was aware of the location of Aishquagonabe's village in that area."[194] Tanner explained the perception that the east shore of the Grand Traverse Bay appeared to travelers in the 1800s to be the north shore as such:

> [Peter] Dougherty's description of the village location notes that it was on the "north bank" of the bay. Similarly, Schoolcraft's description of the proposed location of a reservation for the Grand Traverse Indians in the 1836 treaty specified the "north shore" of the bay. The terminology in both cases comes from the experience of canoeing southward toward the Grand River from Mackinac Island. On that route, the big open-water crossing is the broad mouth of the Grand Traverse Bay, where the geographic perception is that the route south heads up to the tip of the Leelanau Peninsula. Therefore, the Charlevoix side of the mouth of the Grand Traverse Bay was identified as the *north* side.[195]

The 1836 Treaty created over a dozen reservations in the Upper and Lower Peninsulas. Lewis Cass, the secretary of war and Henry Schoolcraft's immediate supervisor, was willing to tolerate the creation of permanent reservations for the Michigan Anishinaabek, but only barely.[196] In addition to the creation of the reservations, the treaty settled the debts of the Anishinaabek, meaning that the fur traders who traveled with the *ogemuk* and Schoolcraft to Washington received thousands and thousands of dollars from the United States government.[197] Henry Schoolcraft and his family members also received over $56,000 out of the $221,000 allocated within the treaty.[198] The *ogemuk* who attended the treaty negotiations also received large cash awards for the purpose of purchasing lands in fee to supplement the reservation land base.[199]

Schoolcraft also knew that the *ogemuk* had not gone to Washington solely to negotiate a land cession and reservation treaty. In the words of Dr. Susan Gray of Arizona State University, "He was convinced that without [Article 13 of the Treaty] the Ottawa and Chippewa delegates would neither have signed the treaty in March nor have accepted several months later the Senate's elimination of permanent reserves."[200] And so Article 13 reserved tribal hunting, fishing, gathering, and other rights "until the land was required for settlement"—language that had never been used before in any Indian treaty.[201] Susan Gray demonstrated in 2004 that a large portion of the 1836 cession area has never been "required for settlement," as the treaty negotiators would have understood that term.[202] "Settlement is equated with occupation with, in the case of whites, good land. 'Good' in this context undoubtedly means agricultural land."[203]

On the day the 1836 Treaty was signed, Schoolcraft wrote a letter to his wife, Jane Johnston Schoolcraft, that likely was intended to reassure her that the Michigan Anishinaabek—many of whom were her close relatives—would not be forced to leave Michigan or otherwise be forced to give up what had been their way of living for many years:

> Particularly well insulated in this reckoning were Indians at the northern edge of the cession like his wife Jane's family. When Schoolcraft wrote to Jane on March 28, the day that the negotiations came to a successful close, he enjoined her to, "Rejoice with me, the day of their [the Indians'] prosperity has long been delayed, but has finally reached them, in their lowest state of poverty, when their game is almost gone, and the country is shorn of all its advantage for the hunter state." He surely meant these words to encourage Jane to consider how his treaty would benefit her family, and it is hard to believe that he would have used such language if he were not himself convinced that white settlement, at least in the Upper-Peninsula portion of the cession, lay far in the future.[204]

Schoolcraft's representations about the likelihood that much of northern Michigan would remain unsettled were remarkably prescient. In fact, as Susan Gray concluded, much of the 1836 Treaty cession remains unsettled, as both the 1836 American and Anishinaabek treaty negotiators would have understood that term. Following the 1836 Treaty and statehood for Michigan in 1837, the ceded territories underwent a kind of historic and abominable systematic deforestation [that] not only did not promote settlement in the cession, but proved antithetical to it. Removal of trees did not, as had been the case before 1850 in southern Michigan, prepare the land for further "improvement" in the form of plowed and fenced fields, dwellings, and town sites. Lumbering camps were by definition impermanent affairs. Such economic development as lumbering fostered in the cession was concentrated in lake ports like Muskegon that became centers of timber processing and shipping. Over time, lumbermen in the cession—the largest operators not infrequently joined in interlocking directorates with railroad and mining interests—found themselves owners of tens of thousands of acres of cutover for which they remained liable for taxes.[205]

In general, efforts to "settle" the 1836 Treaty cession area were failures, with large-scale agriculture all but impossible north of a line across the state near Clare, where the growing season is simply too short. However, the fruit orchards in Leelanau County, for example, proved an exception to this general rule.[206] The year 1930 constitutes the year of the greatest extent of agriculture in the ceded territories,[207] and perhaps "settlement," with much land reverting to the public trust (both federal and state) by 1960.[208] According to Professor Gray, about 37 percent of the ceded land was used for agricultural purposes by 1930—but that figure declined to 20 percent by the end of the twentieth century, and continues to decline.[209]

In 1839, Henry Schoolcraft would describe the purpose of the 1836 Treaty from his point of view:

> This cession was made by these two leading tribes of the Algonquin Stock, on the principle of making permanent reservations of from 1000 to 70,000 acres, at a few points, reserving at the same time, the usufructuary right of living and hunting upon, and cultivating the ceded portions of the soil until it was actually required for settlement. To provide for their advancement, they set apart, out of the ample sum paid to them by the government, for this large territory, funds, for agriculture, cattle, and implements and mechanics tools, the pay of smiths and artisans, education, books, missions, annual supplies of provisions and salt to enable them to engage in the fisheries, besides a heavy annuity in coin. It was the design of these tribes, in the original sale to have these means applied on their reservations, under the expectation that they would find themselves

so far advanced in agriculture, letters, and the acts, at the termination of the 20 years annuity, as to be able to sustain themselves thenceforward without reliance on the chase.[210]

While seething with ethnocentrism, the general description fits the Indian understanding of the 1836 Treaty as well—permanent reservations, rights to use the ceded territory long past the treaty date, and annuities and other resources for the development of territories on and near the reservations.

The Abrogation of the Original 1836 Treaty by the United States Senate

The March 28 version of the 1836 Treaty included provisions for permanent reservations and excluded the possibility of removal of the Michigan Indians to the west.[211] But no treaty is valid under American law until the Senate ratifies it, and so the Senate rewrote Articles 2 and 3 to limit the reservations to five years, and to provide for the optional removal of Indian communities to areas south of the Missouri River in the west.[212] The Senate added the carrot of $200,000 to the bands that chose to remove to these lands in exchange for their reservation lands.[213] The President proclaimed the treaty as amended by the Senate on May 27, 1836.

Schoolcraft finally notified the Michigan Anishinaabek of these unilateral changes in July 1836 at Mackinac, when he summoned the leaders back for a second treaty council to discuss these changes. Andrew Blackbird wrote that the reaction of the L'Arbre Croche Odawa community was complete outrage at the loss of permanent reservations, asserting (though likely exaggerating) that fully half of the Ottawas in the region moved to Manitoulin Island in Canada.[214]

At the Michilimackinac treaty council, Schoolcraft made important representations to the *ogemuk*, according to Helen Tanner: "As Schoolcraft explained [in later writings], it was only his emphasis on the continued use of ceded territory specified in Article Thirteenth, which had no time limit and was therefore considered permanent, that brought the Indians' acquiescence to these changes."[215] The Grand Traverse community had no interest in five-year reservations—they wanted permanent homelands and were willing to try to use their annuities to purchase land for this purpose.[216] The Grand Traverse *ogemuk* likely acceded to the new terms because they hoped that the community would be able to use annuities to purchase a permanent homeland, which Schoolcraft threatened, illegally, to take away if the *ogemuk* did not assent.[217] Moreover, the *ogemuk* predicted that the northern Michigan lands would not be settled for many, many years, if ever, due to the short growing season.[218]

Helen Tanner notes that Henry Schoolcraft sought to bring in surveyors from the south of Michigan to survey the 20,000-acre Grand Traverse Reservation by the spring of 1837; but no surveyor appeared in the region for two years, wasting 40 percent of the proposed time period.[219] Schoolcraft believed that the costly and arduous process of surveying the 1836 Treaty reservations was a waste of time, given their short five-year duration.[220] By 1839, Schoolcraft argued that the only remaining viable provision in the 1836 Treaty protecting Indian rights on their own reservations was Article 13.[221] The operation of the 1836 Treaty in terms of the five-year reservations was a sad joke. It is clear that the American policymakers in Senate and in the White House had no conception of reality in Indian Country or in the Michigan Territory.

Peter Dougherty and the Implementation of the 1836 Treaty at Grand Traverse

The placement of the 1836 Grand Traverse Reservation—one of only two reservations established in the 1836 Treaty that was actually surveyed and declared (the other being the Manistee Reservation)[222]—has a long and complicated history. It starts with the arrival of Protestant missionary Peter Dougherty in 1838.[223] Much of the history of the Grand Traverse Band after the 1836 Treaty and before the 1855 Treaty is told in Dougherty's diaries.[224]

The fourth article of the 1836 Treaty provided funds for the establishment of missions and for the education of Indian children.[225] Schoolcraft, a Presbyterian, responded favorably to contact from the Presbyterian Board of Foreign Missions. The board sent Peter Dougherty to Mackinac Island in 1838.[226] Schoolcraft's brother-in-law, John Johnston, and his wife, Jane Johnston Schoolcraft, greeted Dougherty. At their recommendation, Dougherty traveled to the Grand Traverse Bay. He wrote:

> Mr. Johnston informed me that the Grand Traverse Bay, in point of numbers, of character, as well as freedom from Catholic influences, was the most promising place to commence operation. The Indians are beginning to gather on that reservation. The soil on the Bay is the best in that part of Michigan. . . . He advised [me] to visit the village of Aischquagonabe and, if I could, to go as far as the Manistee.[227]

Henry Schoolcraft agreed, according to Dougherty's diary:

> He think[s] the grand Travers[e] as favourable a point as any to which my attention
> can be directed. He recommends to go and establish under the patronage of the
> government which will give recommendation to the Indians, make the mission
> more independent of the influence from any source against it.[228]

Dougherty traveled first to Aghosa's village, but found it temporarily empty,[229]
and so he moved on to Aishquagonabe's village, situated at Eastport on what
Dougherty called the "north bank." He wrote:

> When I came to the principal village on the Grand Traverse, which is situated up
> the bay about twelve miles, on the north bank; I found the chief [Aishquagonabe]
> was absent, and could do nothing more than see the situation of the village
> and the country around it. His absence, however, was not a thing that very
> much interfered with my object in visiting the place, which was to see, as Mr.
> Schoolcraft advised not to say much about the object of my visit further than
> to say that according to their treaty the President had promised them teachers,
> that it was one of their privileges to which they had a right and I had been sent
> to select a place and build a school house and wished him to point out to me
> the best location, and that Mr. S would explain the whole matter when he went
> to Mackinac. . . .
>
> On the bay there are about four hundred living in three or four villages, at
> different points, but they are gathering Mr. Johnston says on the reservation
> which will bring them all within the sphere of a missionary stationed at the
> village of Esquagonabe.[230]

After leaving Aishquagonabe's village, Dougherty crossed to the lake side of
Leelanau Peninsula and visited what is likely Leland. About that place, he wrote:

> About twenty five miles further up the Lake [*i.e.,* going south] there is a village at
> the mouth of a fine stream of water. It is not quite as large as the one mentioned
> on the bay [*i.e.,* Aischquagonabe's], but the situation, the appearance of the
> soil, the aspect of the village, made a very favourable impression. The chief felt
> favourable toward the establishment of a school and said they were at home all
> the time except when absent on their hunting excursions or in the sugar bush.
> This place is more easy of access to vessels going up and down the lake as they

pass directly in sight and the water is deep so that almost any vessel could run close to the shore. . . . There is less probability of white men settling near this village. There are men, several, at Mackinack who are talking of going in to the Bay to take up lands, out of the limits of the reservation, however, most of them are men of good morals. One is a carpenter, and one a blacksmith.[231]

Because of what he saw at Grand Traverse, and because of the advice of the Schoolcraft and Johnston families in Mackinac, Dougherty chose the Grand Traverse Bay for his mission. He may also have been influenced by the plague of mosquitoes that tormented him in the Grand River Valley, and information from the Manistee Indians that they were unhappy with their reservation and planning to leave.[232] Eventually, the Manistee Reservation, supplied by Henry Schoolcraft, failed.[233]

After wintering in Mackinac, Dougherty traveled to Grand Traverse, where he found that Aishquagonabe had established that summer's village at Elk Rapids, a prime area near a river mouth, with excellent fishing and hunting, and access to sugar groves.[234] Dougherty quickly built a house and a school. However, Henry Schoolcraft, arriving that summer with a government blacksmith, encouraged Dougherty to establish the permanent mission on "the Point," later called Old Mission Peninsula, perhaps at the request of American Fur Company traders, who preferred the friendlier harbor at the Point. Aghosa, the *ogema* there, issued an invitation, and Dougherty moved across the bay.[235] Peter Greensky, Dougherty's interpreter, began teaching classes to Indian children.[236] The new apprentice for the blacksmith Isaac George was Andrew Blackbird, later famed for his history of the Little Traverse Bay Bands of Odawa Indians,[237] who carried the nickname "Jackson."[238] Blackbird would later write of the complaints made by the Ojibwes in the Old Mission community who preferred an Ojibwe blacksmith apprentice rather than an Odawa apprentice—perhaps one of the first demands for tribal preference in employment.[239] Jane Johnston Schoolcraft's brother George Johnston would serve as the carpenter at Grand Traverse in 1839–1840, until relieved of his position after allegations of nepotism were leveled at his brother-in-law.[240]

A few weeks later, Aishquagonabe arrived with three or four families and announced plans to settle at the Point as well. The Protestant mission became an attraction of sorts to Anishinaabe communities, especially those near L'Arbre Croche, because the teacher taught in not only Anishinaabemowin but also

English. The Austrian priests near Little Traverse Bay spoke little or no English, and the Indians wanted their children to speak English.[241]

As missionary and teacher, Dougherty found the Grand Traverse Indians unwieldy. Their seasonal habits of relocating inland to winter camps, reappearing at the sugar camps in the spring, before returning to the summer camps around Grand Traverse Bay undermined Dougherty's attempts to control them and to convert them. In the fall of 1839, Dougherty succeeded in convincing Aghosa to spend the winter at the Point, but as the Indians depleted wintertime food reserves, they desperately scoured the woods for game.[242] Richard White argues that the missionaries generally failed to convert the Grand Traverse Indians to Christian farmers, but "their coming did spur a rather remarkable series of cultural adjustments by the Ottawas which, until they were swamped by White settlers in the 1860s, seemed about to make them a group that, although still distinctly Indian, was yet able to adjust to and profit from the encroaching American economy."[243] One Indian, Ogemawish, told Dougherty he would not go to church because "When I sit down I have to smoke, and I can't smoke in church. That is why I never come."[244] Aishquagonabe told Dougherty that the missionary was too young to teach old Indians, compelling Dougherty to write in his journal that Aishquagonabe was "an old snake."[245]

James McClurken had another point of view on the influence of the missionaries—that the Anishinaabek used them as allies and tools in their attempts to avoid removal:

> Ottawa people understood very well the process of making allies for their own benefit. As part of their campaign to remain in Michigan, they made allies of those missionaries who opposed removal and supported Ottawa efforts to purchase land. In the process, they learned that so long as they attended church services, the missionaries would help them build farms and supply them with food, clothing, and medicine. Some Ottawa adults even went to the missionary schools to learn to read and write so they could conduct their own affairs in American society.[246]

Susan Gray described the importance of white missions near Indian villages: "The Ottawa . . . were far less interested in becoming like white men than in learning to live as Indians in the midst of white settlement. For them, the missions were less cradles of civilization than bases from which to pursue a seasonally migratory economy."[247] Perhaps this explains Dougherty's later frustration with the lack of Indian conversions to Protestantism.[248]

In 1839 and 1840, Dougherty drew the first accurate maps created by non-Indians, showing the shape of the Grand Traverse Bay and the locations of seven Indian villages on the bay: The Point (Aghosa's village at Old Mission), Eastpoint (Aishquagonabe's old village), Northport (later Waukazoo's village), two villages south of Aghosa's Old Mission village, Omena, and Leland.[249] In September 1839, Dougherty issued his first report to Schoolcraft, writing, "In conclusion I would say it be an act of great generosity and kindness on the part of the Government if it would give that little point to those people."[250]

Schoolcraft would follow Dougherty's recommendation. In 1839, the Grand Traverse Bay region surveys were completed, and Schoolcraft wrote to the commissioner of Indian Affairs that the Grand Traverse Band people had chosen Old Mission Peninsula, or "the Point," as the focus of its reservation:

> Sir: The Indians at Grand Traverse Bay have selected their reservation of 20,000 acres under the 2nd Article of the treaty, on the point of land extending North into that bay, being parts of fractional Townships No. 28, 29, 30, in Range 10 West of the principal meridian, which they request to be exempted from sale.[251]

Sadly, Schoolcraft never received word that the national General Land Office in Washington had found that the Point alone did not come to 20,000 acres, and added "a disconnected triangle of land on the southeast shore across the bay from 'the point' selected by the Indians."[252] On August 10, 1840, Commissioner J. W. Whitcomb of the General Land Office wrote the commissioner of Indian Affairs:

> I have to inform you by order of the President the whole of fractional Townships twenty eight, twenty nine and thirty North of Range ten West of the Michigan Mer[idian] in the Ionia district have been withdrawn from the public sale advertised to take place on the 26th of October next, as reserved for the reservation of 20,000 acres of the Ottawa and Chippewa Treaty of the 28th of March 1836 and that the Register and Receiver have this day been instructed accordingly.[253]

The total acreage after this amendment was 20,672.74 acres. And so Schoolcraft apparently never learned of the reservation on the east shore.[254] Federal officials decided by 1840, after a complaint from Michigan Indians spearheaded by

William Johnston (Schoolcraft's brother-in-law) and Augustin Hamelin Jr. that Schoolcraft should be removed from his position as Michigan Indian agent.[255] The first map published that showed the contours of the 1836 Grand Traverse Reservation did not appear until 1899, when Charles C. Royce published his collection *Indian Land Cessions in the United States*.[256]

In the 1840s, the Indians that remained at Old Mission began to adapt to the changing circumstances by harvesting larger agricultural plots and adapting European technology for that purpose.[257] By 1847, Dougherty congratulated himself on helping to build a large and all-but-permanent Indian mission settlement on Old Mission:

> Six years ago the site occupied by the village was a dense thicket. The village now extends nearly a mile in length, containing some twenty log houses and some good log stables belonging to the Indians. During that period they have cleared and cultivated some two hundred acres of new gardens, besides what additions were made to the old ones. They raise for sale several hundred bushels of corn and potatoes.[258]

By 1849, the surplus in corn and potatoes cultivated at Old Mission exceeded several thousand bushels.[259] According to Richard White, "With agricultural surpluses the danger of starvation disappeared, and the destruction of the southern hunting grounds by White settlers gave Indians another incentive to remain at home during the winter."[260] The success of the Anishinaabek at Grand Traverse during the 1840s gave the communities a further incentive to use treaty annuity money to buy land in fee, which they did in significant amounts beginning in 1850.[261]

While the 1836 Treaty's abrogation by the Senate forced the Grand Traverse Band Anishinaabek to live under a cloud of uncertainty as to the permanence of their homelands, the 1840s were a relative period of prosperity for the community.

The Story of the 1855 Treaty of Detroit

fter the United States Senate abrogated many provisions of the 1836 Treaty of Washington without the consent of the Michigan Anishinaabek communities, the 1836 Treaty signatories sought a second treaty. The resulting Treaty of Detroit did little to benefit the Grand Traverse Anishinaabek by creating an allotment system of land ownership within a new Grand Traverse Reservation instead of creating a permanent reservation, but the 1855 Treaty did guarantee as a practical matter that the Grand Traverse Anishinaabek could avoid forced removal to the west.

The Foundations of a New Treaty

There were several reasons that the Michigan Anishinaabek sought a new treaty in the 1850s, including a desire for a guaranteed land base in their traditional homelands and an accounting of the annuity money due the bands from the 1836 Treaty.

Even though the federal government in 1840 officially declared the establishment of the Grand Traverse Reservation under the terms of the 1836 Treaty, the Anishinaabek living at Grand Traverse or anywhere else in the 1836 territories could not feel secure. Nothing felt settled or permanent. Under the terms of the 1836 Treaty, the reservation that had just been established in 1840 would expire in 1841. This uncertainty created the conditions for the near-abandonment of the 1836 Old Mission reservation. According to Richard White:

> The dedication of the Ottawas to agriculture and their success at it, paradoxically, was the major cause of the break up of the Old Mission village. The Ottawas desired permanent title to their lands, and this was impossible at the Old Mission since the lands had not been offered for sale. As a result, the Indians began to seek available land across the bay during the 1850s.[1]

In other words, because the federal land office kept the declared reservation off the public sale list, and because the federal government kept threatening to remove the Grand Traverse Indians west, the Grand Traverse Anishinaabek felt they had to leave the reservation in order to secure a permanent land title in the region.

In 1840, Henry Schoolcraft's contribution to the annual report from the commissioner of Indian Affairs to Congress helped to create the need for a remedial treaty, one that would not come for fifteen years. In the following excerpt, Schoolcraft highlights the bountiful natural resources of northern Michigan, making it ideal in some ways to American settlement, while downplaying the presence of American Indians, even suggesting that they would not be in the area for long:

> Both the climate and the soil . . . are highly favorable to the growth of wheat, flint corn, barley, peas, oats, and other productions . . . the recent discoveries of prime saline waters, gypsum, bog-ore, slaty coal, and shell marl, together with the pineries, the amount of water power of its streams, and the facilities of lake navigation, point it out as a highly and permanently valuable portion of the state . . . the whole area is open to the scrutiny and enterprise of a steadily accumulating population; and it cannot be predicted that the comparatively large number of Ottawas and Chippewas, who are still located here, can maintain themselves for any length of time by hunting. Collisions happen whenever the two races come into contact.[2]

Schoolcraft's enticement to American industrialists—and, a bit disingenuously, agriculturalists—helped to generate demand for Indian lands and to create the kind of conflict he feared. His misrepresentation of the capacity for northern Michigan Anishinaabek to live indefinitely in the area given its natural resources is all but criminal. Similarly, in 1870 the *Atlantic Monthly* published a short article on the agriculture and scenery of the Grand Traverse Bay region without mentioning the presence of the Anishinaabek.[3]

Despite the Senate's amendment of the 1836 Treaty to include provisions meant to persuade the northern Michigan Anishinaabek to move to lands west of the Mississippi and south of the Missouri, the federal government neither persuaded the tribes to leave, nor did they take significant physical action to force them west, despite efforts by Henry Schoolcraft.[4] The "Panic of 1837," the beginning of a major national economic downturn, further reduced American demand for northern Michigan Indian lands.[5] Moreover, the 1837 downturn encouraged unscrupulous non-Indians to seek avenues of acquiring Indian annuity money, perhaps generated a form of dependence upon the presence of Indian people in the region.[6] By the 1840s or 1850s, the federal government ceased trying to remove the Michigan Anishinaabek to the west.[7]

There were at least two significant reasons for the failure of the federal government to convince the Michigan Anishinaabek to move west. First, Anishinaabek scouts who visited the lands in Kansas and elsewhere contemplated for the new homeland were very dissatisfied with the land. In 1838, Schoolcraft took action in an effort to convince the Ottawas and Chippewas to move to Kansas, in accordance with the option removal plan in the 1836 Treaty. He sought to put together a delegation to visit the Kansas lands while the prairie plants were in bloom during the summer, but he could get only a few Ottawas together, and even fewer *ogemuk*.[8] No Chippewas traveled, and neither did anyone from the Grand Traverse Anishinaabek communities.[9] Kansas was prairie land, not woodlands, with little in the way of natural resources that the Indians needed for survival and trade. There were no significant lakes or river waters for fishing, nor the right kind of lands for hunting and gathering. It would have required the Michigan tribes to become large-scale agriculturalists, and probably cattlemen, as well as fighters: "They reported that there were no streams good for fishing, no sugar maples, and the climate was unhealthy—bitter cold in winter and too hot in summer. Nor were they anxious to engage plains tribes like the Sioux in warfare as the Potawatomi who had gone west were forced to do."[10] According to correspondence from Schoolcraft, the Great Lakes Indians considered themselves "woodsmen and watermen," unfit for the plains.[11] As a result, they resisted mightily. In the words of Robert Keller:

> The Great Lakes tribes' attachment to their land resulted in an unyielding opposition to the federal government plan to remove them south of the Missouri River or west of the Mississippi. Their resistance was so strong and their attachment to a particular land so intense that the Chippewa and Ottawa, by sheer perseverance, finally forced the government to reverse its 50 year policy of removing all eastern Indians to the Far West.[12]

Rumors of Indian removal to the west spread throughout Anishinaabe Indian Country in 1839 and 1840.[13] According to James McClurken:

> In May 1839, rumors swept through the population at the Straits of Mackinac: the government, many believed, planned to load the Ottawa on steamboats and send them to western lands without their consent. In response, more than 250 persons from L'Arbre Croche and Cheboygan loaded their canoes and moved

their families into British territory on Manitoulin Island. Others threatened to leave. Schoolcraft responded by deleting those who left from the annuity rolls.[14]

The leading Grand Traverse Anishinaabe *ogemuk*, Aishquagonabe, along with Aghosa, repeatedly sought federal-government guarantees that the Grand Traverse Anishinaabek would not be removed out of their homeland. In 1841, Aghosa told Peter Dougherty that the Grand Traverse Anishinaabek "hold on to this place as a bird clings to a tree ready to fall."[15] Also in 1841, Aishquagonabe and Aghosa, with George Johnston and William Johnston's assistance, sought assurances from the Michigan Indian agent: "We feel such an attachment to this our native place, from whence we derive our birth, that it looks like going to certain death from it, we again beg to remind you that we need your aid and advice. We feel anxious to make a purchase from the government of Lands on this point."[16] In 1843, the Grand Traverse *ogemuk* formally petitioned Congress and the President for federal citizenship and a guarantee that they could remain on their lands: "to remain on our native soil, to buy the lands where we now live."[17] Congress responded favorably to this petition, but recommended that the Michigan Indians seek citizenship from the state government.[18]

Second, geopolitical reasons may have influenced the government's decision not to use the military to force the northern Michigan Anishinaabek west. The Old Northwest in the middle part of the nineteenth century was still relatively a hot spot in terms of potential military conflict between the nascent United States and Great Britain, operating out of Canada. Moreover, the Americans appeared to recognize that Michigan Indians, former allies of the English during the War of 1812, still had an economic, if not military, presence in Michigan that the English could exploit as a means of harassing American interests. In 1815, Michigan Territorial Governor Lewis Cass reported that the Michigan Ottawas and Chippewas were hostile to the United States and remained under the influence of the British.[19] One rumor circulated in Michigan in 1815 that eighteen hundred Indians had met with the British on Drummond Island, receiving presents and weapons to use against the Americans.[20] According to Robert Keller:

> Between 1785 and 1830 the major concern of the new United States was to control the Indian trade by discouraging and prohibiting tribal relations with the British Hudson's Bay Company and the French Canadian Northwest Company. . . .

During these early years, 1785–1830, the United States occupied a weak position both in relation to Canada and to the tribes. It sought to neutralize [Great] Lakes Indians as a military threat and to discourage their trade to the north.[21]

And when the United States threatened to use its military—and then did use its military—to remove southwestern Michigan Potawatomis[22] and Ohio Ottawas west to Kansas and then Oklahoma,[23] many hundreds of Anishinaabek fled to Canada, where they had relatives.[24] The northern Michigan Indians also had relatives in Canada, and some northern Indians fled to Canada at this time as well.[25] This was worrisome to the Americans, who may have decided that it was better to have Indians in northern Michigan than to lose many or all of them to Canada, where they could become formidable enemies. Even so, according to Andrew Blackbird, perhaps as many as half of the Grand Traverse and Little Traverse Anishinaabek moved to Canada between 1839 and 1842.[26] However, recent scholarship disputes this claim as being an exaggeration, with the actual number being closer to 250 Ottawas.[27] Yet it is clear that these movements affected American policy.[28] In 1842, when the uncertainty of the permanence of the Grand Traverse Reservation reached a peak, Aishquagonabe and a large group of Grand Traverse Indians again traveled to Manitoulin Island to receive presents from the British, reviving a longstanding tradition dating back to the War of 1812.[29]

One potential solution for the United States was to use the annuity system created in the treaties to control Michigan Anishinaabek. According to Robert Keller:

> Skillfully manipulated, the annuity system gave government officials a powerful weapon with which to coerce tribal conformity with BIA policy. Ottawa and Chippewa who crossed the Canadian border, for example, forfeited their treaty payments. To achieve what Alexander Ramsey called the government's policy of "breaking and creating chiefs at will," disbursement of annuities was used to restrict the power of traditional chiefs and to enhance the authority of more cooperative individuals.[30]

Henry Schoolcraft's threats to cut off annuity payments during various stages of his work in northern Michigan were examples of this phenomenon.

The 1840s passed without action from Congress or the federal government on the reservation permanence question. The year 1841 was a momentous year for the Michigan Anishinaabek who had been signatories to the 1836 Treaty—it was the year the five-year period on reservations would expire. On May 27, 1841, the date for the proposed termination of the reservations, the *ogemuk* for all the bands gathered at Mackinac Island to draft a petition seeking an extension of the time period. By then, the government had removed Henry Schoolcraft from office because of alleged political activity.[31] He was replaced by a former American Fur Company representative, Robert Stuart. Peter Dougherty petitioned Stuart as well.[32] Silence followed.

Grand Traverse Indians had begun to use annuities paid at the annual Mackinac gatherings to purchase land in the area as early as 1838, following the advice of Peter Dougherty.[33] Rumors about the lands in the region being open to public sale (that is, to non-Indian land speculators) abounded in 1844 and 1849, often spread by George Johnston.[34] Dougherty wrote in 1849 that Indians were talking about

> getting up a petition here praying the government to bring this point into market that the Indians may purchase if they wish. . . . Persons are beginning to look about here for locations. All is uncertainty at present with regard to this land whether it is regarded still by the government as a reservation to which the laws relating to Indian territory apply or not. If a reservation, preemption cannot hold here, hence all improvements are made at considerable hazard.[35]

Dougherty explained that the Grand Traverse Indians, especially those living on Old Mission, had been developing an active agricultural economy, including cattle and fruit orchards.[36]

In 1850, the Grand Traverse post office opened.[37] More significantly, the Michigan Constitution was ratified. It included a provision allowing Indian males to vote, assuming they were "civilized." The provision stated, "Every civilized male inhabitant of Indian descent, a native of the United States and not a member of any tribe, shall be an elector and entitled to vote."[38]

Michigan Ottawa leaders had been petitioning the United States for assistance (and perhaps federal citizenship) since at least 1837 because of the problems they faced with federal homesteading laws.[39] Federal law allowed American citizens to "homestead" land through a process known as "preemption."[40] Any citizen could go to lands held by the federal government, literally trespass and squat on that land for a certain period of years, and acquire that land after the time period expired for a nominal fee, so long as the citizen could prove actual use and improvement of the land.[41] Since the 1836 Treaty, Michigan Anishinaabek *ogemuk* had been purchasing land near the 1836 reservations using treaty annuity money.[42] But by 1850, non-Indian squatters and land speculators had been claiming preemption rights on lands that had been purchased, occupied, and improved by Grand Traverse Indians for as long as a decade.[43] The federal land office in Ionia, where Peter Dougherty had assisted Aishquagonabe and Aghosa in purchasing lands for the Grand Traverse Anishinaabek, opined that Indians could not claim homesteading or preemption rights in these lands, and began to grant them to non-Indians, most of whom had never even seen the lands.[44] Michigan Indians first sought federal citizenship, but the United States refused to grant it.[45] In 1843 and 1844, the Ottawa again petitioned the Michigan legislature for state citizenship.[46] Only in 1850 did the State of Michigan grant state citizenship and the suffrage to some Michigan Indians, but only if they became "civilized."[47] The extension of state citizenship did little to improve Anishinaabek legal standing in Michigan: "In 1860 the Attorney General of the State of Michigan would argue that the framers of the constitution intended to enfranchise only this mixed blood, non-tribal population [living apart from Indian villages], not the entire Ottawa, Chippewa, and Potawatomie population of the state."[48]

Henry Schoolcraft's politics and statements made in the late 1830s, during his last years as Michigan Indian agent, also did little to assist the Michigan Anishinaabek. In 1837, during the American economic downturn, he did little or nothing to continue federal support for the 1836 Treaty-protected hunting, fishing, and sugaring rights.[49] The same year, after three prominent Grand Rapids property owners sought a legal opinion on the meaning of the Article 13 treaty rights, Schoolcraft privately argued that the treaty rights on ceded territory would expire as soon as the land became private property.[50] An April 13, 1837, United States attorney general opinion that Schoolcraft had published in the Detroit *Daily Advertiser* reached the same conclusion.[51] But at the same time, Schoolcraft referred to the ceded territory as "Indian Country,"[52] reflecting his true understanding that Article 13 rights did not expire until the lands in the ceded territory were used for permanent agriculture. In 1840, shortly before being forced out of office, Schoolcraft argued that the United States should compel the Anishinaabek to give up their Article 13 rights, relying upon the expansive definition of "settlement" to mean permanent agricultural improvements.[53]

Schoolcraft also attempted to exploit fears of an Indian war to support his proposal to remove the Indians from Michigan. In 1837, several non-Indians were scalped near the Grand River Valley, with Saginaw Chippewa Indians suspected of the crime, raising fears of a bloody war like that ongoing in Florida between the United States and the Seminole Tribe.[54] Schoolcraft used the event to drum up support for Indian removal, though there was little evidence that any Indians had committed the crime.[55] Later, Schoolcraft admitted that Indians likely did not commit the crime, and in 1841, one of the non-Indians allegedly murdered was located alive in Wisconsin.[56]

Despite these challenges and ongoing threats, the Grand Traverse Anishinaabek took to their education and carpentry apprenticeships well. Despite smaller and smaller federal appropriations, the Indian agent sent a blacksmith to Grand Traverse in 1844.[57] By 1855, the Indian agent reported that Grand Traverse had become a minor shipbuilding center:

> At Grand Traverse the Indians have built and launched three schooners, one of which was completed during the last summer. The work was all done by themselves, and I am told the vessel would do credit to any ship yard on the lakes. The captain and crew are all Indians, and navigate the vessel and transport freight on Lake Michigan and transact all ordinary business resulting from such an [enterprise].[58]

By the time that American and Anishinaabek treaty negotiators sought a new treaty in 1855, the American focus in the Great Lakes had changed a bit, from removal to protection of American economic interests and the collection of Indian debts to American traders:

> Much of the cash appropriated for land fell directly into the American Fur Company bank account, or, on a lesser scale, it went into the coffers of local traders. A Michigan resident [in the Grand River Valley] recalled that at the time of treaty payments, "the Indians would enter the front door . . . sign their receipts, receive their money and walk out the back door, where stood a crowd of hungry traders, who quickly transferred most of the money from the hands of the Indians to their own pockets for payment of old debts. The traders commonly claimed all they could see, and the Indians, as a rule, gave it up without protest."[59]

Just as they had with the 1836 Treaty, non-Indian traders continued to exploit the Michigan Anishinaabek, hoping for a new treaty and another big payday.[60]

In 1850, William Johnston wrote on behalf of "Chiefs of the Ottawa and Chippewa Tribes of Indians, residing in Michigan," for a new treaty to be made that would settle the questions of Indian land permanence.[61] After pressure from Michigan political leaders, the Senate issued a resolution offered by Michigan Senator Alpheas Felch on April 6, 1852:

> That the Committee on Indian Affairs be instructed to inquire into the expediency of making provisions for the amicable arrangement with the Ottawa and Chippewa Indians of all questions arising under the treaty with them of 1836, relative to the continued occupancy of the lands reserved to them and the consideration to be paid for such cession; and also, as to the expediency of making an appropriation to enable the proper Department to consummate such measures as may be necessary for their permanent settlement in the country where they now reside.[62]

George Manypenny, the commissioner of Indian Affairs, asked the secretary of the Interior to seek a congressional appropriation for funds to conduct a treaty council with the Ottawa and Chippewa tribes, "with a view to arranging for them to continue living in their own ceded lands."[63] Henry C. Gilbert, the Michigan Indian Agency superintendent at the time, wrote in March 1854 that when treaty annuity payments ended in 1855, several thousand Michigan Indians might need state subsistence payments, justifying a new treaty from the point of view of the federal government.[64]

Grand Traverse Villages (1840s to 1850s) and the Shifting Character of Tribal Leadership

The focus of the Grand Traverse Bay Anishinaabek community shifted from Old Mission to Leelanau Peninsula during this period. The Indians at Old Mission and elsewhere around the bay had been saving annuity money to purchase lands, and began buying land when the federal government opened up Leelanau Peninsula to public sale.[65] In the 1850s, Aghosa moved his community from Old Mission to New Mission, an area south of Northport still referred to by many Indians as Aghosatown but now called Omena,[66] after a joking nickname given to Peter Dougherty.[67] Aghosa and Dougherty had traveled to the Ionia federal land office to purchase lands in the vicinity in 1851.[68]

By 1850, there were fewer and fewer Grand Traverse Anishinaabek living on Old Mission.[69] There were several villages in the northern half of the Leelanau Peninsula, including the Shabwasson, Nagonabe, and Onomunese bands.[70] By 1863, there were several Indian schools in Leelanau County—near Onawmeceeneville and Eagletown, for example[71]—with attendance encouraged by a hot-lunch program.

In 1852, a community of Odawak at the La Croix mission near Cross Village, led by a man named Peshawbe (or Peshaba), relocated from the north to the area in Leelanau County now referred to as Peshawbestown. They called their village Eagletown.[72] This group moved to the area to take advantage of the English-speaking teachers in Grand Traverse—better, in their view, than the German-speaking Austrians operating the La Croix mission and school. By 1855, Eagletown was one of a small group of Ottawa villages with a Catholic Indian school.[73] According to Virgil Vogel, in 1883 Father Philip Zara named the village after Peshawbe—Peshawbestown.[74]

In 1848 or 1849, a community of Odawak living near Holland, Michigan, at an Indian mission operated by a Congregationalist named George N. Smith,[75] relocated to a village near Northport.[76] Their *ogema* was Waukazoo, and so the town for a period was known as Waukazooville.[77]

Anishinaabe leadership retained its traditional character during this period. According to Richard White, "It is typical of Ottawa social organization that the move was initiated by the villagers, leaving the chiefs and missionaries the choice of following or losing their influence."[78] In 1847, Father Frederick Baraga offered a description of the Anishinaabe leadership and governmental structure:

> The [Anishinaabe] Indians form but one tribe. . . . They live in larger or smaller camps or Indian villages very thinly over an immense tract of land. Every village, camp or band of Indians has one or more chiefs. There is no general chief over the whole tribe.[79]

In the mid-eighteenth century, bands of family or hunting units would congregate in villages for the summer months—villages in places like Old Mission Point, Aghosatown, Northport, or Peshawbestown. Above this level, according to Richard White, the bands in a region might confederate for specific purposes, such as treaty negotiations. In those instances, there might be the Grand Traverse bands, or the Little Traverse bands, or the Grand River bands, for example.[80]

Three lead Grand Traverse Anishinaabe *ogemuk*—Aghosa, Onawmoneese, and Peshawbe[81]—represented the villages at the 1855 treaty negotiations in Detroit, which lasted from July 25 to July 31, 1855.[82] Several lesser *ogemuk* attended as well and signed the treaty—younger Indians educated in American schools, who could speak, read, and write English.[83] The Anishinaabe representatives grouped themselves together as regional confederacies, with five groups: Sault Ste. Marie, Mackinac, Grand River, Little Traverse Bay, and Grand Traverse Bay.[84] The Ottawa *ogemuk* selected Asagon (Aasagan), from Cheboygan of the Burt Lake Band (despite the fact that the Burt Lake villages refused to appear), to speak for them,[85] and the Chippewa *ogemuk* selected Waubojeeg, from Sault Ste. Marie.[86] Asagon explained the legal authority of the tribal delegates as follows:

> The chiefs here present are delegates appointed by those they have left behind them. They were sent to get as far as possible the views of Government relative to this treaty. They got as it were a power of Attorney to come here and transact business. And so it is with you—you are the agent of the [United States].[87]

The Grand Traverse bands chose delegates to the treaty council as village bands (Aghosatown, Eagletown, and so on), signed the treaty as a regional confederacy (the Grand Traverse Band), but negotiated as a tribe (Ottawa, although one of the delegates was Chippewa).[88] George Manypenny, the commissioner of Indian Affairs, and Henry Gilbert, the Michigan Indian agent, represented the federal government.

Professor Ramirez-shkwegnaabi studied the negotiation tactics of the Anishinaabe *ogemuk* in the 1855 treaty negotiations. There was an important change in the manners and speeches of the leading *ogemuk* compared to that of earlier treaty negotiations. "By 1855, the Anishinaabeg of Michigan had been involved in numerous treaty negotiations with the United States. Since the 1795 Treaty of Greenville and through the treaties of 1807, 1819, and 1836 they had learned that they could not count on the United States to honor treaty agreements."[89] He continues:

> In Michigan, by 1855 longer and more constant interactions with whites had given Anishinaabeg a much greater degree of familiarity with non-Indian diplomacy

and financial matters. By this time they understood many American business and financial practices, including the concept of "interest on the principle." The northern Michigan bands, who did not want to be removed to Indian Country and were prepared to negotiate transactions involving permanent sale of their lands in exchange for specified payments and permanent reservations, recognized the usefulness of speaking, reading, and calculating in English and stressed the need for quality mainstream education. Although Anishinaabeg protocol remained important, diplomats now took a new approach that combined traditional ceremony and rhetoric with almost blunt questioning in pursuit of detailed financial information.[90]

Despite this aggressive and well-planned stance, it was clear that the Anishinaabek came to the table without much bargaining power.[91]

The Treaty of Detroit (1855)

In January and February of 1855, the Lower Peninsula Ottawa bands met at Grand Traverse Bay and at the Grand River Valley to plan for treaty negotiations with the American government. "They agreed to ask for a permanent home in Michigan, continued government trusteeship over their financial affairs, and a clarification of their rights under previous treaties."[92] After these meetings, a delegation of Little Traverse and Grand River people left for Washington, D.C., to begin treaty negotiations, but the Grand Traverse delegation refused to accompany them or authorize their actions. A second delegation of Chippewa Indians from Mackinac, authorized and encouraged by the Indian agent Henry Gilbert, arrived in Washington after the Ottawa delegation arrived, adding to the confusion. A memorial dated January 16, 1855,[93] and presented to Congress on February 26, 1855, may have articulated the views of the Lower Peninsula Anishinaabek,[94] but shortly thereafter, the Grand River *ogemuk* disavowed the Washington trip made by the Ottawas, and anything else done there.[95]

Treaty commissioner Manypenny succeeded in convincing the Michigan Anishinaabek to meet in Detroit. And so from July 25 to July 31, 1855, Manypenny convened another treaty council.[96] The Americans negotiated with five separate Anishinaabe bands, representing regions from Sault Ste. Marie, Mackinac, Grand River, Grand Traverse, and Little Traverse, while the Burt Lake communities refused to appear.[97] Despite the different regional or band constituencies, the

Anishinaabek negotiated as tribes, with the Upper Peninsula Chippewa bands and the Lower Peninsula Ottawa and Chippewa bands each speaking for themselves.[98] On July 31, 1855, several *ogemuk* representing the Grand Traverse Band Anishinaabek signed the Treaty of Detroit.

Once again, the United States met in a treaty council with what the American treaty negotiators referred to as the Ottawa and Chippewa "nation," or the Michigan Anishinaabek who were parties to the 1836 Treaty. As in 1836, the government wanted one "nation" to be a party to the treaty "to avoid territorial disputes between the bands and to settle the cession with one treaty instead of many. . . . This group . . . was created for only one purpose—to cede land. It never exercised any political sovereignty outside the treaty councils."[99] The key 1855 treaty negotiators on the American side, Indian agent Henry Gilbert and Commissioner of Indian Affairs George Manypenny, had "no idea how to make meaningful tribal distinctions between the various bands of Ottawas and Chippewas with whom [they] would negotiate."[100] After the treaty was negotiated, the federal government would have no further use for the "nation."[101]

George Manypenny initiated the proceedings without honoring the Anishinaabek with appropriate ceremonies, instead cutting directly to an explanation of the purpose of the treaty council. In return, Asagon sought "time to consult." The time took the rest of the day, ending that day's negotiations and annoying Manypenny.[102] When the Anishinaabek returned after the first day of negotiations, they took aggressive negotiating positions that would continually surprise the Americans:

> However, having learned from experience some valuable lessons on U.S. unreliability in financial dealings, Anishinaabeg leaders were in no rush to commit to Manypenny's plan. Manypenny's opening remarks dismissed concerns over payments for previous treaties brought to his attention the previous winter in Washington, D.C., by two delegations of Odawa and Ojibwe. Aasagan responded to the commissioner by telling him what the Anishinaabeg expected of this council: "I want to speak of the past. Twenty years ago it is, since we treated with you [and] sold you our lands. It is because twenty years are nearly past to settle the business of those years that we are here. We expect justice from you. In regard to what you admonish us that we look to the interest of [our] children, we reply that is our design." Aasagan, Wawbegeeg, and other Anishinaabeg representatives deliberately took the United States to task for failure to fulfill

earlier treaty stipulations. Aasagan's hard-driving series of questions suggests that during the pre-council meetings in Mackinaw the *ogimaag* had asked him to be the heavy, to ask the questions that put U.S. representatives on the spot.[103]

Asagan, who knew the provisions of earlier treaties better than the government negotiators,[104] hounded Manypenny and Gilbert over the government's failure to make treaty payments, and its failure to appropriate money for schools and community improvements, medical care, and other concerns.[105] When Manypenny reacted to this negotiating tactic by threatening to close down the treaty council, Aasagan responded: "Father, you said to me the other day I was rather extravagant in my demands. You seemed to think me a glutton, never satisfied. Now I live only on corn soup at home & you have every luxury of life. It is strange that I should try to get as good as you!"[106]

The United States representatives came to the table in 1855 with interests that deviated far from the Anishinaabek. They wanted to establish a "civilization program . . . which did involve continued recognition of and services to the bands whose members were to be transformed into duplicates of White Christian farmers."[107] And they wanted to do so without incurring state government expense or burden, and without imposing any burden or disadvantage to non-Indians. George Manypenny wrote:

> Suitable locations, it is understood, can be found for them in the State, where they can be concentrated under circumstances favorable to their comfort and improvement, without detriment to the State or individual interests, and early measures for that purpose should be adopted.[108]

Indian Agent Gilbert seconded Manypenny's view, adding that the influx of non-Indian settlers would create conditions of extreme poverty for the Indians, leaving them to be "turned over to the State in the conditions of paupers and will be from year to year a continued source of annoyance to her citizens and expense to her Treasury."[109]

Manypenny's proposal for the treaty was the allotment of Indian lands in severalty, a policy that had recently come into vogue in Washington (at Manypenny's recommendation),[110] but had been around since the beginning of American–tribal relations. From the American point of view, allotment was a way to transform tribal Indians into tax-paying, Christian farmers.[111] However, the historical record is clear that Manypenny could not sell this idea to the Michigan Anishinaabeg—so he simply deceived them on a fundamental level. Moreover, he disregarded the demands made by the Anishinaabek completely, all the while negotiating with them over terms in apparent, but not actual, good faith.

The Michigan Anishinaabek came to the table requesting a permanent homeland,[112] just as they had in the 1836 treaty negotiations. Manypenny offered them allotment, a program in which lands in the public domain would be set aside in areas near traditional Anishinaabek villages and other landholdings.

Allotment was a complicated endeavor. The Anishinaabek heads of household could select parcels of this land at any time within five years and receive certifications, and then within ten years, they would receive patents from the government to prove that they owned their lands in fee simple absolute.[113] In theory, they could retain their interests in lands they already possessed and occupied in Leelanau County and on the east shore, and perhaps on Old Mission Peninsula as well. The new allotments would be in addition to these older lands. But from the beginning, there were problems. At Grand Traverse, "more than 25,640 acres of the 87,000 reserved acres were excluded from Indian settlement by federal laws before the Indians began to select land."[114]

Manypenny was negligent at best—and deceitful at worst—in explaining the legal ramifications of allotment. It is all but certain that the Indians came away from the 1855 treaty council believing that the new reservation lands would be permanently immune from taxation, creating a permanent land base for their communities. Manypenny, when confronted with the taxation question, answered that "'on the question of taxes' he was 'disposed to manage it for your benefit.'"[115] Richard White, for one, opined, "This certainly seemed a promise of exemption from taxation and thus a promise of special status for Indian lands."[116] It is certain that the Anishinaabek who heard Manypenny utter those words believed it to be a promise of tax exemption for all time.

Ironically, Manypenny and Gilbert hoped to use the new reservation lands to group the Anishinaabe bands closer together, so that they would be more accessible to missionaries and teachers, as a means of assimilation. Prior to the treaty negotiations, Gilbert wrote:

> [A new reservation] is the only plan offering any reasonable ground of hope for the improvement of this race in civilization—they are now scattered throughout the whole central and northern portions of the lower peninsula of Michigan

and cannot be effectively reached by teachers and missionaries unless they are colonized and have permanent homes with an interest in the soil.[117]

Instead of offering permanence, the vague allotment provisions offered more insecurity in both their terms and their implementation. While both the Americans and the Anishinaabek wanted to create a place for Indian people to live, allotment was a dramatic and tragic failure. Without a stable land base, federal government officials decided to withdraw many services and end the federal recognition of many Michigan tribes. In Richard White's words, "Cessation of services and the end of federal guardianship were exactly what Manypenny and Gilbert most feared and sought to avoid."[118]

Finally, the bad faith of the American treaty negotiators was demonstrated by the way in which pre-treaty annuity obligations of the United States toward the Michigan Anishinaabek were handled. The Anishinaabe negotiators were unanimous in asking the government to set aside the $200,000 remaining money owed to the Indians, allowing the bands to use the interest on the principal amount for current needs.[119] Manypenny and Gilbert appear to not have responded to these requests, but instead inserted Article 3 of the 1855 Treaty, which released the United States from any pre-1855 claims, without interpreting the provision to the *ogemuk*.[120] Andrew Blackbird would later claim the release was inserted fraudulently,[121] as would the *ogemuk* who signed the treaty.[122]

What is clear from the historical record of the 1855 treaty negotiations was that the federal government's negotiators came to the treaty council with a clear idea of what they wanted in the treaty, ignored most of the demands of the Anishinaabek while appearing to negotiate and compromise, and finalized the treaty by including little of the negotiated compromises. According to Richard White:

> Manypenny and Gilbert achieved three major American objectives: the elimination of perpetual annuities, the continued provision for governmental education programs and technical aid, and the selection of new reservations to be allotted in severalty. All Indian attempts to modify these basic provisions proved unsuccessful, although the chiefs did increase the amount of money they received and eliminated the tribal organization in favor of band organization.[123]

While the government negotiators knew what had been negotiated to a certainty, the Anishinaabek did not: "To the [Indian] delegates it seemed that the treaty had renewed their annuities, guaranteed their landholdings, quieted the last rumors of removal, and assured the bands' status as independent groups."[124]

It was not to be.

The United States made one more effort to negotiate a third treaty with the Grand Traverse Band, but the effort failed due to federal incompetence and pettiness. In 1864, treaty commissioners gathered in southern Michigan to negotiate new treaties, this time with each individual band as the 1855 Treaty had demanded. The commissioner of Indian Affairs responded favorably to Michigan Indian Agent D. C. Leach's request for a treaty council. Leach wanted to concentrate smaller bands on larger reservations; namely, one in Emmet County, the homeland of the Little Traverse Bay Bands of Odawa Indians. Leach succeeded in reaching the Isabella Reservation, where the Saginaw Chippewa Indian Tribe was located, but the winter set in, and the other treaty commissioner, Henry Alvord, could not travel north in the winter.[125] And, over the next two years, the federal government did not engage the Ottawa bands, who expressed hostility toward removing to one reservation, in treaty negotiations. In 1866, Grand Traverse, Little Traverse, and Cross Village Ottawas traveled to Washington for treaty negotiations, but they never occurred.[126] Over the next few years, various 1855 treaty tribes pressured the government for a treaty, but to no avail.[127] Eventually, in 1869, the commissioner of Indian Affairs wrote the secretary of the Interior to inform him that he would not seek a new treaty any longer, and any changes in federal Indian policy in Michigan should be concluded by Congress.[128]

Grand Traverse Band Villages (1860s and 1870s) and Tribal Leadership

The shift in the focal point of the Grand Traverse Band from Old Mission Peninsula to Leelanau Peninsula was completed by the end of the 1850s. Grand Traverse Band villages surrounded the area ostensibly reserved to the Grand Traverse Band Anishinaabek. They stretched from Leland north along the lake side of the peninsula to Northport, and then back down south on the bay side toward Suttons Bay. The villages were at Leland, Cathead Point, Northport, Omena, Eagletown, and Suttons Bay.[129] A separate group, headed by the aging Aishquagonabe, left Old Mission and returned to its roots on the east bay, probably at Elk Rapids within the east-bay boundaries of the 1855 Treaty reservation.[130] The south and western boundary village recognized as part of the Grand Traverse community was at Glen Arbor.[131] Peter Greensky, who had come to the Grand Traverse Bay as a federal blacksmith in 1846, returned to the region in 1859 to start a mission near what is now Charlevoix, the famed Greensky Hill Mission.[132] The *ogemuk* from the Waganakasing and Grand Traverse Anishinaabek communities often met at the Greensky Hill location, at the Council of Trees.[133]

As had been true during the negotiations of the 1836 and 1855 treaties, the leadership of the Grand Traverse Band community remained diffuse, and not centered around any one individual or even one village. In the 1860s and 1870s, there were as many as ten or eleven villages or bands, each with their own *ogemuk*.[134] Some *ogemuk*, such as Aishquagonabe and Aghosa, retained influence among the entire Grand Traverse community for some time after the 1855 treaty negotiations, and participated in a group that traveled to Washington in 1866 to discuss treaty concerns.[135] Kewaytosay, who perhaps succeeded Peshawbe as the leader of the Eagletown community, also traveled to Washington in 1866.[136]

But these *ogemuk* and their communities were not focused on exercising solely political power. In Richard White's words, the villages and their leadership remained primarily economic communities:

> The Ottawa bands that composed the Grand Traverse confederation were not purely political units. Their main function was economic: they were the bodies which organized and governed the winter hunting and trapping expeditions where each band possessed its own hunting territory. The persistence of band organization was inextricably tied in with the hunting and fishing economy.[137]

However, by the end of the 1850s, fishing and hunting were in decline due to overharvesting by non-Indian settlers.[138] As a result, the Grand Traverse Anishinaabek began to rely more heavily on the village communities that existed before the 1855 Treaty and the merging of some Indian villages with white towns.[139] Grand Traverse Band Anishinaabek began to identify as part of these villages, more than as part of a family identified with a particular *ogema*.[140]

The Failures of the 1855 Treaty

The failures of the 1855 Treaty started the day it was signed by the *ogemuk*, and conditions became worse from there. The renewal of treaty annuities the *ogemuk* demanded was written out of the treaty without tribal consent. The permanent homeland, free from state and local taxation, promised by the government was elusive. The continuation of a viable federal–band relationship would soon dissipate into the morass of "administrative termination." The federal government education and technical assistance would be replaced by a state government unwilling to provide adequate or needed services. By the 1970s, the Grand Traverse Band would be on its knees.

Meanwhile, the 1836 and 1855 Treaties paved the way for the establishment of the State of Michigan, and in many ways the state today looks the way it does because of these treaties and the federal and state policy that followed them. The 1836 ceded territory became the situs of some of the worst environmental degradation in American history—the deforestation of Michigan. The Michigan Anishinaabek would barely survive the century after the 1855 Treaty.

Adaptation of the Grand Traverse Anishinaabek to Changing Conditions

The clash of cultures that occurred in the traditional territories of the 1836 Treaty tribes in Michigan is captured, in many ways, by a statement made in a speech by a judge to non-Indians in Benzie County in 1902:

> It would probably be too much to say that the hopes & anticipations of the first settlers have been fully realized . . . but . . . we may well congratulate ourselves on the success attained. Then an unbroken and heavily timbered wilderness challenged the would-be settlers. . . . Now we see . . . broad fields of waving grain, valuable buildings scattered all over the land or grouped into flourishing and busy cities and villages, where the hum of machinery & steam whistles are heard instead of the dismal hooting of the owl or the weird scream of the loon.[141]

This is not what most late-nineteenth-century Indian people would have wanted to happen in their homelands.

Grand Traverse Anishinaabek continued to adapt to the increasingly disruptive presence of the non-Indians. The once open hunting territories began to close as the number of non-Indians increased, along with their slashing of the timber. Indian Agent E. J. Brooks described Anishinaabek living in 1877:

> They lead a nomadic life, subsisting largely by hunting and fishing. When they leave their homes on an expedition of this kind for the purpose of doing a few

days work to supply immediate necessities, the whole family goes together, a temporary wigwam is erected in which they all live, and while the husband is at work the wife and children subsist the family by picking and selling berries, fishing, or making baskets. . . . Most of them have small houses in the old Indian villages to which to repair during the fishing season for the double purpose of convenience and in order that the women and children may be on hand to clean and cure the fish. . . . About the first of March such of them as have been in the village return to their land to prepare for sugar making. Generally I think they remain on the land until about the first of June when summer fishing commences. During the summer they alternate between their fishing grounds and their farms.[142]

They once again modified their seasonal economy and lifeways by beginning to incorporate wage labor as an additional means of subsistence.[143] More and more Anishinaabek were forced to work, ironically, in the migrant lumber camps, contributing to the disappearance of the forests and hunting territories.[144] In Leelanau County, an Ottawa village appeared near the sawmill at Gill's Pier, and there were villages near sawmills at Suttons Bay, Northport, and Leland.[145] However, the Anishinaabek refused to clear-cut their own maple groves, as non-Indians suggested, preferring to save them for their children.[146]

Tragically, a smallpox epidemic at Peshawbestown in 1881–1882 killed thirty-two people.[147] After the local Indian agent accused the local non-Indian communities of quarantining Peshawbestown without adequate help, the *Grand Traverse Herald* opined with words that sound familiar to Indians all across the nation, and especially those Indians who were involved in the treaty rights fight: "The epidemic would only provide an excuse for the Indians 'to take all they can get and just as long as they can get it' from the county."[148] Twenty-five years after Peshawbestown had demonstrated prosperity, by 1889, the local paper described it as "a double line of houses in all stages of decay."[149]

Times were extraordinarily difficult for Michigan Indians during the last decades of the nineteenth century, and in 1885, Edward Allen, the commissioner of Indian Affairs, predicted that Indians would disappear from Michigan in fifty years.[150]

Of course, that would not be the case.

When Indian Agent Horace Durant prepared the rolls of Michigan Anishinaabek in 1908 and 1909, he found the same group of Grand Traverse Indian communities as had been there in the 1860s—Northport, Suttons Bay, Elk Rapids, Omena, Peshawbestown, Glen Haven—with the addition of Barkins Creek.[151] As the label on the Durant rolls and the letters from the *ogemuk* made clear, these villages had coalesced politically to consider themselves communities within the Grand Traverse Band of Ottawa and Chippewa Indians.[152]

CHAPTER THREE

The Story of the Dispossession of the Grand Traverse Band Land Base

The 1855 Treaty of Detroit intended to solidify the Anishinaabe land base did not help at all. In perhaps the worst case of mass fraud and incompetence in American Indian political and legal history, the Grand Traverse Band suffered the near-complete dispossession of their lands.

Anishinaabe Property Rights before the Treaties

The Anishinaabek of the Grand Traverse Bay region lived in a complex system of property and land use for hundreds of years before the negotiation of the first American treaties.

The origin story of the confederation of the several Ottawa villages with two Chippewa villages that would become the Grand Traverse Band of Ottawa and Chippewa villages is instructive. By the eighteenth century, the center of regional trading and Anishinaabe politics was the Mackinac Straits. During this century, the Ottawa and Chippewa informally divided the Lower Peninsula going north and south from Mackinac, with the Chippewa people staying toward the Lake Huron shore and the Ottawa people keeping to the Lake Michigan side. Mackinac would remain a critical summer village where Anishinaabe people and others might congregate for trade and for other reasons. At this time, the villages that would be affiliated with the Waganakising Odawak (the L'Arbre Croche people) and the Grand Traverse Band formed as this group of Ottawa people moved south.

There are two stories as to the possible reason for the placement of two Chippewa villages on the Ottawa side of Michigan. The first, and perhaps less likely, is that some Chippewas assisted the Ottawas who drove out the Mascoutens, who occupied the western half of the northern Lower Peninsula. The Ottawas who then occupied the region rewarded these Chippewas with rights to some territories there. The second story, retold by Andrew Blackbird, the leading Michigan Ottawa historian of the nineteenth century, is that a young Ottawa murdered a Chippewa at Mackinac. The Ottawas chose to avoid retribution from the Chippewas by offering territories in the Grand Traverse Bay region to the Chippewas.[1]

If nothing else, these stories demonstrate the link between politics and territory as to the Grand Traverse Band Ottawas and Chippewas. A brief recap of Anishinaabe land use and history detailed in earlier chapters is necessary here.

The Grand Traverse Bay Anishinaabe land-use patterns were seasonal. During the summer, the Anishinaabek would congregate in fishing and gardening villages along the coast of the bay and Lake Michigan. After harvest and before the snows, the Anishinaabek, dividing into smaller familial hunting units, would retreat inland to lakes and rivers in Michigan. Favorite places included the Manistee and Grand River valleys in mid- and southern Michigan. Many Grand Traverse people would travel by canoe to northern Indiana and Illinois. During the winter, the Anishinaabek would rely on stored vegetables and berries, and some hunting and fishing for sustenance.

In the spring, around early to mid-March, the Anishinaabek would begin returning to the bay area to harvest maple sugar. In March, the food stores would be at their lowest point, and maple sugar could become a major part of the Anishinaabe diet until the hunting and fishing season started in the latter part of spring. The favorite places for sugaring included the swampy lakes area on the east shore of the Grand Traverse Bay. During the sugar seasons, some summer villages that might otherwise be occupied most of the year could appear to be entirely abandoned.[2]

After the six- to eight-week sugaring season ended, the Grand Traverse Anishinaabek would return to their larger summer villages, where the hunting and fishing would begin, and the key crops would be planted for the summer. The summer villages would serve as a base for the summer, but the Anishinaabek would move around the Great Lakes region during this period. Many Indians would travel to favorite hunting, fishing, trapping, and gathering places in the region, while returning periodically to the summer village to tend to the gardens. At this time, the Grand Traverse Anishinaabek would engage in the dynamic and lucrative summer trading season based in Mackinac, but extending as far east as Montreal and as far south as Chicago. The Ottawa, in particular, were well-known as traders.

The governmental and property-rights structure at this time was based in the family or hunting units, and their respective territories.[3] Father Baraga wrote that "Each family of this tribe has a certain hunting region, to which the members of the family have a particular and exclusive right. Intrusions on these tracts are the most common source of disputes among the Indians, and sometimes also of bloodshed."[4] The leading family member of a particular winter village, the *ogema*, would be charged with protecting and enforcing the family's hunting, trapping, fishing, and gathering grounds, as well as sugaring grounds, in all seasons.[5] In the winter, the *ogema* would identify and protect the family's winter village. In the spring, the *ogema* would identify and protect the family's sugaring territories, but with the added cooperation and complication of other families who might share in the same territories.[6] In the summer, the *ogema* of the winter family might become the lead *ogema* of an entire summer village, or might not. The summer villages might include ten, twenty, or more families, depending on the size of the village. The lead *ogema* of the summer village—and there likely would be more than one—would be charged with defining and enforcing the property rights of the entire village, with the input and cooperation of the lesser family *ogemuk*. This head *ogema* would be charged with maintaining law and order, and has been referred to as a civil *ogema*. These summer villages are often described as "bands."[7]

The authority and responsibility of the family *ogema* is captured in the story of how one Grand Traverse region family's traps intruded on the trapping territories of another family, recounted by Henry Schoolcraft:

> Some years ago, a Chippewa hunter of Grand Traverse Bay, Lake Michigan, found that an Indian of a separate band had been found trespassing on his hunting grounds by trapping furred animals. He determined to visit him, but found on reaching his lodge the family absent, and the lodge door carefully closed and tied. In one corner of the lodge he found two small packs of furs, these he seized. He then took his hatchet and blazed a large tree. With a pencil made of a burned end of a stick, he then drew on this surface the figure of a man holding a gun, pointing at another man having traps in his hands. The two packs of furs were placed between them. By these figures he told the tale of the trespass, the seizure of the furs, and the threat of shooting him if he persevered in his trespass.[8]

This ended the dispute. Schoolcraft also described the authority of the *ogemuk*, as he understood it, in the context of a dispute involving an Ojibwe *ogema* from Sault Ste. Marie:[9]

> It is the rule of the chase, that each hunter has a portion of the country assigned to him, on which he alone may hunt; and there are conventional laws which decide all questions of right and priority in stalking and killing game. In these questions, the chief exercises a proper authority; and it is thus in the power of these forest governors and magistrates, where they happen to be men of sound

sense, judgement and manly independence, to make themselves felt and known, and to become true benefactors to their tribes.[10]

Peter Dougherty stated that the penalty for trespassing on another band's hunting territories could be severe:

> Each family has a certain hunting ground and trespass was in former times considered to be a sufficient cause for retaliation on the life of the trespasser. Now the one against whom the trespass is committed has the right to go to the lodge of the offender and take from him property to satisfy himself. In case of trespass by one tribe on the hunting ground of another tribe, the injured party sends a message to the other, and if satisfaction is not rendered it becomes a just cause of war.[11]

Francis Assikinack, an Odawa Indian from Drummond Island who lived at L'Arbre Croche at a young age, asserted that tribal sovereignty originates in these territorial boundary questions:

> Each of these tribes had to maintain a small sovereignty of its own and for its own use. The members of the neighboring tribes had no right to go beyond the limits of their respective districts on their hunting excursions, and encroach upon that belonging to others. Any hunter that was caught trespassing upon the rights of other tribes, or taking beaver in the rivers running through their lands, was in danger of forfeiting his life on the spot for his rashness.[12]

An *ogema*'s rights were not entirely personal. An *ogema* did not own property rights—but he held the property rights of his band in his name,[13] making it easy for Europeans to confuse an *ogema* with their own understanding of property owners.

Another critical element of tribal property rights, important to understanding the provision in the 1836 Treaty of Washington that reserved hunting and fishing rights, was that these property rights were not exclusive.[14] The *ogemuk* had authority to assign certain rights to use the land and its resources temporarily.[15] The violence that could be used to enforce tribal property rights was unusual; a more usual practice was to allow permission.[16] As a result, the territory property structure of the bands created a stable political and economic system well into the nineteenth century.[17]

In terms of international relations, the band political structure easily translated into a viable system for decision making. As the need arose, the summer village *ogemuk* would meet the other summer village *ogemuk* in the Grand Traverse region. There might be military threats from outsiders, such as possible war with the Haudenosaunees or a European nation, or a call for a treaty council with an outside power. The Grand Traverse *ogemuk*, representing each summer village, would meet collectively to discuss how to proceed. In rarer circumstances, the Grand Traverse *ogemuk* would meet in council with other Ottawa and Chippewa *ogemuk* from the larger Great Lakes region.

Negotiating for a Permanent Homeland: The 1836 Treaty

By the 1830s, the Grand Traverse Anishinaabek had participated in many treaty councils, all involving the cession of lands far away from the traditional home-lands of the Grand Traverse Band. But by the 1830s, the American government had come to power in the southwestern Great Lakes, including both the Lower and Upper Peninsulas in Michigan. Congress had authorized the creation of the Michigan Territory, which excluded the Upper Peninsula, but forced the Anishinaabek to acknowledge that American settlers were coming. By this time, much of the southern portion of the Lower Peninsula, as far north as the Grand River, was overrun by Americans. These Americans were clear-cutting southern Michigan with an eye to establishing farms and exploiting timber. Worse, the large confederacy of Indians—Anishinaabe and others—who had long resided in the Detroit area had been removed from there treaty by treaty, after the various disastrous military campaigns beginning with Pontiac's War in 1763 and continuing through the War of 1812. The Potawatomis of southwestern Michigan were under constant threat of removal. It was a bleak time.

So the Grand Traverse Bay *ogemuk* answered the call for a major treaty council in Washington, D.C., in 1836, with an eye toward creating a permanent homeland for future generations, and avoiding the fate of so many tribes in the eastern United States—removal to the west. Secretary of War Lewis Cass appointed Michigan Indian Agent Henry Schoolcraft to be treaty commissioner for the United States in these negotiations. Schoolcraft hoped to purchase the

Anishinaabe lands north of the Grand River, and as far west as the Marquette River in the Upper Peninsula.

The Grand Traverse *ogemuk* came away from the treaty council believing that they had created a permanent homeland of 20,000 acres to be located on the eastern shore of the Grand Traverse Bay, where Aishquagonabe's village was located. They also understood that the ceded territory of the Lower Peninsula remained accessible until the lands "were required for settlement." The *ogemuk* would have understood that "settlement" was decades into the future.

Henry Schoolcraft and the Disintegration of Federal Promises

Henry Schoolcraft took the 1836 Treaty as negotiated to the Senate, where it was unilaterally amended to cut short the permanence of the reservations to a mere five years, and to add monetary enticements to the Michigan Anishinaabek to remove to the west during that period. Schoolcraft successfully convinced the *ogemuk* to accept the newly amended treaty by confirming that the Anishinaabek would be free to continue using the ceded territories as before until "settlement."[18]

Of the reservations promised in the 1836 Treaty, the only reservation actually surveyed and declared was that of the Grand Traverse Band. Schoolcraft sketched a rough map of what he understood to be the bay, with the common error of assuming the eastern shore was actually the "north shore." He placed a rectangular box on the "north shore" to signify the Grand Traverse Reservation. But Schoolcraft did not send surveyors north until 1837, and they did not reach the Grand Traverse Bay for two more years.[19] By then, the center of the Grand Traverse Anishinaabe polity was the Point, now known as Old Mission Peninsula.[20] This place was where the Chippewa *ogema* Aghosa kept his village, and where Rev. Peter Dougherty had located his mission. With Dougherty's prodding, the Grand Traverse *ogema* informed Henry Schoolcraft that they had selected Old Mission Peninsula as the location for their reservation. The General Land Office in Washington declared the peninsula and a smaller parcel on the eastern shore as the Grand Traverse Reservation.

But the five-year time frame in the 1836 Treaty added by the Senate, set to expire in 1841, implied that the declaration of the Washington, D.C., land office meant little to the Grand Traverse Anishinaabek if the federal government was going to proceed with forced removal to the west. Uncertainty reigned in the 1840s as rumors and threats pervaded the entire Michigan region. While the

Old Mission Indians proceeded to populate the peninsula and elsewhere on the bay, developing a broad agricultural base and establishing a strong and livable community under the terms of the 1836 Treaty, they also saved their treaty annuity payments for the day when they feared the government would close down the reservation and terminate the community.

Finally, in the late 1840s and early 1850s, many Grand Traverse Anishinaabe families purchased land in Leelanau Peninsula and on the eastern shore of the Grand Traverse Bay in an attempt to acquire some security in their land holdings, with the hope of acquiring a permanent land base. Of course, over time, these lands would be taxable by the state and local governments, and subject to possible alienation. The hope for a permanent homeland would require a new treaty.

By the mid-1850s, much of the Old Mission Reservation had been abandoned by the Anishinaabek, who left behind large fruit orchards.

The 1855 Treaty and the Failure of Allotment

The Michigan Anishinaabek came to the 1855 treaty council in Detroit with the hope of securing a permanent homeland in Michigan, and of acquiring guarantees that the United States would not seek to remove them to the west. However, as with the 1836 Treaty, the Anishinaabek would come away with the understanding and belief that they had indeed secured a permanent homeland,[21] only to be deceived and defrauded by the federal government on that question.[22]

The federal government treaty negotiators, Commissioner of Indian Affairs George Manypenny and Michigan Indian Agent Henry Gilbert, came to the table with the expectation that there would be new reservations set aside for the 1836 Treaty tribes, but that these reservations would be established through a process called "allotment." Allotment was a mechanism that Manypenny believed would help to force the Anishinaabek to become Christianized farmers, based as it was on agriculture and private property ownership. If perfected, the allotment process would be the equivalent to a permanent homeland, perhaps, in the mind of the government treaty commissioner Manypenny. However, rather than creating a smooth transition from an inalienable reservation to an allotted reservation, the federal government officials who implemented Manypenny's vision created a bureaucratic and cultural horror for the Grand Traverse Anishinaabek and other Michigan Indian communities.

It is difficult to describe with accuracy the extent of incompetence and criminality that pervaded the implementation of the 1855 Treaty at Grand Traverse. At every step along the path of the treaty language relating to the establishment of the Grand Traverse Reservation—*at every step*—federal government incompetence and criminality, coupled with private or individual criminality, served to deprive the Grand Traverse Anishinaabek of what they had negotiated for in good faith. Since records are spotty—and because abuse of federal and state legal process was part and parcel of the criminality—there is no way to detail each case of incompetence and criminality. But the evidence that is available paints an appalling and shocking picture.

The 1855 Treaty established a complicated means for the Grand Traverse Anishinaabe to acquire land. First, the government officials would create four lists of eligible Anishinaabek by July 1856. The lists would include heads of household, single males over twenty-one, and two classes of orphan children (single, or more than one sibling). In the treaty, the government had set aside an area, for a five-year-period, in the Grand Traverse Bay region—the northern two-thirds of Leelanau County and a portion of Antrim County—within which each of the persons on the various lists could select 80 acres. Once the eligible Anishinaabek selected their parcel and took possession, they would receive a certificate from the federal government indicating that the parcel would be held in trust by the federal government for the benefit of the Indian person. These certificates would be inalienable. Then, at the expiration of ten years, the government would issue a patent to the landholder, who then would acquire the land in fee simple absolute.[23] Despite these promises, the federal government did not allow the Grand Traverse Anishinaabek to complete their selections until 1871, ten years later. Some band members received their patents in 1872, and a few others in 1875 and 1876.[24]

The first complication in the treaty was the fact that much of the land set aside in the treaty for the Anishinaabek to select under the allotment process was already occupied by squatters, or claimed by railroads, such as the grant to the St. Mary's Canal Company.[25] Moreover, many acres of lands set aside went to the State of Michigan under the federal Swamp Act, which reserved "swamp" lands to states.[26] Over 26,000 acres reserved under the 1855 Treaty were already excluded by federal laws.[27] And according to Richard White, "In 1859 officials at the General Land Office estimated that of the 102,645 acres reserved for the Ottawas and Chippewas that they had examined, prior claims existed for 35,695 acres."[28] That acreage likely was 19,584.[29] Sadly, the federal officials interpreted the treaty to allow these prior claims to trump the Indian claims. In this way, much of the reservation land described in the 1855 Treaty was illusory, creating a possible legal claim for reformation of the treaty to meet the expectations of the Anishinaabek and the United States.

The next instance of betrayal was the diminishment of the reservation on the Leelanau Peninsula by the Senate to exclude Northport.[30] The Senate took this action, and other actions like it, around the 1855 Treaty territories in Michigan, due to political favoritism. Coupled with this unilateral amendment of the previously negotiated reservation boundaries was the Senate's failure to promptly ratify the treaty. It was not until September 10, 1856, that the President finally signed the treaty.[31] By that time, some deadlines in the treaty had passed and others were fast approaching.

The next round of incompetence, and perhaps even criminal corruption, was the failure of successive Michigan Indian agents to compile the four lists of Anishinaabek who would be eligible to select lands under the terms of the treaty. The agent was obliged to complete the list within one year of the signing of the treaty, that is, in July 1856. Michigan Indian Agent Gilbert did not even appear in the Grand Traverse Bay region to draft the lists until July 1856, the same month the treaty promised the lists would be complete.[32] Grand Traverse Band Anishinaabek made their selections quickly and the agent forwarded their selections to Washington in April 1857, but the first lists generated by the Indian agents contained incorrect land descriptions.[33] The national office would send the lists back to the agent for correction, but by then Agent Gilbert had been replaced by a new agent (who did little to correct them), and then by a second agent, D. C. Leach, who did nothing at all.[34] Time passed—years—without any effort to correct the lists.

Eventually, the government demanded that Leach start over. And it was not until June 1863 that Leach finally prepared a new list and sent it to Washington. This list was also horribly flawed, and its corrections were not hammered out until February 1866. Once again, this list excluded selections made by many Grand Traverse Anishinaabek.[35] The final list used by the federal government was so far from complete as to be laughable, if it were not so catastrophic. It is very possible that the various Michigan Indian agents (starting with Henry Gilbert) who generated these lists had some personal financial stake in the lists. Worse, the considerable delay—which can be attributed to federal official incompetence—allowed time for American squatters to begin to crowd out the Anishinaabek on land that was supposed to be reserved for Indian use only. Between 1844, when the first American squatter arrived,[36] to 1865, over one hundred non-Indian families settled on the Grand Traverse Reservation.[37]

Moreover, some Indians who represented the interests of land speculators in Chicago and elsewhere made selections far in excess of their allowed 80 acres, with the illegal compliance of federal officials, only to immediately turn those selections over to the land speculators. Indian agents alleged that they had interpreted the 1855 Treaty to allow Indians to select more land only if every eligible Indian had already done so,[38] but "eight young men from the Grand Traverse bands—Francis Blackman, John Aghosa, Peter Nawnebowe, Mitchell Negawnesay, John Eaton, Mitchell Francis, Lorris Remicum, and John Remiswamishkang—succeeded in purchasing 12,000 to 16,000 acres of reservation lands at the Grand Traverse land office."[39] Agent Smith described what Blackman and Aghosa told him they did:

> The lands purchased by them were not purchased for themselves nor for Indians but for whitemen who furnished the money and paid for the lands—that they signed a good many papers for plenty of lands and for doing which the whitemen paid them some money as well as their expenses.[40]

Agent Smith had heard of these frauds and reported them to Washington in August 1865, after which the federal government suspended all entries at Grand Traverse.[41]

Lumber interests also used fraud and theft to exploit the timber resources at Grand Traverse. By 1869, timber theft on Indian lands was widespread.[42] On occasion, lumber speculators paid Canadian Indians to impersonate Michigan Indians and sell timber rights, or bought timber rights from Indians who held a trust certificate but no patent, meaning they had no authority to sell those rights yet.[43]

Moreover, the *ogemuk* wanted to include a list for the male children of the heads of household—that is, the next generation of Anishinaabek. The number of years that passed from the signing of the treaty to the time that the federal government issued patents to Grand Traverse Indians—sixteen—meant that many Grand Traverse Indians who were very young in 1855 had grown to full maturity.[44] The 1855 Treaty did nothing for these young people, creating a great deal of concern for the Anishinaabek.

The next major stage of official incompetence and public and private criminality is even more complicated. During this stage, Anishinaabek who were eligible to select land parcels could go and select their lands. At that point, the federal government should have recorded that selection and issued an inalienable certificate to the Indian landholder. The problems generated from the previous stage carried over here, as many Indians who were indisputably authorized to make a selection were not allowed to do so. Indians who did make selections would be forced to travel a distance to record those selections and receive a certificate. This process was a miserable failure for many Indians, who never received a certificate for various reasons.

Moreover, the *ogemuk* who negotiated the treaty had received some assurance from George Manypenny that their lands would remain immune from taxation. This was a critical component of the treaty negotiations, as the *ogemuk* sought tax immunity for their lands as a means to secure a permanent homeland. But local governments taxed Indian lands anyway. Richard White wrote:

> In August of 1866 Whites stopped Grand Traverse members living around Bingham, Michigan from voting because the Indians had become dissatisfied with tax assessment procedures and decided to vote against the assessor. Obviously taxes were already being levied against lands owned by members of the Grand Traverse bands; just as obviously the Indians believed these taxes to be discriminatory or even illegal. A few years later, Agent James Long protested against the taxation of Indian lands since most Indians had never received patents for these lands. . . . The Indian reaction to the situation was most often a refusal to pay taxes. In 1880 Agent George Lee reported that only about 12 percent of the Indians in Michigan actually paid the taxes on their lands. The result was widespread loss of Indian lands to the counties because of the tax delinquency.[45]

Unfortunately for the Grand Traverse Anishinaabek, the 1855 Treaty is silent as to taxation of the lands. With the exception of the original trust period, which made clear the inalienability of the lands,[46] the treaty as drafted by Manypenny apparently does not contain the assurance that Manypenny agreed to with the *ogemuk*. It may be that Manypenny did not intend to include the language as he had promised to the *ogemuk*, indicating that he committed an act of simple fraud. However, the omission of the tax immunity language, or other language that would guarantee a permanent homeland, may have been inadvertent, which means that the 1855 Treaty could be reformed to include such language.

Yet another stage of incompetence and criminality occurred in the issuance of patents at the expiration of the trust period for the initial selections. Once again, the problems of previous stages carried over into this stage. In short, by the time the government issued patents, to far too few eligible Indians, the process had become so corrupted by incompetence and illegality as to be a sad, twisted joke.

Even the issuance of patents and certificates did little to grant security to the Grand Traverse Anishinaabek. The means by which non-Indians acquired the land interests of the lucky Anishinaabek ostensibly protected by the 1855 Treaty, whether protected by a certificate or a patent, were nothing short of brilliant and barbaric.

From time to time, the federal government delayed the process in order to study the problems or to use the time to correct some problems, but these delays did nothing to solve any of the problems. In 1877, the government sent E. J. Brooks to investigate land frauds as a special agent.[47] In January of that year, Michigan Indian Agent George Lee, who was already investigating land frauds, extended his investigation to Grand Traverse, where he found forty cases of fraud in the Grand Traverse Land Office alone.[48] Tellingly, non-Indians in the region complained that the federal government should not investigate land frauds in Michigan because the Indians there were state citizens and therefore not subject to federal supervision.[49] In all, the investigations uncovered only a tiny fraction of the likely criminality, and in the end, nothing came of it.

It would become apparent to all the parties involved in the treaty implementation that either a new treaty or congressional action would be required to correct the failures of the 1855 Treaty itself, and of its implementation. Federal officials hoped for a new treaty to solve the lands-dispossession problem, and delayed allotment hoping for authorization, but it never came.[50]

Land speculators pressured Michigan and federal officials to conclude the allotment process and free up the remaining Grand Traverse Indian lands for public sale. Michigan's congressional delegation pressured the secretary of the Interior to validate non-Indian land acquisition on the reservation, while the Michigan legislature passed a resolution urging the same.[51] Michigan lawyers and judges advised the Michigan Indian Agent James Long that they would recognize all of the land transactions dispossessing Indians of their lands, regardless of the federal opposition to such transactions.[52] The pressure worked, and in 1871, the federal government resumed the process of allotting Indian lands.[53]

In April 1871, the 1836 Treaty tribes petitioned the government not to issue patents for lands bought by Indians acting on behalf of non-Indian land speculators:

> [Such purchases] were made by a few of our young men . . . against the wishes of us all . . . in the interest of the speculator, comprising thousands of acres of the most valuable land on our reservation which we had hoped to secure by homestead or entry for our young men who have become of age since the time of making selections.[54]

The government failed to heed this petition. Agent John Knox met with the Grand Traverse Indians at Northport that fall to finalize the patent list.[55] He forwarded the concerns of the Grand Traverse community about the young adults to Washington, but he added arguments favoring the issuance of patents to the non-Indians who had already settled on the Grand Traverse Reservation in violation of the treaty.[56]

On June 26, 1872, the government issued 290 patents to Grand Traverse Indians and delivered them on August 6.[57] However, the number of patents issued was far less than the number of Indians who had selected lands under the treaty, and did not include the young adults.[58] Indian Agent George Betts estimated that there were at least one thousand certificates generated by the agency for which no patent had been issued.[59]

Local officials seemed to want the whole process to end as soon as possible, to the benefit of the non-Indians.

The Remedial Statutes and the Federal Government's Betrayal

With the ongoing failure of the United States to enter into new treaty negotiations, the Michigan Ottawa tribes, including the Grand Traverse Band, began to look to federal homestead laws to resolve the land question.[60] Homestead laws allowed American citizens to select lands in the west, technically owned by the United States government (usually ceded by Indian tribes in a treaty).

The individuals would then use the land for some purpose, usually agriculture. After a period of time, the government would sell the lands to the individuals for a tiny amount. While this theory had merit for the Anishinaabek in Michigan, federal officials declined to allow most Indians to take advantage of these laws. And when Congress did allow Indians to apply for homestead lands, they lost them anyway.

Instead, Congress chose to enact three pieces of legislation as a means to "correct" the 1855 Treaty implementation problems. And so, in 1872, 1875, and 1876, Congress took action, but it appears that Congress passed these statutes as a means of ratifying the illegality that had taken place.

The first statute, enacted in 1872, was titled "An Act for the Restoration to Market of Certain Land in Michigan."[61] Section 2 of the statute authorized Indians who had reached adulthood since the 1855 Treaty to select lands—in addition to other Indians who were otherwise entitled to select land but had not done so yet—for a mere six months after the enactment of the statute.[62] Section 3 ratified the settlements of "actual, permanent, bona fide settlers"—which would by its terms exclude land speculators and others not actually residing on the land.[63] The first clause in section 4 directed the secretary of the Interior to issue patents to Indians who had made selections and received trust certificates in accordance with the 1855 Treaty.[64] The second part of section 4 ratified the purchases of lands made by non-Indians that did not conflict with the selections made by Indians in accordance with the treaty.[65] Section 5 opened up the unsold and unpatented lands on the reservation to public sale at the expiration of six months.[66]

The 1872 Act was deficient in several ways and, like the 1855 Treaty before it, was implemented in the worst way possible for the Grand Traverse Anishinaabek. First, the statute did very little to cancel the fraudulent acquisition of lands by non-Indians and land speculators. In fact, despite vague language, it was interpreted by non-Indians to be a clear ratification of their illegal acquisitions.[67] Second, the statute did little for Indians who had trust certificates for lands that a non-Indian or a land speculator had illegally acquired. Third, as Secretary of the Interior Columbus Delano reported in 1873,[68] many Indians had made selections that were not "reported or recognized as valid" by federal officials, even though they were legitimate, because of the incompetence of federal officials.[69] Fourth, the statute offered no relief to married women who had come of age since 1855.[70] Moreover, "imposing cultural standards of residence and use designed for White farmers on the Indians was both inherently unfair and a fecund source for later controversy."[71] Finally, there simply was not enough unoccupied land on the Grand Traverse Reservation to satisfy the unmet needs of the Anishinaabek.[72]

The government incorrectly implemented even the specific and clear terms of the 1872 Act. Despite the six-month waiting period of the act, non-Indians began to encroach on Indian lands even before the end of 1872.[73] In January 1873, the secretary of the Interior suspended some of the provisions of the 1872 Act—provisions that would have created intratribal conflict—but did nothing about white depredations.[74] Congress might have intended to enact a statute to remedy the situation on the ground, but the federal officials in Michigan would not or could not help Indian people.

Additional legislation followed. In 1874, the House of Representatives drafted Bill 1700, which would authorize the secretary to issue patents to an additional 320 Indians who had certificates, and allow Indians who had reached the age of maturity since the 1855 Treaty to make selections of land for one year.[75] This bill passed in 1875, authorizing the issuance of patents to 320 Indians and opening up the remainder of the reservation for one year.[76] Once again, the 1875 Act did nothing to resolve the problem of fraud and other illegal land transfers, and many other Indians holding valid certificates did not receive a patent.[77] In 1876, Congress extended the homestead period indefinitely.[78]

The 1875 Act and the 1876 Act, both requiring that Indians follow American homesteading laws, generated yet another round of fraud, often consisting of non-Indians claiming that Indians had abandoned their lands, a typical challenge under homestead laws.[79] Agent George Lee claimed to have discovered forty cases of fraud in February 1877, writing:

> I have given in the foregoing list only a few of the numerous complaints in this Grand Traverse District, of these people who have been thus driven from their homes. They can be deprived of their land, but they cannot except by force be driven from the Neighborhood. It is the home of their Childhood, and their parents and Grandparents, before them. It is robbery and cruelty in the extreme, and the greatest mistake our government has made in their case, was the opening of this reservation to the occupation of white settlers.[80]

Forcing Indians to comply with the rules of American homestead laws was deeply unfair, as was requiring the Anishinaabek to resort to non-Indian legal processes in order to contest the land fraud. According to Richard White:

The Indians were vulnerable under the Homestead Act because the act set strict requirements as to how long the claimant had to live on the land during the years before he or she received title. Whenever Indians left their homes for hunting or fishing, work, or to spend part of the winter in one of their old villages, Whites would claim the land had been abandoned. E.J. Brooks, the special agent sent to assist Lee in investigating land, explained why Indians could rarely successfully contest these claims.

> These Indians are very poor. They reside 75 to 150 miles from the local offices. A contest with them implies not only the fees of the officer in the case but the transportation of themselves and their witnesses to the office and their support during the hearing and also the pay of an interpreter, an expense which the major portion of them are entirely unable to meet. I am of the opinion that the knowledge of this fact has induced a contest against an Indian claimant in several cases where the contestant would not have thought of contesting a white.[81]

Grand Traverse Anishinaabek, as well as other northern Michigan Indians, attempted to maintain a modified form of their economy (as practiced in the 1840s and earlier) during this period, further prejudicing them under the homesteading system, which rewarded large-scale, American-style agriculture. Indian Agent Brooks reported that these Indians showed no interest in American-style farming, but instead sought "a place on which to make sugar in the spring, raise a few potatoes and sufficient corn to supply their bread during the year, and to have a home upon which they may at any time return."[82] Grand Traverse Anishinaabek retained their summer homes at villages in which Indians had purchased lands prior to the 1855 Treaty.[83]

Non-Indians also resorted to many other fraudulent tactics to deprive Indians of their homestead lands, according to the Lee and Brooks investigation. Brooks referred to a "class of sharks" who would get Indians drunk and then have them sign over their lands.[84] Other non-Indians tricked Indians into mortgaging their land, with the money due during a time of the year when the non-Indian knew the Indians had no cash.[85] Agent Lee's investigation revealed another tactic of selling sewing machines and parlor organs to Indians on credit, with their lands used as collateral:[86]

Designing Agents have been among them selling cheap sewing machines and Parlor Organs, articles for which they have no use, and taking in payment mortgages on their lands many times the value of goods sold in confident expectation, as is almost invariably the case, that the Indian will fail to meet the payment and thus forfeit the land.[87]

Some family-owned and operated stores in Suttons Bay and Northport were adept at obtaining Indian mortgages and then foreclosing on them.[88] Yet another tactic was for a non-Indian to offer to purchase a small amount of timber on an Indian's land, then inducing the Indian landowner to sign a contract purporting to be for the sale of the timber, but which was actually a warranty deed for the land.[89] Finally, patents owned by Indians would simply be stolen by non-Indians and then assigned to a white man, sometimes with the consent of the Indian agent.[90]

The remedial statutes enacted by Congress did little to benefit the Grand Traverse Anishinaabek. In the end, non-Indians continued to resort to the same acts of fraud and intimidation to exploit Indian people.

Termination and the Dispossession of South Fox Island

The story of the dispossession of Indian lands on South Fox Island occurred during the first half of the twentieth century. South Fox Island has long been an important place for the Grand Traverse Band Anishinaabek, serving as a haven for fishing and trading canoes.[91] Grand Traverse people also used the lands for gardening and for gathering important plants and other materials.[92] Indians would typically live there in the summertime, and spend their winters on the mainland.[93]

In 1847, when the first American surveyor visited South Fox, he found no one there at the time, and so the government opened up the island for sale.[94] Mormons and others moved onto the island, but by 1860, they had abandoned it.[95] Other non-Indians attempted to live there over the next several decades, but the only permanent residents were the lighthouse keepers and their families.[96]

By the turn of the century, "Grand Traverse Band members secured nineteen public domain homestead allotments on South Fox Island."[97] In the early 1880s, a smallpox epidemic in Peshawbestown had claimed the lives of dozens of Grand Traverse Band Anishinaabek, and so some families moved to South Fox Island as early as 1881.[98] Other families followed in the years to come. It is likely that these families claimed the lands in accordance with the remedial acts of Congress from the 1870s, discussed above, and in 1862 and 1884 statutes.[99] A total of twenty-two Grand Traverse Band members selected lands on South Fox, with nineteen completing the homesteading process in some fashion.[100]

During the first half of the twentieth century, federal officials properly exercised their obligation to protect the Anishinaabe homesteads on South Fox Island. In 1919, for example, federal investigators confirmed trespasses on South Fox and pressed for monetary damages.[101] In 1922, after Leelanau County added the homesteads to its tax rolls, the government ordered them to be removed.[102]

In the 1930s, though, with the downturn in the American economy, the South Fox Anishinaabek spent more and more time on the mainland for economic reasons.[103] Lumbermen then petitioned the federal government to remove the trust status of the lands so that they could extract the timber on South Fox.[104] In the 1940s, federal officials began to recommend that the South Fox homesteads be sold.[105] However, the government also knew that the original homesteaders had walked on, and they needed the permission of the heirs to sell the land.[106] The government under the Roosevelt and Truman administrations did not pursue the sale option, but with the advent of the Eisenhower administration's embrace of the "Termination Policy" in 1953, everything changed.[107]

And so in 1953 and 1954, the United States sold eleven of the fifteen homesteads to Sterling and Eva Nickerson, and four homesteads to others, who likely sold them to the Nickersons.[108] One trust patent remains to this day unaccounted for and may still be owned by the heirs of the owner William Shawawabenesey.[109] However, in at least two instances, the government sold the lands without *any* of the owners consenting to the sale.[110] In the case of the other sales, the government sold the land with the consent of *some* of the owners, but not all.[111] In legal terms, this is referred to as a "Secretarial transfer" of Indian lands, and is almost certainly illegal.[112]

According to James McClurken, who researched the history of the Grand Traverse Anishinaabek on South Fox Island:

> The events by which the United States conveyed title to the South Fox Island
> trust properties took place less than fifty years ago. The events are still fresh in
> the memory of living Grand Traverse Band members who were directly involved
> in the search for heirs and know that their parents and grandparents refused to

sign away their title claim to the South Fox Island homesteads. John Bailey's mother was an heir to South Fox Island property. He reported that she refused to sign her consent, saying:

> They had a fear of the government coming back and taking something, or more, and then they. . . . She said whatever the amount of money was, that they were talking about, her and my dad, was not enough to even bother about it. Was one of the comments. Now, I don't think it said anything in the letter about money. It might have, but they were talking about it not being worth the effort and then even if she did consent and send in the form, she'd probably never get the money anyway. So, the old story about waiting for Indian money, was one of the things that was a factor in her decision not to send it in. Because she said it probably wasn't a significant amount or it wouldn't amount to much anyway. They'd probably never get it anyway. So.
>
> I know they didn't send it in. She didn't sign it and they put it away. Fact is, I do recall the letter was around the house for probably a couple of years before it might have finally got thrown out or just disappeared or whatever, but I know they kept it for awhile. But, they never sent it in.

Eva Petoskey, a descendant of Jeannette Oliver, the wife of Benjamin Ance, actually owns the letter that her mother received from the Bureau of Indian Affairs regarding an heirship claim on the Sam Bird homestead. The letter gave heirs thirty days, "[to] show cause why the rejection of the application of Sam Bird should not be made final and the case closed." Although Eva's family members who received this letter were literate, they did not know what the letter meant or why they received it. They do know that the federal government passed title to the Bird homestead to others; they received a check for approximately five dollars in payment for their property. A bureau official hand delivered a similar letter to the home of Eva Petoskey's uncle, Jay Oliver and his mother Isabelle, seeking consent for sale of a second parcel the family claimed on Beaver Island. The story of Isabelle's reaction to the letter is still told in the family. Eva retold the story, saying:

> There is a story that my Uncle Jay Oliver would tell about. . . . this occasion. An Indian agent from Ashland actually came here to . . . Charlevoix. I don't know what they were doing over here. If they were in the business

of terminating people's land rights or whatever, but they made a trip over here. The person from the bureau went to see my grandmother, Jay's mother, who was Isabelle Willis originally, but is Isabelle Oliver when they came to see her. It seemed to me that that was more related to the parcel on Beaver Island. That they were trying to . . . this was in the 50s also . . . that they were trying to get her to relinquish that parcel because she was probably one of the few people still living that had some direct connection there. Her and her children as descendants of Joe Oliver. Jay said she listened for about twenty minutes and then she threw the man out.

She [Isabelle Oliver] was a tiny little woman, but she went on a tirade I guess and said, "Don't ever come here again." You know, I don't know what she. . . . I wish I could have been there. She threw him out of her house and said, you know, "Don't ever come back. You know, we've all suffered enough injury and if you think I'm going to relinquish anything, you're crazy." Basically, that's what the tone of the conversation was. She threw him out. I often wonder well, maybe that's why [the Oliver Allotment on Beaver Island] that's still a U.S. Government lot, because they didn't get anywhere. She never signed anything. She wouldn't take money. She wouldn't take anything, she just threw them out.

Darrel Wright, grandson of Emaline Ance, the daughter of Benjamin Ance, acknowledges that his mother signed the sales consent form during the 1950s but alleges that she was misinformed about the meaning of the document she signed. Wright said:

What they swapped mostly was the selling of their timber out there. Most of them signed contracts to sell their timber. A lot of them, when they signed the contract, didn't know what they were signing. They also signed the land away.

But, I find out now, they weren't supposed to do that. You know, that was trust land. I think my mother might have signed one of those deals. But you know all she got for her tract was $1500. So, I . . . when I saw the price, what she got, I thought, "Well, that's alright for the timber, you know." But when I heard she might have signed something to give away her land, I didn't think that's great, you know. So, that's when I started checking in to could they do this to her, you know. I'm hearing now that no, they couldn't have done this to her. But that remains to be seen.

Wright, like many other Grand Traverse Band members call for a reinvestigation of the legitimacy of the South Fox Island land sales. The emotion with which Wright and other modern Grand Traverse Band members speak of this issue is a sign of their continuing sense of ownership and cultural ties to South Fox Island.[113]

On South Fox Island, there remains a cemetery of Anishinaabek remains on the homestead owned by the Alex Cornstalk family until 1955.[114] David Johnson, a non-Indian land developer, purchased the lands around that homestead in 1989 and now forbids Grand Traverse Band members to visit the cemetery.[115] Again from Dr. McClurken:

Every family who lived on the Island during the late nineteenth and early twentieth centuries left the bodies of their relatives in the South Fox Island Cemetery. They visited their ancestors graves freely until David Johnson bought South Fox Island property in 1989. Johnson prohibits Grand Traverse Band members from crossing his property to the cemetery. Descendants of the people buried there resent his actions and are seeking to restore their access to the South Fox Island and its spirit inhabitants. Darrel Wright said:

> [M]y biggest thing . . . I can't say it's my biggest, but it's a big thing . . . I want to be able to have access to that cemetery. I think that's my right because I have somebody buried there. I don't think he should be able to prevent me from going there. Right now, he is. That's what started it all. When I took everything to the tribe and says, "Can you help me? Can you do something? I want to go out there."

Rose Ogemagegedo echoed Wright's sentiment, saying:

> I really don't know what's going on about how they're . . . you know, how they . . . who owns it or anything, but it behooves the people, who have ancestors buried there, to do something and to keep that cemetery so that they can travel back and forth to visit it. . . . the cemetery should be able to be opened to the ancestors, or to those that are living, you

know, so that they can visit it . . . so that they don't trap it in there, you know, trap them . . . trap it . . . I feel like they're trapped. You know? I don't know. So. I said a . . . I did say a prayer to free the spirits, which I don't understand, but that was a prayer that just come out when I was praying. So, at the fire, that I was able to do that.

These are statements of people who still feel an ownership of South Fox Island. Theirs is an ownership beyond that of legal land title. They own a stake in the Island's inhabitants and culture in history and in the present. . . .

John Bailey focused specifically on the continuing relationship between Grand Traverse Band members and their relationship with ancestral spirits, saying:

Well, I think that there ought to be some considerations in this development of the island of . . . of course, not only the environmental, but the cultural. There's people buried out there yet. I did visit that cemetery. I left tobacco when I was out there. Probably some of my ancestors, my mother's side, lived out there . . . buried out there I should say. You can see the remnants of the village yet. I think that ought to be preserved for future generations. It's be nice if we could even do a little bit of building out there and commemorate that with a plaque and maybe a shop or something, just to let people know that this is where we lived. This is how we lived in this Great Lakes Region. That they. . . . Maybe 100 years . . . 200 years from now, anthropologists will say, "Well, the Ottawa and the Ojibwe and the Potawatamie, the three fires, lived here, but they've since disappeared." Like the Hopewell and the Mound Builders, all those groups, they say, "They disappeared." But I think we're still their descendants. Our technology changes over time. I think that's what they fail to understand, that when our technology changed, we changed, our modes changed, how we lived. But we are still here. We haven't disappeared. I think if we keep that history alive for our descendants, or grandchildren, I think they'll be appreciative of that as well.

Eva Petoskey also focused her comments on the Island's physical environment—on the quietness and distance from the mainland culture that Grand Traverse Band members have valued for generations. Like John Bailey, Eva Petoskey sees protection of the island as a critical component in the Grand Traverse Band's effort to preserve the Band's access to the spirits of their traditional cosmos. She said:

> I would have liked to have seen the tribe own all of the stone circle on Beaver Island, all of . . . South Fox, and to build places there where people can go and enjoy the land where some of the natural habitat is undisturbed, the plants, and the animals, and even the shoreline, because we need that. Even to go and spend time there . . . even if you go and just walk around if you don't do anything. But ideally, even to have spiritual retreat places for people to visit so people could have solitude, a place to camp, or to go on a vision quest. Now, if people want to go on a vision quest here, it's pretty hard to find a space. So, not too many people are doing it. I mean, I know people who have gone out and camped right out in the middle of the circle as part of the vision quest. But, even there, you've got a road going up and down. So, the loss of place and, you know, of place of solitude is much greater . . . is huge because of the lost opportunity to learn about the . . . ability to develop that relationship with the plants and the animals and a spiritual relationship with the earth, which is really part of our culture. I don't mean that in a philosophical way, it really is. If you had someone like my grandfather. . . . If you really talked to him, I'm sure, you know. . . . He could swim like that because he had a deep appreciation for the fish. There was a relationship there. There . . . there's so much like that, that we don't fully understand because most of us haven't lived like that. We can't quite grasp the depth of the relationship. I think the farther and farther we get away from that, you know, the greater the losses. . . . I don't advocate that we all move out there and live like we used to, but we need to have that in our lives today and everyone benefits. . . . Certainly [at] South Fox, there's an opportunity to set some of that land aside for everyone to appreciate and have available to them. Certainly, I would hope that some land could be set aside for people who wanted to do vision quests and retreats, spiritually. So they could do it out in a place that was appreciated by our ancestors. You know, in the old days too. . . . Jay [Oliver] told me. . . . they saw it not only to cut wood there, but even in the generation before that [they] kind of sought sanctuary out there because of all of the efforts even toward removal and certainly

toward . . . assimilating us . . . all becoming farmers. So, a lot of people sought sanctuary out on Beaver and the Foxes and Garden Island. In a sense of wanting to continue their lifestyle that was so rapidly changing on the mainland.

The Grand Traverse Band's claims to South Fox Island are unlike those that any other group of people can raise. The non-Indian population of the Grand Traverse Bay region, or of Michigan in general, can raise issues of environmental degradation and perhaps issues over land title. The Grand Traverse band can raise both of these issues as well. No other group of Michigan citizens has a longer continuous record of using and preserving the natural resources of South Fox Island than do members of the Grand Traverse Band. On the issue of land title, they have federally preserved legal claims to Island properties to adjudicate for heirs of homestead owners who once occupied South Fox Island. No other group, however, can claim a long historical and cultural tie to the spirits who inhabit the Island. This cultural property, handed down to them from their ancestors is one that cannot be bought or sold, but it is one valued as highly as the fish in waters surrounding the Island, the land title, and the valuable plants on South Fox Island. Spiritual properties of South Fox Island, though imperceptible to the broader Michigan population, are real relationships that members of the Grand Traverse Band of Ottawa and Chippewa Indians . . . hope to preserve for future generations.[116]

In late 2001, the Grand Traverse Band sued David Johnson and his company Mirada Ranch, as well as the Michigan Department of Natural Resources.[117] The DNR owned about half of South Fox Island, and David Johnson and his company owned most of the rest. They proposed swapping lands on the island as a means of consolidating properties, which the DNR asserted would increase access to the public lands. But Johnson and his company had a long history of developing pristine northern Michigan lands, making him a millionaire. And there was significant evidence that Johnson intended to develop South Fox Island as yet another of his profit-making properties. He had already added a small runway to the island. Tribal people believed Johnson was going to destroy South Fox Island for the Anishinaabek.[118]

Unfortunately, the lawsuit failed to prevent the transfer. In 2002, Judge Thomas G. Power declined to prevent the transfer, citing permissive state laws allowing and encouraging these kinds of transfers. Sadly, to this day, Grand Traverse Band Anishinaabek cannot visit the graves of their ancestors because of David Johnson's personal control of access points to the cemetery.[119]

The Indian Claims Commission Cases

In 1946, Congress passed the Indian Claims Commission Act, which created a commission of non-lawyers to judge the merits of Indian land claims, treaty claims, and various other claims.[120] The act required tribal claimants to prove a continuing or long-standing aboriginal right to lands that had been ceded to, or taken by the United States before the commission would recognize compensable tribal rights to the land.[121] In the Great Lakes region, where the Haudenosaunee people had invaded in the seventeenth century, displacing dozens of tribal groups, including the northern Michigan Anishinaabek, proving this historical nexus was no simple feat.[122] Northern Michigan Ottawas filed at least two major claims before the Indian Claims Commission. The first was dismissed on procedural grounds. The second resulted in a settlement award from the United States.

On August 22, 1949, Robert Dominic, on behalf of the Northern Michigan Ottawa Association and others, filed a claim under the Indian Claims Commission Act of 1946, *Dominic v. United States*.[123] In this claim, Dominic and his co-petitioners asserted the right to file a claim on behalf of the Ottawa tribes that signed the Treaties of August 3, 1795; July 4, 1805; November 17, 1807; September 29, 1817; and August 29, 1821. However, each of these treaties had been executed by Ottawa Indians residing in southeastern Michigan, northern Ohio, and scattered other areas far south of the northern Michigan region. William Vernon Kinietz testified that the Ottawa bands did not hold to a single leader, as each band had its own leadership.[124] As such, the Indian Claims Commission dismissed the claim.[125]

However, Dominic also filed claims under the rubric of the Ottawa and Chippewa Indians of Michigan under the 1836 Treaty—claims that eventually reached a successful conclusion in 1968. In 1959, the commission agreed that the various Ottawa and Chippewa bands that executed the 1836 Treaty were jointly and severally entitled to whatever rights or award the commission would recommend to Congress.[126] For whatever reason, the commission did not pass upon the damages phase until 1968, where it concluded that the 1836

Treaty–ceded territory had a fair market value of $10,800,000 on March 28, 1836.[127] After some procedural wrangling and the taking of additional evidence, the commission recommended a final award of $10,109,003.55 in 1972.[128]

Since the only federally recognized Indian tribe in 1972 that was a signatory to the 1836 treaty was the Bay Mills Indian Community, it was not until 1997 that Congress appropriated money to pay the judgment.[129]

The Preserved Land Claims

Many individual and tribal land claims remain preserved as listed in the *Federal Register*. How these claims have been identified and preserved is an important story.

In the late 1970s, the federal government asked Michigan Indian Legal Services to research and prepare a list of potential land claims that might arise out of the 1836 and 1855 Treaties relating to the dispossession of the Grand Traverse Band's lands.[130] After years of attempting to complete the research, federal government officials informed MILS that it no longer had funding for continued research on the fishery claim, and would not respond to requests for information on potential land claims.[131] Meanwhile, the federal statute of limitations on these claims was set to expire at the end of 1982.

In late 1982, the Native American Rights Fund sued Interior Secretary James Watt on behalf of the band and several other tribes. The Grand Traverse Band tribal council enacted a resolution that identified two classes of potential claims that it believed existed, and that it believed the federal government was obligated to prosecute: the loss of treaty fishing habitat and land claims exceeding 10,000 acres.[132] In *Covelo Indian Community v. Watt*, the plaintiffs claimed that the secretary had failed to prosecute the land and treaty claims of the tribes and of individual Indians, and that the federal statute of limitations on these claims was set to expire on December 31, 1982.[133]

The court agreed with the plaintiffs, and ordered the secretary of the Interior to either file land claims on behalf of the tribes or seek legislation from Congress extending the statute of limitations.[134] And so Congress extended the statute of limitations for these kinds of cases indefinitely.[135] In March 1983, the federal government published a list of potential land claims that are preserved under the 1982 statute.[136] Despite their listing, the United States has not made any effort to prosecute the claims.

In 2007, the Grand Traverse Band tribal council passed a resolution formally requesting the United States to take action on these land claims.[137] Representatives of the Grand Traverse Band, led by chairman Robert Kewaygoshkum, personally presented the resolution and request to United States Attorney General Alberto Gonzales on August 14, 2007, but still the government has taken no action.

CHAPTER FOUR

The Story of the Federal Recognition of the Grand Traverse Band

T he story of the federal recognition of the Grand Traverse Band of Ottawa and Chippewa Indians begins with the end of treaty times, when
federal government bureaucrats, including the secretary of the Interior,
practiced a policy that would later be called "administrative termination"—where
federal officials illegally refused to acknowledge the government of the Grand
Traverse Band beginning in the 1870s. No act of Congress, no treaty, and no
agreement—nothing—authorized this action. And yet it was sufficient to deprive
the Grand Traverse Band community of its bargained-for trust relationship
with the United States for over one hundred years. Perhaps in large part due
to the egregiousness of administrative termination, the Grand Traverse Band
became the first Indian tribe to be formally acknowledged by the Bureau of
Indian Affairs's administrative recognition process in 1980.

Federal Government Recognition of the Grand Traverse Band in Treaty Times

The United States' dealings with the various Indian political units during the mid-nineteenth century, when the two major treaties involving the
Grand Traverse Band were signed, were very complicated. The Anishinaabek

understood their political authority and often tried to explain it to the baffled Americans, who just wanted one big tribe and a few big leaders with whom to negotiate. But Michigan Anishinaabek politics were not so simple. As the *ogemuk* and their speakers explained, again and again, the combined Ottawa and Chippewa "Nation" did not exist as a viable political unit. There were two different "tribes," Ottawa and Chippewa, who really were peoples grouped by language and culture. These "tribes" elected speakers during treaty negotiations to represent them *in their language* only. The most significant political unit in treaty negotiations, from the point of view of the Anishinaabek, was the regional confederacy of villages. Hence, the treaty signatories on each treaty are differentiated by region: the Grand Traverse Bands, the Little Traverse Bands, the Grand River Bands, and so on.

Henry Schoolcraft, the Michigan Indian agent from 1822 to 1841, understood the political structure of the Anishinaabek enough to know that the regional confederacy was the key political unit for dealing with outsiders, such as in a treaty negotiation, but that the real political power lay with certain important village *ogemuk*. At Grand Traverse in 1838, for example, Schoolcraft knew that Aishquagonabe was the most visible and respected *ogema* in the region, followed by his nephew Aghosa. For this reason, he sent Peter Dougherty to these men first to secure a mission in the Grand Traverse Bay region.

George Manypenny and Henry Gilbert took extra time to learn this political structure during the 1855 treaty negotiations, but they did eventually learn. They agreed in the treaty to dissolve the organization known as the Ottawa and Chippewa nation or tribe, a legal fiction, and to deal with the regional confederacies—often called bands—from then on. And these men, and their successors, did so for a decade or more after the ratification of the 1855 Treaty.[1]

Michigan Indians as Michigan Citizens

In 1850, the State of Michigan amended its constitution to include a provision that would create unintended complications for the Michigan Anishinaabek. The constitution of 1850 extended state citizenship and voting rights to Anishinaabek, provided that they were "civilized male[s]" and "not a member of any tribe."[2] According to Richard White, "In 1860 the Attorney General of the State of Michigan would argue that the framers of the constitution intended to enfranchise only this mixed blood, nontribal population [living apart from Indian villages], not the entire Ottawa, Chippewa, and Potawatomie population of the state."[3] The language of the provision, using the words "civilized" and invoking tribal membership, could reasonably be read in the 1860s to draw the line in the way the state attorney general argued. But the provision usually would be interpreted in ways that would be much more detrimental to the Michigan Anishinaabek.

While the 1855 Treaty dissolved the fictional Ottawa and Chippewa nation, it was most certainly intended to preserve the political status of the various bands. The 1850 Michigan constitution complicated that intention. One area of complication was voting. Right away, Henry Gilbert, the Indian agent, organized and encouraged Anishinaabe voting in state elections, while others sought to keep the Indians out of the polls. Both used the treaty documents and the language of the constitution to support their arguments about the eligibility of Indian voters.[4]

These same arguments would also be used to set the stage for the administrative termination of the Grand Traverse Band and other bands.

Administrative Termination

The federal government's schizophrenic treatment of the Grand Traverse Band after the 1855 Treaty led to the administrative termination of the band as a federally recognized tribal entity, as those terms are now understood; but the government would also continue to recognize and classify the tribe and its members in different and conflicting ways depending on the political interests of the various government officials involved. Moreover, the government extended many federal services to half-blood Michigan Anishinaabek during this time.

The focal point of this federal policy was American citizenship, as complicated by the 1855 Treaty and the 1850 Michigan constitution. No act of Congress granted or extended American citizenship to Grand Traverse Band Indians in the nineteenth century, and so federal officials would not recognize them as American citizens, even if they were or could be citizens of the State of Michigan.[5] As such, one federal official ruled that Indians who were party to the 1855 Treaty could not be drafted during the Civil War. After the Civil War, in 1871, another government official opined that Michigan Indians were not citizens and therefore not eligible to secure lands under federal homestead laws. In 1872, the secretary of the Interior opined that Michigan Indians *could* secure lands under federal homestead laws because the tribal organization of the Ottawas and Chippewas had been dissolved under the 1855 Treaty—the first major federal action using this misinterpretation of that provision, ironically attempting to benefit the Anishinaabek.[6] But in 1875, the General Land Office opined in the opposite direction on the same question.[7]

It is useful to note that the 1872 opinion of Interior Secretary Columbus Delano, while ignored by other agencies in the federal government and even contradicted by Congress the same year in the first of the remedial acts,[8] became the touchstone for federal officials for nearly 108 years.[9] In 1887, for example, Indian Agent Mark Stevens propounded the same theory, arguing that state citizenship was equivalent to the termination of federal supervision.[10] In Richard White's words:

> Despite the weakness of their premises, opinions such as Long's and Stevens' would gradually pervade the Bureau [of Indian Affairs]. A quick and superficial reading of the Treaty of 1855 seemed to support the belief in the dissolution of all Ottawa political organization, and no one within the Bureau investigated the matter much further. Bureau officials apparently never consulted the minutes

of the treaty council which made the actual meaning of Article five, the clause that dissolved the Ottawa and Chippewa Tribe (not the bands themselves), quite clear. As a result, the belief in the dissolution of the bands took on a legitimacy within the Bureau that it never deserved.[11]

More discussion of Delano's opinion is required.

On March 27, 1872, Secretary Delano wrote from Washington, D.C., to opine on the status of the Grand Traverse Band of Ottawa and Chippewa Indians, and other bands that had executed the 1836 and 1855 treaties. He was called to interpret a provision in the 1855 Treaty that stated, "The tribal organization of the said Ottawa and Chippewa Indians, except so far as may be necessary for the purpose of carrying into effect the provisions of this agreement, is hereby dissolved."[12] Did this mean the Ottawa and Chippewa *ogemuk* had agreed to abandon their tribal relations upon the completion of some of the terms of the 1855 Treaty? Secretary Delano believed it did.

It is important to note the context of the request for the Department of the Interior's opinion on the status of the 1855 Treaty signatories. The request came from the Mackinac Agency at a time when the process for the establishment of a tribal land base was about to be complete. But the process had been a terrible failure. In Delano's words at the beginning of the letter:

> Under the treaty provisions, allowing Indians to purchase lands additional to their individual selections, a large amount of land has been entered but ... that *the entries were made in the interest of white men*, [and] they have been suspended by order of the Department. ... Since the ratification of the treaty, *a considerable number have come of age and are heads of families and are without legal homes.*[13]

The Mackinac Agency had asked Delano for an opinion about whether the Ottawa and Chippewa Indians who had been unable to acquire land under the 1855 Treaty were citizens of the United States. If they were American citizens, then these Indians could acquire land under other federal statutes called Homestead Acts.

Delano wrote that in order for the Ottawa and Chippewa Indians to be American citizens, they must have abandoned their tribal relations. In order to reach the conclusion that the Michigan Anishinaabek could take advantage of the Homestead Acts, he wrote that the 1855 Treaty had terminated the tribes:

The fifth Article of the treaty referred to expressly provides that—"The tribal organization of said Ottawa and Chippewa Indians except so far as may be necessary for the purpose of carrying into effect the provisions of this agreement is hereby dissolved."

Upon full payment being made tribal relations will be terminated.

The inquiry which I have presented, involves a consideration of the civil status of Indians after all tribal relations are dissolved. Are they citizens of the United States and as such entitled to share in the public lands?

I think they are. . . .

These Indians were born in the United States. They therefore come within the [Fourteenth Amendment] provid[ing] they are "subject to the jurisdiction thereof."

While tribal relations exist they are not "subject to the jurisdiction of the United States," because they are "domestic dependent nations." . . . When the reason for the rule ceases the rule itself ceases. When the nationality ceases, then the consequences which have sprung from such nationality cease.

When tribal relations have been dissolved *with the consent of the United States*, then there is no longer any dependent nation, and those who composed it are merged in the mass of the people of the United States and subject to its jurisdiction. . . .

My conclusion is that when an Indian tribe is dissolved and all tribal relations with it ended, and this done with the consent of the United States, then the members of such tribe become *ipso facto* citizens of the United States, and, as such, entitled to all the privileges and immunities of such citizens.[14]

Secretary Delano, despite his good intentions, was almost certainly wrong on a number of points, but the most important point involved the "tribal organization" of Ottawa and Chippewa Indians that signed the 1855 Treaty. This "tribal organization" was purely a legal fiction. As the United States had done in innumerable other instances, its treaty negotiators needed to find a tribe with which to treat. With tribes that had a clear military or political leadership, usually tribes with which the United States was at war, there was a recognized tribal political entity to sign the treaty. But the Ottawa and Chippewa bands were not at war with the United States, nor was there an obvious dominant political leader that satisfied the American treaty negotiators. As the Indian Claims Commission noted in 1958:

But each [Ottawa and Chippewa community] has been divided into separate
units, groups, or bands, acting autonomously and independently of any central
authority. Each separate unit was early identified with its geographic location,
and the United States has dealt with such separate units as political entities,
particularly with respect to land purchases. Since time immemorial it has been
a common custom among each of these units to confer membership upon those
individual Indians residing with any one band or group. A permanent change of
residence from the land of one band to that of another constituted a corresponding
change in membership and an abandonment or waiver of right to participate in
property or other rights of the group or band, in which membership was formerly
held. In like manner, and through intermarriage, members of one nationality
were readily adopted into bands of another.[15]

The very fact that dozens of Ottawa and Chippewa leaders signed the 1855 Treaty
demonstrates that the United States knew that there was no one leader or even a
small group of leaders with authority to bind all of these tribal communities. The
"tribal organization" created for purposes of negotiating and signing the 1855
Treaty might "dissolve," but the actual Indian political communities—including
the Grand Traverse Band—would not.

In short, the intended meaning of the treaty provision dissolving the "tribal
organization" was nothing more than to require a new kind of negotiation in
the event the United States or the tribes chose to amend the treaty terms—a
tribe-by-tribe negotiation instead of an omnibus tribal treaty negotiation. A
January 29, 1869, letter drafted by the Commission of Indian Affairs demonstrates
that the United States government knew the difference:

The Ottawas and Chippewas have for several years been anxious to make some
new arrangement whereby they can procure allotments of land for their children
for whom no provision was made by the treaty of 1855, which omission they say
was an oversight. The same oversight occurred in the Treaty with the Chippewas
of Saginaw, Swan Creek and Black River of August 2, 1855 which was remedied
by the Treaty with these Indians of October 18, 1864. This desire on the part of
the Indians seems but just and proper, but in as much as the terms of the 5th
Article of the Treaty of 1855, dissolves the tribal organization of the Ottawas
and Chippewas, negotiations with them can now only be had by said Article,
therefore, should it be determined to accede to the wishes of the Indians in

this respect, it is suggested that this end can be more readily accomplished by Congressional enactment than by treating with the numerous bands of these Indians, and certainly with far less expense to the government.[16]

In 1878, federal official E. J. Brooks, an Indian agent appointed to study the land frauds occurring under the 1855 Treaty,[17] further reported that the Anishinaabek did not consider the 1855 Treaty to be a termination treaty:

> It is without doubt the fact that at the date of the treaty the Indians had no conception of the position in which they were placed by the dissolution of their tribal relations. I know that they accepted the conditions and obligations of citizenship reluctantly and even now many among them claim that the constituted authorities have no jurisdiction over them.[18]

In 1886, Mark Stevens reported that the Michigan Anishinaabek continued to appoint *ogemuk* to conduct all tribal business, despite being considered tribes that had abandoned their tribal relations by the government.[19]

From the 1870s on, the communities of Ottawa and Chippewa Indians living in the Grand Traverse Bay region continued to band together for political, economic, and family reasons. But the federal government generally refused to assist the community in preserving its land base and in improving living conditions on the grounds that the trust relationship between the United States and the tribe had been severed.

The Durant Rolls and the Annuity Distribution of 1910

Of note, the Grand Traverse Band participated in the treaty annuity judgment distributions of the first decade of the twentieth century that led to the creation of the Durant Rolls of 1908 and 1910. For years prior to the distribution, James M. Paul of Omena took several trips to Washington, D.C., to argue for it.[20] In 1900, several Odawa *ogemuk* visiting Washington learned that the 1855 Treaty obligated the federal government to pay treaty annuities that, by the turn of the century, had accumulated to $538,400.[21] Since the United States refused to pay on the theory that the Michigan Anishinaabek nations had been "dissolved" by the treaty, the Indians sued the government in 1905.[22] The lawsuit was settled, with the government agreeing to pay the Ottawa tribes in Michigan $131,000, to be divided up per person.[23] Prior to the settlement in 1905, the government sent Charles McNichols to determine how many Indians would be beneficiaries of a settlement, expecting a few hundred Indians at most; McNichols found thousands of eligible Indians and gave up.[24]

The government then sent Henry Durant to prepare a new roll of Indians eligible to receive the distribution by band in 1908 and 1909.[25] His instructions were to enroll "the Indians that are found to be living in tribal relation[. T]he certificate of the chief or head men of a band is to be accepted by you as prima facie evidence of the right to enrollment of any Indian belonging to such a band."[26] Durant noted the continued importance of traditional tribal leadership in the form of *ogemuk* as he responded to their opposition to enrolling descendants of certain "half-breeds" on the 1870 roll.[27] Grand Traverse *ogemuk*, unlike others, sought to include these descendants.[28] The commissioner of Indian Affairs recognized that the Anishinaabek still considered their *ogemuk* to be the proper representatives of the community:

> [Durant's] reports show that the various Indian communities and groups still recognize chiefs and headmen and to some extent have maintained their tribal organization notwithstanding the treaty of 1855 by which such organization was to be dissolved.[29]

Still, the government refused to agree to the requests of the Grand Traverse *ogemuk*, recommending that Durant exclude the contested descendants.[30]

During this period, the presence of the Grand Traverse Anishinaabek was surprising to the non-Indians living in the region. In 1910, when many Anishinaabek traveled to Traverse City for the distribution:

> Whites viewed them as exotics. Residents of Traverse City crowded the payment office, gawking at the Indians, acting, as Charles Dickson, the distribution agent, said, "as though they had never seen an Indian before." The curiosity was hardly friendly. Dickson's wife told a reporter:
>
>> We found the worst conditions in Michigan. There is more prejudice against these people in Michigan that in any state we have been in and it is senseless.[31]

The experience of the Anishinaabek during the Traverse City annuity distribution was terrible in other ways as well. The Indians had little money to pay for travel, and they were forced to wait for days for the payments to arrive, losing the remainder of their funds on lodging and food expenses. Two Indians died in a train accident along the way.[32]

The 1910 distribution marked the beginning of major changes in northern Michigan Anishinaabek economics and politics. The timber industry, upon which many Grand Traverse Anishinaabek depended for wages, was at last sputtering to a halt in Antrim and Charlevoix Counties.[33] By the 1920s, Grand Traverse Anishinaabek no longer could rely on the industry that exploited and destroyed the precious northern Michigan forests, and many Indians were forced to become migrant wage laborers.[34]

Early Attempts to Secure Federal Recognition (1930s)

Richard White reported that during the Great Depression of the 1930s, neither the federal government nor the State of Michigan nor the local units of government would take any action to assist the Grand Traverse Band Anishinaabek.[35] Leelanau County relief agencies discriminated against Indians, and federal employment was unavailable.[36]

By 1939, Peshawbestown was the largest Grand Traverse Band community, with forty or more families, but delinquent tax payments had undermined the security of the village, according to Richard White.[37] Aghosatown (now Omena) numbered six families, seven families lived in Traverse City, and another eight families lived in the Elk Rapids and Kewadin area.[38] Other than four Kewadin families—"advised" by Ben Mamagona, who had purchased land and ran successful farms—the Grand Traverse Anishinaabek were all but destitute.[39]

The people of the Grand Traverse Band believed that the enactment of the Indian New Deal, often called the Indian Reorganization Act or the Wheeler-Howard Act,[40] would allow the tribe to reorganize into a tribal government that the United States would recognize. The act allowed Indian tribes to organize as a constitutional system of government, with optional corporate charters to be sued for economic development purposes.[41] Grand Traverse *ogemuk* and tribal members wrote to John Collier, the architect of the Indian New Deal, on August 22, 1934:

As members of the Ottawa and Chippewa tribes of Indians of the State of Michigan, we gratefully petition you for help on behalf of the Wheeler-Howard Bill.

Since the majority of parents and children of the above named tribes have attended and depended for an education on our Government school at Mt. Pleasant, Mich. which is now abolished we ask,

(1) An educational system be established for our younger generation where-in they may have the privilege of a professional or business education as well as the grade schools.

(2) That communities be established for self government, where in we might be self supporting and respectable citizens. These communities being provided with homes, farm lands suitable for raising corn, potatoes, truck garden and fruits, horses, milch cows and poultry.

(3) That we have access to timber and lakes for fuel, fishing and hunting.

(4) Where in we may be provided with a central meeting place for socials, churches, public schools, social service from the U.S. Government, hospitals with professional and other necessary equipment for caring of our sick, crippled, blind and needy members.[42]

Other Michigan tribes, including the Little Traverse Bay region Odawa community, did the same.[43]

As if in a "cruel joke,"[44] the regional federal Indian officers at Tomah Agency in Wisconsin first began to secure options on 7,000 acres of land in Emmet County for the benefit of the Grand Traverse Band Indians and the other Ottawa bands, expecting the federal government to allow the tribe to reorganize under the act.[45] Frank Christy, the superintendent of the Tomah Indian Agency in Wisconsin, wrote:

If the Indian Re-organization Act is to fulfill its primary purpose—the rehabilitation of Indians in need of such rehabilitation—its provisions should be extended to Indians such as these Ottawas and Chippewas. Certainly there are none in more need of economic rehabilitation.[46]

In 1935, Christy and M. L. Burns drafted a plan to assist the Michigan Anishinaabek:

Elk Rapids, Traverse City, Northport, Brethren, Honor, Hart, Pentwater, Muskegon—Location of a large community of Ottawas, drawn from the points listed above and from other outposts of the tribe, at Peshawbytown on Suttons Bay. Acquisition of land necessary for subsistence farming, fruit raising (this is a cherry district). Small canning factory; purchase of facilities for commercial fishing.

A fact which so persistently came to the attention of your representatives during the survey is the rapid disappearance of the black ash from which most of the Indian baskets are made. This was taken up with the American Legion representatives who indicated their intention of taking up with the State Department of Forestry the matter of reforestation for their essential source of raw materials upon which many of the Indians depend for ready cash.[47]

The hopefulness and optimism of Christy and Burns's plans faded over time. By 1938, Christy informed the tribe that Congress had not appropriated money for the purchase of the requested land:

Only one individual raised the question of land and this was answered with the statement that Congress had failed to appropriate an adequate amount of money for the purchase of land for those already organized, and it was believed that our office could do more for them at this time by interceding where necessary with county and state officials where relief and emergency work was needed, that appropriations under the Indian Reorganization Act were not being made by Congress in amounts called for by the Act, and that it would probably be some time before additional groups could be assisted to any great degree under the Act.[48]

Burns and Christy later turned to a plan to purchase land in the Upper Peninsula for the Anishinaabek, and then operate Civilian Conservation Corps camps around the land. But the Lower Peninsula Michigan Indians had no wish to abandon the villages of their grandmothers and grandfathers, so the plan went nowhere.[49]

John Collier's letters to Robert Dominic of Cross Village and to Ben Shawanesse demonstrated the lengths to which the government had to go to deny reorganization to the Grand Traverse, Little Traverse, Grand River, and other Ottawa bands.[50] The letter to Shawanesse offers a definition of federal recognition that appears to be written in such a manner as to exclude the Michigan Ottawa tribes:

A recognized tribe is one with which the government at one time or another has had a treaty or agreement or those for whom reservations or lands have been provided and over whom the government exercises supervision through an official representative.[51]

It was true, Collier had to recognize, that the Michigan Ottawa tribes had been treaty signatories, and even that the tribes had reserved lands under the two treaties, but the last phrases in the definition excluded the Anishinaabek. There was no federal official on site to "supervise" the Indians. Of course, none had been provided for, requested, or needed in the 1855 Treaty.

Around the time of the enactment of the Indian New Deal, there was conflict in the Grand Traverse Bay and Little Traverse Bay regions, as was true on many Indian reservations nationwide,[52] over whether the tribe should organize under the act. Father Aubert, a Catholic priest working out of Petoskey, rallied against the Indian Reorganization Act (IRA).[53] He formed the Michigan Indian Defense Association, hoping to earn federal recognition under this entity.[54] But, according to Richard White: "After being informed that such an organization would not be eligible for federal recognition under the IRA, Aubert apparently saw the IRA as a threat both to his own assimilationist beliefs, and to his influence and that of the Michigan Indian Defense Association."[55] His activities created a kind of split between the Ottawa groups, with Ben Peshawbe being the leader of the group supporting the Indian New Deal.[56] The Grand Traverse Anishinaabek, not succumbing to Fr. Aubert's influence, forwarded their petition for reorganization to Washington over Aubert's objections.[57]

John Collier, after meeting with Ben Peshawbe in the fall of 1935, ordered a series of public meetings to be held in the Michigan Ottawa communities.[58] Meetings between federal officials and the Ottawa communities took place in March 1936 at Petoskey, Suttons Bay, Cross Village, Manistee, Muskegon, and Grand Haven.[59] Fr. Aubert appeared at three of these meetings in an attempt to disrupt the proceedings, although he appeared to have little impact.[60] However, contemporaneous memoranda drafted by M. L. Burns suggest that federal officials continued to misunderstand the 1836 and 1855 treaty organization, and the terms of the treaties themselves.[61]

In May of 1937, regional Bureau of Indian Affairs (BIA) officials met to discuss the Michigan Ottawa petitions, and formally agreed not to "proceed to enroll and organize these Indians until such a time as the Federal Government was ready to follow through on a comprehensive program of rehabilitation."[62] But the government did nothing. Within the federal government, perhaps only Peru Farmer, who had visited Peshawbestown in 1938, knew the real situation there. He objected to John H. Holst's report, but to deaf ears.[63] In May 1940, John Collier formalized the decision not to extend the benefits of the Indian Reorganization Act to the Michigan Ottawa and Potawatomi tribes.[64]

There were some heroes during these dark times. Emelia Schaub, the first female Leelanau County prosecuting attorney,[65] wrote a letter in March 1937 to Eleanor Roosevelt seeking relief for the Leelanau Indians:

> Many of them cannot earn their own living; they find it particularly difficult to get work with equal pay . . . and they have not adjusted themselves readily to civilized life and many will never be able to do so. . . . May I ask you to assist us by urging the Department of Interior or the Re-settlement administration to formulate some plan to rehabilitate these Indians, some program specially suited to the problems of the American Indian, he must have a special program as he cannot take care of himself.[66]

Assistant Commissioner of Indian Affairs William Zimmerman responded to Schaub's letter by arguing that the Michigan Indian problem was peculiar, and that the federal government was not eager to assist:

> Although a way has been opened to us to extend aid to Indians who, as in Michigan, have not in recent years been under Federal jurisdiction, we are not anxious to assume responsibility for Indians who have adapted themselves in anything like an adequate manner in their present communities. For this reason, it seems best not to make a blanket policy with each group as its legal status and economic needs require.[67]

In other words, since the government had ignored the Michigan Ottawa communities for so long (illegally) and this inaction had created such hardships for the Indians, for that reason the federal government would refuse to assist.

In 1935, Frank Christy himself would begin to oppose reorganization for the northern Michigan Ottawa tribes because he believed they were too poor for federal help, or perhaps too assimilated into American society.[68] Moreover, in a letter with Orwellian overtones, he worried that state and local governments would end whatever government services provided.

> I have consistently maintained that it would be unwise for the Indian Service at this time to make any gestures that might be interpreted as evidence that it

was about to assume responsibility for the welfare of these Indians. At present local and State municipalities regard them in the same light as other citizens and extend to them without discrimination all the advantages in the way of direct relief, employment relief, and health facilities that are enjoyed by other citizens of a similar economic status. In my judgment it would be exceedingly unwise to disturb this arrangement until and if the Indian Service is prepared financially and otherwise to assume full responsibility for them. Naturally the local county and township governments while under present conditions they are willing to discharge their responsibilities toward the Indians, would welcome the opportunity to transfer responsibility to the Federal Government.[69]

This letter is a complete turnaround from Christy, who only a year earlier agreed that the Michigan Ottawas needed the benefits of reorganization as much as any tribes nationally. He touts the state and local government services to Indians while ignoring the reality on the ground, as expounded by Emelia Schaub, that there were no state and local services benefiting the Anishinaabek. In 1937, BIA anthropologist H. Scudder Meekel studied the Michigan Indian situation and reached the same conclusion as Christy, that reliance on state and local government services was the best bet for the Anishinaabek.[70] Part of this federal policy position came from the 1934 transfer of the Mt. Pleasant Indian School to the State of Michigan.[71]

Richard White reported that in 1938 in Peshawbestown, nearly everyone was out of work, only two out of thirty remaining families had members employed in federal works programs, and only two more received state and local relief.[72] County old-age-assistance programs often denied assistance to Peshawbestown elders.[73] Peru Farver, the Tomah Indian Agency superintendent, visited Peshawbestown in July 1938 and concluded that county authorities discriminated on a massive scale against the Anishinaabek.[74]

The Grand Traverse Band's pursuit of federal recognition hit a dead end when the Office of Indian Affairs commissioned John H. Holst, supervisor of Indian Schools, to report on the demographics of Michigan Indians in 1939. In the survey, Holst repeated the recommendation that non-recognized Michigan Indian tribes were better off non-recognized, so that they would be eligible for state and local services.[75] Holst concluded that around 1812, Michigan "tribal organizations crumbled never to revive again."[76] Holst perpetuated the myth that the Michigan Ottawa tribes had self-terminated in accordance with the terms of the 1855 Treaty. Finally, he wrote that "the Indians of lower Michigan have gone far in the way to effective assimilation."[77]

However, as the Grand Traverse Band's petition for federal acknowledgment filed in 1979 demonstrated, Holst's conclusions were utterly false. Eleesha M. Pastor of the Michigan Indian Legal Services, the primary author of the petition, wrote:

> One can only wonder at Holst's motivations for writing his report in this manner. Certainly, he misrepresented the condition of the Ottawas. They still practiced their traditional crafts, as other Indian agents had reported Ottawa basketmaking accounted for much of the case for entering the communities in the 1930's. U.S. Officials even recommended U.S. planting of Black Ash trees to replenish the crop taken by lumbermen so the Ottawas basketmaking crafts would continue uninterrupted. Other traditional activities, such as berry gathering, fishing, and acting as guides for white people continued.[78]

Even the Catholic Church in Peshawbestown assimilated Anishinaabe *mide* ceremonies into the Liturgy (although the assimilation may have gone both ways):

> Because the Indian people were reluctant to enter into the Church community—we found it necessary to go to the Indian people and in a very real [*sic*] join the Indian community. The Mission of Peshawbestown established in the 1830's by Franciscan priests has become an extra-territorial parish for the Indian people throughout the diocese because they feel it is their church. We have attempted to have the Peshawbestown church speak something of and to the people who share Eucharist here. The Church has incorporated the Ancient Ottawa *mide* rites into the Liturgy. We have retained the sacred signs and symbols of the Indian people. In a very real way, we have made sacramentals of the Indian pipe and tobacco, the turtle rattle, the Sacred hoop, sweet grass, cedar boughs and birch bark. The Indian relationship to nature and the desire for harmony with all living things is incorporated in prayer and attitude. We have centered the Diocesean wide ministry in Peshawbestown because it is a center of Indian people with a long and rich history of maintaining its Indian identity.[79]

Richard White added:

Unless Holst expected to find people fishing from birch bark canoes and living in bark lodges on the shores of Grand Traverse Bay, it is hard to know what to make of these statements. It was the equivalent of complaining in 1855 that since log cabins and ship building were "unIndian" the Ottawas had lost their culture. . . . Holst later in the report commented on the weakness of Indian leaders, but this, if anything, was proof of the persistence of native political patterns. Ottawa chiefs had never possessed much coercive power and dissident factions had always played a major role in decision making. . . .

Given the existence of exclusively Indian communities such as Peshawbestown, the assertion of Leelanau County officials such as Ms. Schaub that the Indians composed a separate and distinct class within Leelanau County, the reluctance of county officials to aid the Ottawas through programs designed for all citizens, and, finally, the persistent attempts of the Ottawas of the region to organize and get reservation lands and federal assistance, Holst's conclusions are incredible.[80]

The federal government's refusal to fulfill its treaty-guaranteed responsibilities to the Grand Traverse Band—and its refusal to allow the band to reorganize under the Indian Reorganization Act—created unbearable hardships on the Ottawa and Chippewa people around the Grand Traverse Bay.

In Peshawbestown, many of the titles to the lands owned and occupied by the Anishinaabek had become clouded by delinquent taxes, with some land being foreclosed upon by the State of Michigan.[81] At the recommendation of Emelia Schaub, later to become an honorary member of the Grand Traverse Band,[82] county supervisor Russell Bolton recommended to the Leelanau County Board of Commissioners in 1943 that the county petition the State of Michigan to secure title to the remaining Indian lands in Peshawbestown in trust for the benefit of the Grand Traverse Band community:

Certain real estate of the plat of Peshawbestown located in Suttons Bay Township, Leelanau County, Michigan consisting of small homes and garden sites is now and always has been occupied by Indians, mostly of the Ottawa and Chippewa tribes, and whereas, most of the residents of Peshawbestown either have been or are now on welfare rolls of this county and by reason of such poverty have lost title to their respective lands, and, the title to the same is now in the State of Michigan, and whereas, the keeping intact and preservation of such Indian community is to the best interest of such [sic] Indians, the county taxpayers and the general public therefore, be it resolved, that application be made to the Michigan Department of Conservation to obtain title to the parcels of land in Peshawbestown ... from the State of Michigan to vest in the County of Leelanau as an Indian Community for the use and occupation by such Indians as a home and garden site.[83]

The county completed the purchase of 72 acres of tax-foreclosed land in June 1944.[84] The county purchased additional lands for the benefit of the Peshaw-bestown Indians in 1954 and 1971.

The 1944 land purchase by the county did little to ease the hardships faced by the Peshawbestown Indians. The county quickly lost interest in providing services to the Indians, and the county permits to use the land could be revoked at any time.[85] Also, if an Indian built a home or made any improvements to the county land, the county owned those improvements.[86]

Participation in the Northern Michigan Ottawa Association

In 1948, Robert Dominic from Cross Village organized the Northern Michigan Ottawa Association (NMOA).[87] Delegates from Peshawbestown and Northport appeared at formal meetings in 1951.[88] The Bureau of Indian Affairs, with J. C. Cavill as the general superintendent of the Great Lakes Agency, quickly added the association to its list of "Indian groups."[89] The NMOA eventually consisted of eleven units, with the Grand Traverse Band as Unit 2, and its primary goal was to bring claims under the Indian Claims Commission Act, passed in 1946.[90] Those claims finally reached fruition in 1970 with a judgment favoring the tribes for more than 10 million dollars.[91]

In 1975, the NMOA expanded its goals to include federal recognition, and filed papers with the Bureau of Indian Affairs seeking the right to organize under the Indian Reorganization Act.[92] The BIA refused to recognize the NMOA, forcing the various Ottawa bands to independently seek federal recognition.[93] Eventually, Robert Dominic, who had served as the director of the NMOA for decades, walked on, and was replaced by his spouse, Waunetta.[94]

In contrast, and while years passed before the Indian Claims Commission finally issued a judgment in the *Dominic* claims, the Grand Traverse Anishinaabek continued to pursue federal recognition, without success.[95] The 1950s and 1960s were the era of termination of federal supervision over Indian tribes, not an era of extending federal recognition.[96] In 1954, a House subcommittee recommended that the Bureau of Indian Affairs cease all activity in Michigan.[97] In 1954 and again in 1970, Leelanau County acquired land in and near Peshawbestown that had been lost to tax foreclosures.[98] By the 1970s, the director of Leelanau County Social Services controlled these county-held lands, and often exercised a form of arbitrary, capricious, and absolute power over the Peshawbestown Indians.[99] Former chairman Joseph C. (Buddy) Raphael noted that administrative termination meant that Peshawbestown "was run as a DSS fiefdom for many years."[100]

Leelanau Indians, Inc. and the Federal Recognition of the Grand Traverse Band*

In 1972, a group of Grand Traverse Band Indians—elders and young people—formed the nonprofit corporation Leelanau Indians, Inc.[101] At the time, the traditional leader (*ogema*) of the community was Fred Harris, but the nonprofit corporation was useful for securing grants, contracts, or other funds from government and private agencies.[102]

In 1974, state officers arrested Arthur Duhamel, exercising Grand Traverse Band treaty rights, for the first time.[103] According to Arthur's son Skip Duhamel, the strongest push for federal recognition in the 1970s came from the treaty fishers:

> There was no organized tribe as such when we first came here. Tribal government was kind of a fallout from my father fishing. Because we had to be licensed, you had to have a bureaucracy or government to license. Then you had to have a tribal council and you had to be federally recognized. All those things are things that he orchestrated. . . .
>
> My dad's first ticket was in 1974, in December. The initial result was ninety days in jail for dad, but they were able to get an injunction through the federal court systems and he was released after a week. The end result of it was federal recognition for this tribe, decent housing, and jobs, not to mention further refinement of the treaty right itself. The whole tribe here is based on fishing. When we first came here we found a community in despair. We found a community that was used to frequent visits from locals who tossed beer cans at its inhabitants. There were beatings in taverns that still had "No Indians" signs in the 1970s; there were outhouses and poor sanitation. Now we have our own water plant. Anybody in this community who needs a job can have a decent

paying job, employed through their own community. Everybody has housing. We have seen a return of our traditional ways. We have seen hope again. That is basically what was the end result of that ticket.[104]

Arthur Duhamel recalled what it was like in Peshawbestown when he brought his family to live there in 1972:

> When Babs and I came back here after years of working in the outside world, the people here had little self-respect. They had very little drive or ambition. That is the way they felt about themselves. Let us pick our cherries. Let us chop our wood. Let us trap a few muskrats. Indians just did the shitwork and survived. They were afraid to hope for anything better.[105]

Leelanau Indians, Inc. became the focal point in the pursuit for federal recognition, as well as serving as the de facto corporate body of the tribe. The board of directors of the corporation served as the business and governmental leaders of the community, applying for and receiving grant funds as well as implementing the projects funded by the grants. The nonprofit corporation succeeded in securing federal grants for sewer and water facilities in 1976, administered a CETA Title VI grant in 1977–1978, and participated in other activities in the Peshawbestown community.[106] In 1978, L. John Lufkins, regional Bureau of Indian Affairs superintendent, informed Leelanau Indians, Inc. that he would support a request to take land into federal trust on its behalf.[107]

In 1975, Congress created the American Indian Policy Review Commission.[108] Part of the commission's charge was to identify the Indian tribes that the federal government refused to recognize for whatever reason—bureaucratic negligence, accidents of history, and so on. Task Force Ten, the part of the commission that researched terminated and non-recognized Indian tribes, identified the Leelanau Indians, Inc. of Suttons Bay as one of the several non-recognized tribes in Michigan.[109]

After the commission released its report, Congress began to study the question of federal non-recognition of Indian tribes—in particular, the question of how to recognize Indian tribes. Rather than allow Congress to generate its own process, the Bureau of Indian Affairs attempted to head off Congress by promulgating its own process for the administrative recognition of Indian tribes.[110] These regulations created the Branch of Acknowledgment and Research

(BAR) to administer a complicated process that would allow non-recognized tribal communities to petition for federal recognition. This process is known as the federal acknowledgment process (FAP).

Arthur Duhamel noted in 1980 that there was no consensus among the board members of Leelanau Indians, Inc. about whether to petition for federal recognition, and that some Peshawbestown people actively opposed federal recognition:

> After I thought about tribal recognition and talked to people, I decided that recognition was the thing to do. I went to Leelanau Indians, Inc. They were our representatives then—a business corporation that had been formed to look after our interests. I made my pitch for recognition and they appointed me to head up a campaign for federal acknowledgement. . . .
>
> Apathy was our biggest problem. Most of the older people, people my age and older, were indifferent. They did not care. They did not oppose us but they did not help us either. We had to try to overcome their lack of interest and that was hard to do. Some of the board members of Leelanau Indians were not very supportive of recognition either so I tried to get the people to elect board members who were sympathetic to recognition. In time, the board came around to our side. I guess we won them over.
>
> Some people really fought to prevent recognition. People who owned property in the village worried that they might lose it. Others thought that we were selling out to the feds and that recognition would have the BIA (Bureau of Indian Affairs) running our lives. Some people still feel that way and a few families are still working against recognition.[111]

Arthur explained that he understood federal recognition to be a compromise, but a worthy one:

> I can see why some people think that we have to conform to white institutions in order to be recognized. They are right. We do have to abide by BIA guidelines. We do have to create a government patterned after non-Indian institutions. But I believe those are compromises worth making. Without recognition, we would just exist as we always have without control over our own lives—powerless. With recognition, we can exert ourselves and take initiative. We can be sovereign people as we were long ago.[112]

Years later, Joseph C. "Buddy" Raphael would comment that it was treaty fishing that gave the Grand Traverse Band "the push" to become federally recognized:

> After the 1979 Fox decision, you needed to be a federally recognized tribe. Quite frankly, that was the instrument here. That was the push. And that was the motivation from the standpoint of economics, also. They were fishing. They were making money. Arthur and that following he had here in the village [Peshawbestown]—they were making money, exercising what they considered to be the treaty rights. And they were right.
>
> I don't believe without *U.S. v. Michigan* and treaty fishing it [federal recognition] would have ever happened.[113]

On May 19, 1978, Leelanau Indians, Inc., represented by Michigan Indian Legal Services, formally petitioned the federal government for federal recognition on behalf of the Grand Traverse Band of Ottawa and Chippewa Indians, the fourth tribal group nationwide to begin the Federal Acknowledgment Process (FAP). Ardith (Dodie) Chambers, the chair of Leelanau Indians, Inc., drove with three others all night to Washington, D.C., to deliver the petition to the Department of the Interior, only to be turned back at the lobby.[114] On October 18, 1979, the Bureau of Indian Affairs published a notice in the *Federal Register* indicating its preliminary determination that the Grand Traverse Band should be federally recognized.[115]

On May 27, 1980, the Grand Traverse Band officially became the first petitioner to earn federal recognition under the FAP,[116] bypassing three earlier petitioners. In a real sense, the Grand Traverse Band was the perfect candidate to be the first. The band is a treaty tribe. As Vine Deloria Jr. wrote (writing in relation to the Little Traverse Bay Bands of Odawa Indians and the Little River Band of Ottawa Indians, tribes that were in the same boat as the Grand Traverse Band):

> Never has there been such a clear case of malfeasance and misadministration in the dealings of the United States with Indian tribes. These bands once controlled the major parts of the Great Lakes region and had treaties with France and England long before the founding of the United States. In post-Revolutionary decades the Ottawa and their allies possessed great land areas and constituted a powerful military force in what was then known as the old Northwest. Their representatives were present at numerous treaty negotiations held by the

Chippewa, Odawa and Potawatomi—the famous "Three Fires" confederacy. Indeed it was the presence of these Indian nations that inspired the class phrasing in the Ordinance of 1787 wherein the United States promised to exercise the "utmost good faith" in dealing with the Indian nations.[117]

Much of the Grand Traverse Band's documentary evidence involved direct contact between the *ogemuk* and federal officials, as shown in letters between the federal government and the band. In the BAR's recommendation to acknowledge the Grand Traverse Band, the BAR relied upon the fact that the band's ancestors had signed the 1836 and 1855 treaties, participated in the creation of the 1908 and 1910 annuity rolls, and made at least two efforts to seek federal recognition under the Indian Reorganization Act. The anthropological report accompanying the proposed finding mirrored the band's petition, with no serious objection to any of the band's assertions.

Many members of the Grand Traverse Band at the time of federal recognition were poor, undereducated, and desperate. Members of the Grand Traverse Band community, as well as other Michigan Anishinaabe communities with which the federal government stopped dealing, who were one-half blood, had received federal services in accordance with the Snyder Act and the Indian Reorganization Act.[118] But Michigan Indians were in no sense receiving the same benefits as members of federally recognized tribes. Years later, in the federal court trial over the legality of the Turtle Creek Casino in 2002, former Grand Traverse Band chair and Leelanau Indians, Inc. chair Dodie Chambers testified:

> Back in the 1950s and 60s, there may have been ten homes, maybe 20 people. [Peshawbestown] was quite prosperous—or larger, I'll say, not prosperous but larger at one time, but because people moving away and houses burning down and no economic opportunity, people left. . . . At least once a month for I'm going to say a couple years seemed like at least once a month there was a house burning down in the village because of the wood stoves, the chimney fires, the newspapers that were used for insulation and other things. And [Suttons] Bay was the closest village, but it was five miles south of us and responded, I guess, the best they could, but our homes burned.[119]

One of the first tribal government employees brought in to establish the Grand Traverse Band's government operations, Barry Burtt, testified that "one of the worst case situations, one that we talk about, was an older fellow that was literally living out of a root cellar. There were several gentlemen that [were] homeless. They literally had several poles in the ground that they have plastic draped over and some canvas."[120] Lack of federal recognition had all but devastated the band and its people. Ms. Chambers testified about exactly how she had learned the meaning of federal recognition:

> Well, coming from Peshawbestown, I didn't realize . . . that we were considered poor. I mean so what, we went without this and that, but to us we weren't poor. But when I met the other kids from the other tribes and even within Michigan from Mt. Pleasant and Baraga, they had better housing. They had running water in their house, and our tribal people didn't. I didn't know how our village and the other villages in the area could not have that. So in talking to the kids during and after school, I had asked, "Well, why is it your people—your tribe has water? Why do you have these septics and bathrooms and not modern houses but definitely better homes than we had?" And they simply said, "Well, our tribe gets money from the government." And I said, "What are you talking about, you get money from the government?" And the kids all stated, "Well, we're federally recognized by the government, and we get services from Indian health. We get services from HUD. We get services from the Bureau of Indian Affairs because we're acknowledged, federally acknowledged by the government."[121]

In the words of Vine Deloria Jr., discussing "administrative termination": "The Odawa 'lost' their federal rights to services simply because low level federal bureaucrats refused to carry out their responsibilities."[122]

CHAPTER FIVE

The Story of the Grand Traverse Band's Treaty Rights Fight

The right to resort to the fishing places in controversy was a part of larger rights possessed by the Indians, upon the exercise of which there was not a shadow of impediment, and which were not much less necessary to the existence of the Indians than the atmosphere they breathed.[1]

During treaty times, the Grand Traverse Band Anishinaabek negotiated to preserve their right to stay in Michigan and their way of life, including the right to access the Great Lakes and inland fisheries and hunting and gathering grounds. But by the early twentieth century, overfishing dramatically reduced the fisheries on the Great Lakes, and increasing non-Indian property ownership on and near the Grand Traverse Band reservations reduced tribal access to inland resources, creating incredible hardships for the Grand Traverse Band people. By the 1950s, the State of Michigan and its Department of Natural Resources had all but prohibited Indian people from exercising their treaty rights both inland and on the Great Lakes, all in favor of non-Indian sport hunters and fishers.

In the early 1970s, Grand Traverse Band fishers led by Arthur Duhamel began to stand up to the State of Michigan by exercising their treaty fishing rights. Eventually, the federal courts recognized these treaty rights in the watershed case *United States v. Michigan.*[2] Since 1979, when the Grand Traverse Band earned federal recognition and intervened in the ongoing *United States v. Michigan* case, the people of the Grand Traverse Band have been involved in commercial and subsistence fishing, hunting, and gathering, as well as the conservation and protection of these valuable and limited resources.

Usufructuary Treaty Rights in the 1836 Treaty of Washington

Indian people have been living in the Grand Traverse Bay area for at least 11,000 years. From those times immemorial to 1836, when the Grand Traverse Band *ogemuk* negotiated and signed the Treaty of Washington, many things changed.[3] By 1836, Europeans had been present in Michigan for approximately 200 years. Tribal economies changed as the Europeans brought different goods into the region, such as advanced blacksmithing tools and weapons, demanding furs, food, and other goods from Indian people in return. These Europeans also brought whiskey and disease with them, creating additional means to control and weaken tribal people. By 1836, the French had been replaced by the British, and the British had been replaced by the Americans, who arrived in force in northern Michigan in 1815. By the time the Michigan tribes entered into the 1836 Treaty, these enormous changes—for better or worse—were pervasive, and were still ongoing. Of note, the Americans, far more so the French and the British, began to interfere with the delicate fabric of the Great Lakes fishery by the 1830s.[4]

But many things remained the same, including the expectation that Michigan Anishinaabek would continue to retain the right and ability to utilize and maintain the natural resources of the region as a means of survival and commercial advantage. Indian people continued to fish, for example, both for subsistence and for commercial reasons, long after the 1836 Treaty ink was dry.[5] The 1836 Treaty is a land cession treaty, in which the Michigan Ottawa and Chippewa tribes ceded much of their rights and claims to about one-third of the current land mass of the State of Michigan. The treaty also created permanent reservations for the tribes, but the Senate rewrote that portion of the treaty to delete the permanent reservations without the consent of the tribes. These treaty terms have faded from importance over time, leaving the hunting, fishing, and gathering rights intact.

It is useful to start with the powerful words of Article 13 of the Treaty of Washington: "The Indians stipulate for the right of hunting on the lands ceded, with the other usual privileges of occupancy, until the land is required for settlement."[6] This sentence contains the most important words in the 1836 Treaty. In short, the stages of litigation that constitute the *United States v. Michigan* saga derive from this sentence. The right to fish both inland in the ceded territory and on the Great Lakes for subsistence and for commercial profit is contained in the phrase "other usual privileges of occupancy." The right to hunt and gather inland in the ceded territory is contained in the phrase "the right of hunting on the lands ceded with the other usual privileges of occupancy, until the land is required for settlement."

It is to be remembered that the treaty negotiations of 1836 between the Michigan Anishinaabek communities and the United States involved two languages, with each side likely misinterpreting much of what the other side said and understood. No translation is perfect. And the fact that the governing language of the treaty itself is English lends itself to great difficulty for the

Michigan Anishinaabek. The sense of what the Michigan Indians believed they were executing in the treaty language may be restored through careful ethnohistory, and through a linguistic analysis of the treaty language in light of Anishinaabemowin.

Frankly, the federal courts that have interpreted this treaty language cannot engage in this sort of analysis. So they have created rules for the interpretation of Indian treaties—rules that restore much of the meaning of the treaty language as it would have been understood by the Indian treaty negotiators. In essence, if there is any ambiguity in Indian treaty language, it is to be interpreted for the benefit of Indian people and Indian tribes in the way that they understood the treaty terms.[7]

What is clear from the great weight of ethnohistorical authority is that the 1836 tribal negotiators successfully preserved their rights to hunt, fish, and gather on the ceded territories in Michigan and on the Great Lakes. Henry Schoolcraft, the longtime Michigan Indian agent (1822–1840) and the federal treaty commissioner during the 1836 treaty negotiations, provided much of the strongest evidence that Article 13 means (and was intended to mean) that the Michigan Anishinaabek had reserved all rights of occupancy in the Great Lakes *and* on the ceded territory until the lands were permanently developed, usually in the form of large-scale agriculture.[8]

But recognition by federal and state authorities of these rights would take more than a century.

The Disintegration of Treaty Rights (1830s to 1970s)

In the mid-nineteenth century, a problem developed: the system of hunting, fishing, gathering, and trading that the 1836 and 1855 treaties intended to preserve largely broke down within a few short years after the *ogemuk* signed the treaties. The land base that the treaty negotiators hoped to preserve, much smaller than the lands upon which the Grand Traverse Bay Anishinaabek roamed for hundreds of years, dissipated quickly due to fraud, other illegalities, and politics. With the dispossession of the treaty land base came the disintegration of the way of life for the people of the Grand Traverse Band. Perhaps the most damaging blow to this way of life was the destruction of the fishery.

Michigan Indians had maintained a fishery in the Great Lakes and on the inland lakes and rivers throughout the region. The skills of the Anishinaabe gill-netters "were second to none" in the entire hemisphere.[9] The Grand Traverse Band Indians fished Lakes Michigan, Huron, and Superior from canoes made of cedar, using gill nets in both the shallows and the deep waters.[10] During the summers, the Grand Traverse Bay itself provided abundant fish to the people in the region, necessitating the location of villages on Old Mission Peninsula, the east shore of the bay, and the Leelanau Peninsula. The relatively calm waters of the bay, protected from the winds and raging storms that could ravage the Lake Michigan waters, offered easier fishing.

The east shore inhabitants also fished on the inland lakes and rivers. For example, Torch Lake and Torch River are named after a fishing practice of the Grand Traverse Band Anishinaabek. Since the waters are so shallow, the best means of harvesting fish included spearfishing. Indians would take canoes out onto the water at night, when the fish were active, and illuminate the bottom of the lake or river with torches or a fire basket held aloft over the water. The fish could be seen easily, and then harvested.

In the winter, in the inland camps ranging from places like the Au Sable, Manistee, Muskegon, and Grand Rivers, and Houghton and Mullet Lakes, Indians would break through the ice to fish, often using gill nets even when ice fishing. Samuel de Champlain described the practice as used by the Hurons in 1615.[11]

The Grand Traverse Band people fished the big lakes as well. Massive sturgeon could be caught using canoes and 40-foot-long spears far out into Lake Michigan.[12] Indian fishers also used gill nets in the open water—sometimes anchoring them to other canoes, and sometimes anchoring them to deepwater reefs.[13]

The Great Lakes fishery changed with the arrival of Europeans in the seventeenth century, who brought with them a demand for a commercial fishery. Subsistence fishing by the Michigan Anishinaabek came first, but fish always had been an important currency of trade. The European demand for fish exceeded their ability to catch fish, by far. Indian fishing expanded to accommodate this market demand. Although more fish were taken, no one ever expected the Great Lakes fishery to diminish.

By some estimates, the major change came in the years 1810–1820 with the American Fur Company's expansion into commercial fishing.[14] The company hired Indian and non-Indian fishers to camp along the shores of Lake Superior, fishing at locations until no more fish could be found, then moving to another location. The amount of fish these commercial fishers caught was staggering for the times and created an oversupply in the market. Within two decades, the company's fishing enterprise went bankrupt.[15] Once the market stabilized, however, the stage was set for the eradication of the resource.

In 1848, the first white settlers in Harbor Springs, on the Little Traverse Bay, were attracted to the area by the abundant fishery and the commercial possibilities. They hired local Indians to perform much of the fishing work, but Indians also fished for themselves, as evidenced by their request for fish barrels and other supplies in the 1836 Treaty. These independent Indian commercial fishing enterprises paled in comparison to the large and growing non-Indian commercial industry, which took tons of trout and whitefish using large boats and crews to fish vast swaths of the Great Lakes at a time. Indian fishers benefited very little from this new industry, except as laborers. By 1870, many Indians in the northwest Lower Peninsula were forced to survive as rowboat fishermen.[16]

The fishery was not the only victim of American exploitation. By 1900, both the Upper and Lower Peninsulas had been completely and utterly deforested of their virgin timber.[17] Deadly fires would rage over the northern part of Michigan for decades, fueled by the waste and materials left behind by the lumbermen.[18] Grand Traverse Anishinaabe men without recourse to their own winter hunting and fishing camps often joined the lumber camps in the winter, working as wage laborers.[19] As the timber industry declined in the early decades of the twentieth century, so too did the meager fortunes of the Anishinaabek, who resorted to doing odd jobs in the region as migrant laborers.[20]

The arrival of the American commercial interests also brought incredibly wasteful hunting practices. A region overflowing with game was all but stripped of its biggest animals, such as elk, moose, and even deer. Local predators all but disappeared as well. There are stories of an amazing hunt of passenger pigeons in Little Traverse and Grand Traverse Bay. In 1878, some claim hundreds of millions of passenger pigeons were slaughtered by hunters near the Little Traverse Bay,[21] and also at Northport in Leelanau County.[22] Robert Keller reported that "100,000 beaver, 2,000 bear, 5,000 fox, 6,000 lynx, and 700 elk could be taken near Lake Superior in a season, rates of kill which insured the death of the trade by the 1830s."[23]

At Grand Traverse, the historical record demonstrates that the Grand Traverse Anishinaabek relied heavily on their treaty-protected on- and off-reservation hunting, fishing, and gathering rights.[24] Ruth Craker wrote that Anishinaabe men from Omena would travel as far as Illinois to hunt and fish in the winter.[25]

During the summer, the Grand Traverse Bay region served as a rich source of fish, with significant fisheries on Lake Michigan, the bay, and the inland lakes, rivers, and streams.[26] The east bay region served as an excellent source of the maple sugar that the Grand Traverse Anishinaabek relied upon with greater and greater intensity as the nineteenth century progressed.[27]

Ironically, given that relatively little of the land in the 1836 treaty area throughout Michigan Indian Country was ever used for permanent agriculture,[28] or "required for settlement" by non-Indians, the treaty cession area had few resources left for the Michigan Anishinaabek just a few short decades after the arrival of the Americans. The Michigan Indian commercial fishing industry, which was just getting started, had all but expired by 1850, overwhelmed by non-Indian commercial fishing.[29] The inland hunting rights meant little after the deforestation of Michigan, which tended to destroy the game as well.[30] The dispossession of Indian lands meant that there was little or no opportunity to engage in agriculture, or to hunt and fish on privately owned tribal lands.[31] Without the resources supposedly reserved to the Anishinaabek in the 1836 Treaty "until the land was required for settlement," by the 1920s, many Indians had no choice but to leave the lands of their grandmothers to live in the cities.[32] The Anishinaabek that remained in the area served as cheap wage labor for timber, shipping, fishing, and other industries owned and controlled by non-Indians.[33]

Enforcing Conservation Laws against Anishinaabe Fishers and Hunters

The State of Michigan has a long and distinguished history of being at the forefront of environmental protection and conservation laws, but that history is marred by the discriminatory impacts it has had on treaty hunting and fishing. The state's first conservation agencies began in the 1850s,[34] while the first ban on commercial hunting came in 1881.[35] The ban impacted Anishinaabe hunters more than anyone.[36]

In 1866, local township election officials began to discriminate against Grand Traverse Band members on the basis of their treaty rights. According to Gregory Dowd:

> An organized group of Indians, led by John Ance, Peter Ance, and Joseph Chippewa, attempted to cast votes in an election at the township of Bingham, Michigan (between Sutton's Bay and Traverse City on the Leelanau Peninsula).

The local board of electors refused to allow them to cast ballots. Among the reasons the electors cited was that "they were not citizens, they were receiving pay [annuities] from the Government and were consequently minors, besides they were not subject to the Draft, *neither did the Game Laws of the state prohibit their killing Deer and other wild game.*"[37]

The state government's concern about whether or not it had political authority over Ottawa and Chippewa Indians in Michigan arose in the context of the debates over a proposed third state constitution after the Civil War.[38] Michigan voters rejected the proposed constitution in 1867.[39]

As early as the 1880s, the state began prosecuting Michigan Indians for hunting, fishing, and trapping in accordance with the 1836 Treaty. According to Charles Cleland:

In the 1880s, it became apparent that non-Indian hunters and commercial fishers were grossly overharvesting to supply distant urban restaurants. Indians bore most of the brunt of the crackdown. State wardens entered reservations and searched homes for meat and hides, traps and guns were confiscated, and Indians were fined and jailed. Their protests to agents, the Commissioner of Indian Affairs, and their congressional representatives went unheeded. Federal officials agreed with the contention of the states that allotted Indians were citizens of their respective states and would therefore have to abide by state law. The federal government was only willing to protect Indian treaty rights on the few parcels of allotted land still in Indian hands. Starvation now stalked many Indian families.[40]

One Chippewa *ogema*, Kawbawgum, was arrested in 1892 or 1893 while fishing on an Upper Peninsula lake named after him in ceded territory, though the local judge released the 93-year-old man.[41] In 1896, Louis Micksauby, an *ogema* from Charlevoix, complained to the United States that the State of Michigan had prohibited him from subsistence fishing in traditional fishing waters without a state license.[42] The government responded by instructing the Ottawas to comply with state law, whatever it might be.[43]

In 1930, the Michigan Supreme Court held in *People v. Chosa* that Michigan Indian people were not entitled to exercise their treaty rights because Congress had extended American citizenship to them in 1924.[44] *Chosa* ended whatever remained of Anishinaabe large-scale tribal commercial fishing in the Great Lakes. According to Grand Traverse Band member James Raphael:

> My grandfather fished out of Peshawbestown. I barely remember him. He used to pole fish. We could not commercial fish at the time, probably in the 1920s and 1930s. He would go pole fishing at the back of the village where the marina is. He would bring in eight, ten fish and there would be people waiting to buy them on the shore.[45]

By the 1950s, thanks to ignorant and ineffective conservation practices and the introduction of invasive species, the Great Lakes fishery was again in tatters.[46] Commercial fishermen had long engaged, since the 1830s, in the practice of overharvesting the fishery.[47] But sea lampreys and alewives all but finished the upper Great Lakes fisheries upon which the Anishinaabek depended.[48] The State of Michigan's responses to these problems were partially successful. Commercial fishing gave way to sports fishing, and the invasive species of the 1950s gave way to coho salmon and, to some extent, lake trout.[49] Indians that did fish tended to follow state laws.[50] But in the 1960s and 1970s when Michigan conservation policy restricted subsistence and commercial fishing in favor of sports fishing, the people harmed the most were Indian fishers.[51] Indians began to assert their treaty rights.

In the early 1970s, the Michigan Supreme Court decided *People v. Jondreau*,[52] in which the court recognized the treaty rights of the tribes who had signed the 1842 and 1854 treaties.[53] In 1965, Michigan conservation officers had arrested William Jondeau, a member of the Keweenaw Bay Indian Community (then known as the L'Anse Band of Chippewa Indians) for harvesting lake trout on Keweenaw Bay. The Michigan Court of Appeals had upheld his conviction, based on the *People v. Chosa* precedent.[54] The Michigan Supreme Court reversed the decision and overruled *Chosa*.[55]

Litigation in the 1836 Treaty area began heating up as the United States brought suit on behalf of the Bay Mills Indian Community (the only treaty signatory federally recognized at the time) in 1973. In 1976, the Michigan Supreme Court ruled in *People v. LeBlanc* that the 1836 Treaty preserved fishing rights.[56] By the end of the 1970s, several tribes had adopted tribal fishing regulations, approved by the Department of the Interior, and employed their own conservation officers.[57] The federal government also promulgated regulations in 1967 that the tribal fishers followed.[58] But the State of Michigan refused to honor the decisions of its own supreme court.[59] Arthur Duhamel commented:

> Jondreau's case was decided in 1971. There was a lot of fishing activity. I came up and visited people and talked to them. Pretty soon the attorney general said: "Well, O.K., Jondreau can fish but nobody else." So then Abe LeBlanc went to court and it came out in the state supreme court that perhaps Abe LeBlanc could fish, fine, but nobody else.[60]

Arthur added that local Department of Natural Resources (DNR) officers continued to enforce state laws against treaty fishers as a result:

> My cousin Albert and I had set nets off Gull Island near Northport, in May 1975. Indian people from Bay Mills were fishing and the Michigan State Appeals Court had upheld treaty right fishing. So we were within the law, within our rights, to be fishing out there. We would drive from here and camp on the island so we could lift our nets early in the morning before the wind came up. . . .
>
> Coming in to my place in the fog, we saw there were two DNR boats. They caught us out on the water. Albert was hard of hearing and his motor was loud too. He kept chugging along. The guy yelled, "Stop, shut that boat down or I will blow you out of the water." This was that DNR from Benzie County, a hard-nosed lawman, who thought he was John Wayne.
>
> After they threatened to blow Albert away, I came on in. I heard that, so I came on in. I was not evading them in any case. We came in and you know how conversations go—"Got you again, didn't we! See you are fishing some more." I said: "Yeah sure, that's right. We were fishing."[61]

Vigilantism by non-Indians against treaty fishers was an old, bad habit, but in the 1970s, non-Indian vigilantism reached a violent peak. John Alexander said:

> So we been fishin' all over: Lake Superior, Lake Michigan, Lake Huron. We got hassled lots of times. They'd try to block the road. They'd saw trees so they'd fall across the road. They put big rocks in the middle of the road—put some nails in the road. We had a lotta flat tires. We've had sand in our gas tank. Screwin' with the motor—took the distributor out and threw it away. Just all that kind of hassle. Then out on the lake sometimes they'd try to swamp us.

Around Petoskey and Charlevoix that stuff happens all the time. Unless you find a good spot like Glen Haven, you're going to get hassled. Around Cheboygan and Alpena they mostly get you on the lake—cut your buoys and drag your nets.

I remember one night sittin' at the beach there by Petoskey. It was about twelve o'clock at night. We had a boat tied to the trailer, but the trailer was half way in the water. We were waitin' till about two o'clock, and then we were going to lift. Some guy started—they had a rifle up there [on the bluff above us], and they shot it at us. That was probably about the closest time. When they hit the water, it was only about three feet from my legs. It was a pretty good-sized rifle. Then we heard the car take off.[62]

The fishing wars were on. Amazingly, non-Indian sports fishermen began to assert personal property rights over fishing in the Great Lakes.[63]

One of the more racist organizations was called the Stop Gillnetting Association (SGN). SGN proponents spoke about "hitting the beaches" to stop Indian fishing, and often asserted that Indians were "greedy" and "irresponsible."[64] The *Traverse City Record-Eagle* eventually labeled the group "racist."[65] Ron Paquin, an Indian fisher from St. Ignace, wrote about

that group what got started in Charlevoix and Traverse City—Stop Gill Netters. SGN they called them. Now, them guys was talking violence against us. The Traverse City newspaper said they ought to put on sheets and join the Klan. People in the [Michigan Department of Natural Resources] helped them SGN guys. They gave them stuff and talked at their meetings. SGN was handing out Wanted posters with an Indian's picture on it. That picture was took by Myrl Keller. He works for the DNR. Them guys passed out bumper stickers: "Spear an Indian and Save a Fish." The FBI and the federal marshals sent here from Judge Fox's court in Grand Rapids stopped that stuff.[66]

Paquin added that even after SGN's activities declined, other groups formed:

Them guys wasn't through when SGN busted up. The ones from Traverse City got another group going, the Grand Traverse Area Sportsfishing Association (GTASFA). They wasn't no better than them first ones. This one guy, a public relations man from Lansing, flat denied there was any Indian rights, and he was talking violence. Hit the beaches, he said. John Scott, who ran the Great Lakes

Fishery for the DNR, gave a couple speeches to GTASFA. And Judge Richard L. Benedict, that judge from Leelanau County who convicted an Ottawa Indian, Art Duhamel, went to a few of them meetings, too. Art went to jail for treaty fishing. All of them guys was in it together. In cahoots they was. Put the boots to the Indians—that's their message.[67]

James Raphael noted that there were "a handful, a vocal, violent, vandalism-prone minority who ends up with the sport group organizations. They talk about it day and night."[68]

Arthur Duhamel

The key figure in the treaty fishing fight for the Grand Traverse Band was Arthur Duhamel. A pipe fitter who had worked on the construction of the Mackinac Bridge in the 1950s, he returned to Peshawbestown in 1972 and began exercising his treaty rights.[69] The Michigan Department of Natural Resources had banned all commercial fishing in Grand Traverse Bay by 1974, and Arthur fished anyway.[70] He was arrested several times and even served a jail sentence after being convicted by Hon. Richard L. Benedict in Leelanau County District Court of violating state fishing laws.[71]

Duhamel's early life history and connection to his community is detailed in a legal pleading filed by William Rastetter, who has represented many tribal fishers and the Grand Traverse Band on treaty rights issues since the 1970s.

From the Memorandum of Support of Plaintiff's Motion for Summary Judgment in *Duhamel v. Michigan Department of Natural Resources,** drafted by William R. Rastetter:[†]

On November 8, 1924, Buddy Chippewa was born in the Indian village known as Peshaw-bestown, located on the shores of Grand Traverse Bay in Leelanau County. By this point in time—seven decades after his ancestors were promised "permanent homes" in the Treaty of 1855—most of the 87,000-acre "Leelanau reserve" had passed from the ownership of the families of the Ottawa and Chippewa allottees. The local Indians had fallen on hard times and economic opportunities were nonexistent.

Like other Indian youngsters in Michigan during that era, Buddy was sent to the boarding school at Harbor Springs when he was five years old. For several years he endured the regimented lifestyle and loneliness of the institution, sometimes going for an entire school year without a visit from his family or returning home.

When Buddy was nine, his life was affected even more dramatically by the then-prevailing policy towards Native Americans, which presumed it was in the Indians' best interests to become assimilated into the dominant white society. Ignoring the extended-family aspect of Indian communities which resulted in children like Buddy being taken care of notwithstanding their parents' inability, Leelanau County authorities separated Buddy from his family and sent him off to a white foster home in Grand Rapids. This was followed by a succession of non-Indian foster homes and difficult adjustments for Buddy. Apparently it never occurred to the authorities that his problems at home and school could be related to an assimilation policy which fragmented families and destroyed tribal communities. During his early teenage years Buddy got only an occasional opportunity to return briefly to Peshawbestown, where he found himself subject to ridicule by his cousins Albert and Russel as well as other Indian kids for dressing like a white man in his stiff wool suit, white shirt with necktie, and shiny shoes.

As a teenager he finally achieved some stability in a Big Rapids' foster home, the Duhamel family, which explains how Buddy Chippewa became Arthur Duhamel. Nonetheless, when he finished school, Buddy essentially was adrift between two cultures. Despite the dominant society's attempts to assimilate him, he was an outcast in the white world, and by the late 1930's there was no realistic possibility of relocating in his tribal community: Indians there were virtually "without means of livelihood," and "pervasive poverty" gripped the community.

After a succession of post-war jobs, Plaintiff established himself as a pipefitter, ultimately becoming a journeyman welder. His work took him all over the world, from the American West to Africa and Persia (and later Alaska). During this period, Mr. Duhamel evolved into a worldly person figuratively as well: long stretches in remote locations enabled him to begin to satisfy his unfulfilled desire for learning through extensive reading. The unsuccessful student of the 1930's matured into a self-educated and learned man.

In the 1950's Mr. Duhamel returned to his native Ottawa homeland for several years to work as a welder during the construction of the Mackinac Bridge. This reestablished times with his native roots and influenced his decision to return to Peshawbestown in the 1970's with his wife Babette in order to establish a permanent and stable home for their son's high school education. Mr. Duhamel wanted his son to be able to become a member of the Indian community, and he himself longed to return to his extended family and his Ottawa/Chippewa heritage. Coincidentally, the Duhamels' return to Peshawbestown in

1972 occurred at the same time that the community began its reemergence as a political and tribal entity.

By this time William Jondreau's case had already been decided by the Michigan Supreme Court, and "Big Abe" LeBlanc's 1971 arrest for illegal fishing was itself en route to that court. In 1973 the United States Departments of Justice and the Interior brought the *United States v. Michigan* litigation in order to vindicate fishing rights of "Big Abe's" tribe, the Bay Mills Indian Community, and residents of the long-forgotten Ottawa/Chippewa community at Peshawbestown knew that their Tribe was entitled to similar status as successor to signatories to the Treaty in 1836. The problem they faced was how to reestablish these treaty rights which had once provided their community with a means of livelihood.

Arthur Duhamel and his family were gradually welcomed back into the fold upon their return, and eventually the elders of the community turned to Buddy for help. These elders, who were among the first generation of Ottawa and Chippewa born after the Treaty of 1855, had witnessed the transformation of their culture from a proud, self-sustaining people to a dependent community. But as evidenced by Congress' 1974–75 statement and declaration of policy embodied in the Indian Self-Determination Act, federal policy had reversed itself: the termination era of the 1950's was replaced by a new era of Indian self-determination. This change of policy reflected a national mood which incited consciousness within the local community. Determined not to be ignored as it had been during the 1930's, the community turned to the articulate and worldly Buddy Duhamel to enter the fray and lead the fight on behalf of the Ottawa and Chippewa of Grand Traverse.

It never occurred to the Peshawbestown community in 1973–74 that the struggle would be so arduous. Unlike William Jondreau's and Abe LeBlanc's tribes located in the Upper Peninsula away from major tourism areas, Peshawbestown was on the shores of Grand Traverse Bay, in the midst of Michigan's tourism "gold coast." Anchored by the Michigan Department of Natural Resources' management of the Great Lakes' fishery resource for the benefit of the sportsfishing/tourism industry, state policy operated to the detriment of the state-licensed commercial fishing industry and to the exclusion of Indian treaty fishing.

*No. G84-1186, 1987 U.S. Dist. LEXIS 15721 (W.D. Mich., Jan. 21, 1987).
†Memorandum in Support of Plaintiff's Motion for Summary Judgment 1–5, *Duhamel v. Michigan Dept. of Natural Resources*, No. G84-1186, 1987 U.S. Dist. LEXIS 15721 (W.D. Mich., Oct. 13, 1985).

Arthur began fishing in 1973 at the behest of his father, Geep Sands (Joseph Sands). According to Arthur's son, Skip Duhamel:

My dad moved us back to the community, back to . . . Peshawbestown . . . , so I would grow up and know the heritage. My grandfather was Geep Sands. Good old Geep was the one who got us going. At that time, we were not gill netting because you would promptly be arrested and jailed.

During the 1970s, the old man would come down and he would bug my dad. He had three boxes of nets. He would tell my dad we have got to put them in. He would tell him the time of year was right. We told my dad he had to do it. We knew it was going to mean jail. And finally my dad said, "Well that's it. Let's go put them in." He just could not stand the old man bugging him. It got to him. Geep told my dad that he owed it to the people to do this and this is what he was supposed to do. And so my dad did it. We loaded her up. We sat and promptly got arrested. I cannot even count how many times they took our gear.[72]

Skip added that the confiscation of Arthur's equipment and the destruction of his property by vigilantes did not deter Arthur:

The day they took his first boat [e]nsured that he would buy another two. The day they stole the first nets [e]nsured he would buy ten more. From time to time, he would have to go back to work on a pipeline to get more equipment so that we could continue to fish. Then they would confiscate that equipment. He had several boats sunk, chopped up, with axes by vigilantes.[73]

Arthur added: "People, vigilantes, have harassed us, smashed our boats, torn up our nets. The sheriff will come out and investigate, but he never finds anything out."[74]

Tribal fishers usually had no insurance for the equipment they lost. In the words of Ron Paquin, "You could not insure your rigs because people were shooting holes in them and stealing your nets. What insurance company in their right mind would give you insurance? I could not even get life insurance because I was fishing in a sixteen-foot rowboat."[75] Arthur Duhamel noted that "We could not fish without spending two or three thousand dollars for equipment which would just get confiscated next time they came around."[76]

For all the advances he made on behalf of the Grand Traverse Band, Arthur did not enjoy much of the fruits of his sacrifice. According to Skip:

My father knew the implications of his work absolutely. But, no, he never saw the payoffs. What it meant for him was a life of hardship, struggle, and disappointment. He knew the implications of listening to Geebo's counsel. He knew what it all meant for us. During the 1960s, my dad was making $50–60,000 a year pipeline welding, top of the line. We wanted for nothing. And then he took the next ten to twenty years of his life and invested it in attorneys, not to mention jail time, incarceration, loss, and hardship you could not even fathom.[77]

Skip added that Arthur could not invest much into any particular piece of equipment because of the threat of government confiscation and vigilantism:

> My father's boats were about twenty-foot, open boats. Most were made of door plywood. He had old craft with an old Evinrude on it. It was really quite like a joke. Anyway, he had about eight different boats all with the same name. Of course, he did not want to put a lot of money into them because they were gonna come and take them. Then someone took an axe to my father's boats in Northport Harbor. They whacked them up and sunk them.[78]

Skip also noted that he and his father would find men stealing or destroying their equipment, but that Arthur would avoid confrontation and seek relief from local prosecutors, usually to no avail:

> We were too afraid to launch down here in Leland because of the violence, so we launched at an open sand beach at Sugarfoot. We set ten nets. Then we went down the beach and set ten more. By the time we came back, there were two men in the boat lifting the first nets that we had already set. I was about seventeen and pretty hot-tempered. I wanted to put the boots to them, but my father would never allow something like that. He felt that was not the way to go. You should try to seek prosecution. He really believed in that. My father told me we would report it. They promptly went to shore and got a gun and trained it on him as we tried to repair the damage they had done. They never did fire the weapon, but we were real close to shore. They trained it right on us the whole time we were there. We reported it. Of course, nothing was done. The prosecutor's people were the people that were doing it. So that was the man in charge of prosecuting choosing not to prosecute his own family. At that time the feds were not taking a very active role as far as the FBI reporting. He considered us more of a nuisance. Just go away. And so that did not happen either. Nothing, nothing happened except that we got our nets ruined and they pointed guns at us.[79]

On occasion, however, Arthur would become more aggressive, and was convicted of resisting arrest and obstruction of justice arising out of a May 1975 incident.[80] According to John Petoskey:

> One time Art was arrested for fishing. He said, "Well, let me take a piss before I go off to jail." He was taking a piss. The DNR individuals were standing behind him, and they said something to him, and Art turned around, still pissing, and pissed across their legs, in a very nonchalant manner, saying, "Oh, did you say something?" But that's the type of character he is.[81]

In another incident, John Petoskey recalled an even more aggressive action by Arthur:

> At the time, I had a pony tail that was down to my butt, so Art made me lay down in the truck when we were going to Paradise because there were a lot of non-Indians who were actively against Indians. We were fishing Whitefish Bay and along the Upper Peninsula. We had pulled the boat up and were camped in the woods.
>
> We were outside Paradise somewhere, I don't remember exactly where, but we were pulling the boat to the launch site. A DNR guy pulled up. He took one look at us, because of my long pony tail, he stopped and asked what we were doing.
>
> Art said something to the effect, "We're sports fishermen." The DNR guy said, "You guys wouldn't be Indians, would you?"—something to that effect. Art reached around, grabbed the DNR guy—who was still sitting in his car—and pulled him halfway out. And said something to the effect, "It's none of your business who we are or what we are or what we're doing. We're fishermen." He dropped the guy.
>
> That was obviously a physical assault. The guy scrambled back into his car, fish-tailed down the road, and took off. We knew that reinforcements were going to be coming shortly, so we fishtailed the other way, and got out. The DNR never caught up with us.[82]

In the late 1970s, Arthur appeared before Congress to testify against various bills introduced by anti-treaty lawmakers seeking to abrogate the 1836 Treaty. In one remarkable incident in 1978, Arthur testified:

H.R. 12531 seeks a political solution to an entirely legal problem. We have faith and confidence in the higher courts of the nation to arrive at a rational conclusion with respect to our petitions for recognition of a basic Indian right and therefore we are entirely in opposition to legislation which seeks to circumvent the great promise that only the United States can fulfill. If the United States will not, or by devious political legislation, cannot—fulfill its fiduciary trust relationship then this, to us, means the very end of a once magnificent group of people.[83]

According to Arthur's testimony, the bill would reward the illegal activities of the state and the non-Indian private actors:

We view [the "potentially explosive problem"] as merely the reaction of those groups and agencies who form the greater portion of Mr. Ruppe's constituency, and the only solution to the acts of vandalism and vigilante goonism by non-Indians is the proper enforcement of existing criminal and civil laws.[84]

Of particular note were Arthur's court appearances before Leelanau County judge Richard Benedict. Skip Duhamel recalled his father's conflict with the judge:

They arrested him and brought him before Judge Benedict, the judge in Leland who is retired now. He ordered the old man not to fish in Lake Michigan under court order, so we went to Lake Superior. This was not the first time. This was just one of many. They found out what the old man was up to in Lake Superior, they hunted him down and dragged him back here in handcuffs.[85]

Arthur had very little respect for Judge Benedict. He said in 1980:

Judge Richard L. Benedict of the state's 26th District Court prosecuted me at every turn. He did his best to bury us, but he did not succeed because of the law. Even though he is a representative of the law, and a very poor one in my estimation, there was other representatives of the law who devoted more thought and less passion to my case. I respect the law. That is why I broke it, you know.[86]

Arthur recounted how Judge Benedict wanted the trial to go quickly because the judge wanted to be able to go fishing the next day:

Everyone came to see Judge Benedict and my trial. The courtroom was packed. Lots of Indians came. They flocked in. Benedict tried to hurry it up a bit. He stated from the bench that he wanted to go fishing the next day. I did not realize it then, but that statement said a lot about Benedict's commitments.... Benedict certainly revealed his sympathies when he tried to hurry the trial along so he could go fishing. His sport fishing was more important than my trial.[87]

Helen Tanner, a respected academic who is now a senior research fellow at the Newberry Library in Chicago, and who would later serve as the leading expert witness in the *United States v. Michigan* trial before Judge Fox, described Judge Benedict's behavior:

I actually testified in two state fishing rights cases before I became involved in *United States v. Michigan*. The most aggravating case was heard at the circuit court in Leland, Michigan in about 1975. It had to be completed in one long Friday marathon because the judge had already chartered a boat to go fishing on Saturday morning, so there was a great deal of pressure from the beginning at 8:30 a.m. I remember being acutely resentful at what I thought was the court's less than courteous treatment of [Waunetta] Dominic, a devoted leader of the Northern Michigan Ottawa Association, as she answered queries about the tribal licensing procedure and punishments for infractions of the tribal fishing code. By about 8 o'clock at night, the situation was clearly falling to pieces. I told the prosecuting attorney that they should have listened respectfully to every word that Mrs. Dominic said; that she was the expert on this subject, though that was apparently not recognized by the court. By that time, it was clear that the judge did not want to hear any historical background at all, either about fishing or the Treaty of 1836. He said that he had a copy of this treaty and anything he needed to know was "in the four corners of the document." I had never heard such a stupid assertion in all my life. Treaties are very complex and often obscure documents, but it was clear that he was not going to hear any more testimony, and planned to just read the treaty and render a decision.

Then, apparently, he thought a little more and he turned and asked me a question. I wish I could remember what it was. I took a deep breath and started to answer, when he broke in and stated, "I order you not to answer that question." I looked at him in utter amazement, and the prosecuting attorney looked rather confused and said "'[w]ell, I'd like to hear the answer to that question." Then the judge just roared, "[s]he can't answer that question in my hearing." So, I looked around to see what would happen next, and somebody in the audience stood up and said, "[w]ell, we'd like to hear the answer to the question." Then the judge shouted, "I will charge you with contempt of court if you say another word!" After that explosion, everything quieted down, but the lawyers and prosecuting attorney were all talking at once, as I understand that the transcript at that point drifts off into incomprehensible fragments. I am not sure about the decision, but I believe it was appealed and the higher court found the transcript inadequate. Anyhow, the experience reinforced my belief that you can never tell from one court to the next exactly how historical information will be received.[88]

Arthur added that Ms. Tanner's testimony "probably would not have made any difference. Benedict was not going to pay much attention to her testimony anyway."[89] Babette Duhamel Patton, Arthur's wife, recalled:

Helen Tanner was our expert witness. Her testimony was really important to our case. We needed her to establish the legitimacy of the treaty and Ottawa rights guaranteed by the treaty. She was put on last. Everybody was very tired. She was tired. She was a nervous person. It was late at night, but Benedict insisted that she testify. He insisted she testify because fishing season opened the next morning and he was not going to miss opening day.

All during the trial when witnesses were up on the stand, Benedict would slump back in his chair with his eyes shut, just contemptuous of the whole proceeding. . . .

During the trial, Benedict insulted Mrs. Waunetta Dominic, chairwoman of the Northern Michigan Ottawa Association. He ridiculed her position and the organization. He demeaned the [NMOA] identification cards, and the association's conservation code. . . .

Judge Benedict would only let the jury decide on the state law; nothing was said about the treaty. Now that is the whole issue, the treaty. When he charged the jury, he told them they should just decide did it happen or not, and pay no attention to any treaty.[90]

Arthur noted that the judge believed his decision would catapult him to fame and power:

Well, Benedict was aware that this was not an ordinary case. He wanted to make a landmark decision—a decision of landmark quality. Benedict said so in a speech he gave to the Grand Traverse Area Sportsfishing Association at the Holiday Inn in Traverse City. This was in the spring of 1978. The newspaper said, "Benedict expressed hope that his decisions would ultimately come to be regarded as landmark quality."[91]

Virtually everyone in the Grand Traverse Band community that exercised their treaty-protected right to fish in the Great Lakes fished with or worked for Arthur Duhamel after he began fishing in August 1974.[92] "To younger fishermen and Band members, Duhamel is legendary."[93] Ed John said, "I started commercially fishing with Art Duhamel, who broke into the fishing for the Grand Traverse Band. I worked gill nets with him for about five years. I started fishing for a living in 1975 or 1976."[94] James Raphael said:

I came up here around 1981, 1982, or 1983. It has probably been about sixteen years now. There was not a whole lot of work. I looked around for work but could not find a job. Somebody directed me to Art Duhamel—Skip's father. They said, "Go down and see him. He fishes and can probably put you to work." Art was my cousin. Skip was my cousin too.

I went down there and that was my first involvement with fishing. I introduced myself and he said, "Oh, you are my cousin." He had a crew of people working at the time. He was kind of old; he did not do a whole lot himself. When Art could, he would go out. . . .

I worked with Art for a few years. Pretty much everybody worked for him. Art Duhamel was the man as well as a couple of other gentlemen up north—tribal people—who fought for our fishing rights during the 1970s.[95]

In 1984, represented by William Rastetter, Arthur Duhamel brought suit against the Michigan Department of Natural Resources in an attempt to recover the property that the state had taken from him over the years since the treaty fight began.[96] The suit was not successful.[97] The suit, heard by Judge [Richard] Enslen, read in part:

In the present action, plaintiff seeks to enforce the rights and duties this Court declared in its 1979 opinion. Specifically, in the remaining count of his complaint, plaintiff requests the Court to declare that defendants have violated his constitutional rights by having failed to expunge his arrest and prosecution records, and to return his confiscated fishing equipment and gear and/or to compensate him for the loss of such equipment and gear, as required by this Court's 1979 decision. In addition, he requests the Court to award him nominal and punitive damages for defendant's failure to have abided by that decision.[98]

Judge Enslen was sympathetic to the claim, but denied it. He wrote:

The issue . . . is how to compel defendants to abide by the duties the Court established in its 1979 opinion and order. The present case suggests one way to compel compliance: Allow the Indian fishermen who are the beneficiaries of that opinion and order to initiate separate suits against defendants seeking relief under the theory that defendants' failure to have complied with the Court's opinion and order violates the fishermen's constitutional rights. Specifically, the Court could find that defendants' failure to have expunged the fishermen's criminal convictions and records violates the privileges and immunities that the Court recognized in its 1979 opinion, and violates the fishermen's liberty interests because defendants are maintaining the records unlawfully. Presumably, then, every Indian fisherman who has a fishing-related criminal arrest and conviction that falls within the scope of the Court's opinion and order would be entitled to sue to enforce his right to have that arrest and conviction expunged, and to recover damages for defendants' noncompliance with such opinion and order.[99]

But instead of ordering the DNR to comply, Judge Enslen decided instead:

Given the circumstances of this case, however, I do not believe that plaintiff's way is the proper one. The Court finds, rather, that plaintiff should raise his compliance issues in the ongoing *United States v. Michigan* proceeding, and should seek to compel compliance through the contempt process or by other appropriate means in that proceeding.[100]

In 1989, after yet another incident in which vandals destroyed his fishing equipment, Arthur left Peshawbestown.[101] He swore he would return in time to participate in the negotiations at the expiration of the 1985 Consent Decree in 2000, but he walked on in 1992.[102]

Grand Traverse Band Anishinaabek continue to fish in the Great Lakes and in Grand Traverse Bay because of the influence of Arthur Duhamel. Skip Duhamel said:

> My dad is dead now, but he raised me, him and Geebo. Their influences were paramount to my growing up. I returned home to make sure that my father's work was done. We have been doing the best I can with the help of my crew and my brothers and cousins. And we are going to continue to do the best we can. There are many hard times ahead, but we look forward to the time when our children may not have to endure such hardships in order to make a livelihood on the Great Lakes.[103]

The Fox Decision: *United States v. Michigan* and the Grand Traverse Band

At its heart, the litigation over the treaty right to fish in the Great Lakes involved the fundamental question of whether Michigan Indian people retained rights of self-government, or whether the State of Michigan and its citizens had been successful in destroying those rights.

At the outset of the treaty fishing controversy, the State of Michigan argued that its regulations limiting the fishing rights of Indian people were nondiscriminatory laws, applying equally to all citizens of Michigan.[104] Many non-Indians who opposed tribal treaty fishing argued that treaty rights were violations of their right to equal protection, and that state regulations created a level playing field.[105] Moreover, the state and its allies argued that Michigan Indians learned gill-netting from the French, and that the treaty protected only the technologies that were unique to Indian people.[106] Judge Noel Fox dispelled these myths with a short statement in the beginning pages of his mammoth opinion in *United States v. Michigan* recognizing the continuing validity of treaty rights preserved in the 1836 Treaty of Washington: "Michigan would take the Indians' subsistence and livelihood, their right to fish, and divide it by a modern-day lottery, the Indians being permitted to compete for licenses equally with those who have taken their rights away from them."[107] From these words, it was apparent that the people of the Grand Traverse Band and the other 1836 treaty signatories would retain their rights to make their own laws and be ruled by them, at least in Judge Fox's court.

The lawsuit began on April 9, 1973, when the United States sued the State of Michigan in federal district court to enjoin the state from interfering in the treaty rights of the federally recognized treaty signatories to the 1836 Treaty of Washington. At that time, the only tribe that met that category was the Bay Mills Indian Community, which intervened in the lawsuit in 1974. The Sault Ste. Marie Tribe of Chippewa Indians had attained federal recognition and intervened in 1975. It would not be until October 1979, after federal recognition and nearly two years after the *United States v. Michigan* trial began on February 9, 1978, that the Grand Traverse Band would be allowed to intervene in the case. In 1994, the Little Traverse Bay Bands of Odawa Indians and the Little River Band of Ottawa Indians also intervened after Congress reaffirmed their status as federally recognized Indian tribes.

The trial began with the United States attorney for the Western District of Michigan, James Brady, giving an opening statement to the effect that the United States and the 1836 Treaty tribes were not asking for new rights, but simply the preservation of reserved rights contained in the treaty:

> In this case the testimony will show that the Indians gave up many things, including most of the land area of the State of Michigan and a substantial portion of the Great Lakes, and reserved very little to themselves; but they did have the foresight to reserve their fishing rights, the key to their continued cultural integrity and very existence. And what did the Indians receive from the United States?
>
> The terms of the Treaty show they got practically nothing.
>
> So we ask this Court not to give the Indians anything, but only to allow them to keep what they already have—a right to fish in the ceded waters of the Great Lakes. For it must be remembered that it was we, the non-Indians, that took from them their land, much of their culture, and much of their integrity.
>
> This court need not give the Indians anything, but simply prevent the State of Michigan from taking any more from these people.[108]

The State's opening statement, by Assistant Attorney General Gregory T. Taylor, was not as smooth. Taylor noted that the State's primary expert witness, Dr. Philip P. Mason of Wayne State University, would testify that the 1836 Treaty was a removal treaty, meaning that the Indians who signed the treaty understood that there would be no reserved rights beyond a few years because the treaty provided that the Michigan Anishinaabek would be forced to leave

Michigan.[109] Judge Fox interrupted Mr. Taylor to state the obvious: "But there was no removal."[110]

On May 7, 1979, Judge Fox issued a ninety-page opinion that upheld all the major claims made by the plaintiffs.[111] Judge Fox first underscored the controversial character of the litigation by taking the unusual step of discussing some of the activities of the defendants and their non-Indian supporters. He noted that, in violation of the Federal Rules of Civil Procedure and general notions of fair play, sports fishermen (likely represented by formal groups that participated in the litigation as *amici curiae*) had circulated petitions urging the court to strike down tribal treaty rights.[112]

The first key holding made by Judge Fox was that the *ogemuk* reserved rights under the 1836 Treaty of Washington, and not that the United States granted those rights.[113] It is a fine point, but one of a critical character. It meant that Judge Fox recognized that the Indian tribes that signed the treaty already possessed the full panoply of sovereign rights prior to the execution of the treaty. As such, the United States was in no position to *grant* the rights contained in the treaty. The tribes already possessed them, and in fact had exercised them since time immemorial.

Judge Fox then found that commercial and subsistence fishing rights on the Great Lakes had also been explicitly reserved in the treaty.[114] The plaintiffs offered mounds of evidence that Michigan Indians had relied upon fishing the Great Lakes for over 10,000 years, and that after the arrival of the Europeans, Michigan Indians used their fishing capabilities to trade for the newest goods available.[115] In addition, the Indians who signed the treaty believed that the treaty had preserved their rights to use the land that the treaty ceded to the United States.[116] They believed this because Henry Schoolcraft, the lead treaty negotiator for the United States, told them exactly that. He said, after the Senate had made unilateral amendments to the treaty to change the import of the reservation creation provisions, that "they could continue to use all their lands as before, leading them to understand that this use would go on without limit."[117]

Judge Fox applied longstanding rules relating to Indian treaty interpretation in his finding that the 1836 Treaty reserved fishing rights. In short, Indian treaty provisions that are vague or ambiguous are to be interpreted as the Indians of that time would have understood them. Judge Fox noted:

> The treaty was imposed by subtle, invidious and insidious negotiators who sought only signatures without regard for whether they were a product of free

consent; the treaties binding the Indians were written in English, although the Indians knew no English and their language arose out of a hunting and fishing tradition without a concept of property; interpreters could only describe general outlines of the agreement; details were left to the good faith of the drafters; the final version of the treaty was drafted behind closed doors by Henry Schoolcraft and the traders who escorted the Indians to Washington; these men had conflicts of interest and each was rewarded handsomely by the treaty, altogether receiving over a quarter of a million dollars.[118]

The final major holding made by Judge Fox was that the 1855 Treaty of Detroit did not, and was not intended to, abrogate the fishing rights included in the 1836 Treaty.[119] According to Judge Fox, the United States intended the 1855 Treaty to concentrate Indian people on smaller amounts of land, not abrogate the 1836 Treaty fishing rights.

Judge Fox's decision was not popular with the non-Indian sports fishermen, or with state politicians. The Michigan United Conservation Clubs, with a strong influence on the people and policies of the Michigan Department of Natural Resources,[120] continued a public campaign against treaty fishers. Glen Sheppard's *Northwoods Call*, out of Charlevoix, printed vituperative columns rallying against Grand Traverse Bay treaty fishers, and even went so far on at least one occasion as to issue veiled death threats in print against treaty fishers and Judge Fox.[121] Vigilantism against treaty fishers increased as well, and state and local officials often refused to prosecute.[122] Governor William Milliken and Attorney General Frank Kelley made a lot of noise criticizing the Fox decision, the federal government, and treaty fishers.[123] According to Ron Paquin, the state and the non-Indians perpetuated the myth that tribal fishers were unregulated:

> Now, the DNR messed up people's minds in this town. They're always saying there's no rules, no limits. *Unregulated* is the word they used. These Indians is unregulated, just lawless, they say. Local people believed them lies after a while, and it made things bad for us. The newspapers printed this stuff, too. Indians is raping the lakes, they said. The *Weekly Wave* in Cedarville, Michigan, was probably the worst, but other papers said things like I'm telling you now, and for a long time none of them told the truth or give us a fair shake.[124]

Tribal fishing regulations were—and are—at least as rigorous as state regulations. According to James Raphael:

We follow our conservation rules—they are right on us daily. We have heavy-duty fines and have been in [tribal] court many times for not turning in a catch report. So the things that are talked about as far as unregulated fishing are totally untrue. We follow all the rules and regulations. If I did not, I would be in a brand new house. We would have more fish. We would be making more money than we do in the middle of all the struggles.[125]

Anti-treaty, anti-tribal people argued that tribal fishers were depleting the fishery in the Great Lakes. But Ron Paquin responded with simple math: "If you take a small number—100,000 sportsmen—and they catch three fish a day—that is low, too—how many fish are you going to catch in a day? Now multiply that into a year. That is a lot of fish. They cleaned this area out right over here."[126]

After Judge Fox issued his major opinion in May 1979, the State of Michigan appealed to the Sixth Circuit Court of Appeals. But the state also took steps to delay the court order's effective date or otherwise subvert Judge Fox's decision, including issuing its own proposed regulations for treaty fishing.[127] Judge Fox refused to grant the state's motion for an order delaying the effective date of the decision, and the Sixth Circuit issued a stay on the implementation of Judge Fox's injunction.[128] In the meantime, the Department of the Interior, through the United States Fish and Wildlife Service, issued regulations intended to settle the dispute, largely favoring the tribes.[129] The Sixth Circuit later remanded the appeal back to Judge Fox for his consideration on whether the Department of the Interior's fishing regulations preempted the state regulation.[130] In April 1981, following a campaign promise from President Ronald Reagan, the new secretary of the Interior, James Watt, allowed the federal regulations to expire.[131]

In the appeal, the Sixth Circuit affirmed Judge Fox's order except for one question—the state's authority to regulate off-reservation treaty fishing for conservation purposes.[132] One argument the state had been making all along was that Indians exercising their treaty rights were to blame for much of the decline in the Great Lakes fishery.[133] Although this claim had little factual validity, based on the state's own reports, the argument had rhetorical sway for non-Indians who opposed treaty fishing. Like the federal courts in the Washington State treaty fishing cases, the Sixth Circuit allowed the State Department of Natural Resources to issue minimal fishing regulations as a means of conserving the resource, but mandated that the expired federal regulations be restored as the valid interim regulations.[134] The negotiations over off-reservation treaty rights began at that point, and would not conclude for four years.

In addition to the machinations of the state government, anti-Indian groups continued their political, legal, and rhetorical assault on Indian rights. The Grand Traverse Area Sports Fishing Association argued that the Grand Traverse Anishinaabek were ruining the bay and its lake-trout fishery with their gill-netting.[135] They brought suit against seven fishers in 1979 and convinced a Traverse City judge to enjoin treaty fishing in the bay.[136]

During the legal wrangling after the Fox decision, the competition for the fishery between the tribal fishers, the commercial fishers, and the sports fishers may have begun to deplete the overall fishery, with tribal fishers unable to compete with the large numbers of sports and commercial fishers.[137]

> In an attempt to save the basic stocks of fish, the tribes, the state, and the United States agreed to close the fishery each year as soon as a certain amount of fish had been caught. As the competition increased, closure occurred earlier and earlier each year, and the tribes took a smaller and smaller percentage of the catch. The tribes could not compete technologically with the state commercial fishers, nor were they numerous enough to compete with the burgeoning state sports fishers.[138]

Ron Paquin described the impact of the closures on his business and livelihood and objected to the rationale:

> Then the closures started. You couldn't fish here. You couldn't fish there. They shut the waters, and I couldn't earn a living no more. For a while I had figured that I would be a fisherman. Fishing would be my job. The closures ruined that. I couldn't plan. I didn't know what to do. Get in? Get out? Buy more stuff? Sell everything?
>
> Bureaucrats closed parts of the lakes because they thought so many fish was being caught in them places that the fish was being depleted till they couldn't reproduce. This is mostly bullshit.[139]

The relatively late arrival of the Grand Traverse Band into the *United States v. Michigan* litigation and negotiation was not welcomed by the parties to the dispute. The Grand Traverse Band, with its obvious and extensive interest in the Grand Traverse Bay, pressured tribal and federal negotiators to preserve gill-netting in and around the bay.[140] Until the intervention of the Grand Traverse Band, it appeared that the *United States v. Michigan* plaintiffs were willing to give up the bay.[141]

Prior to the negotiation of the consent decree in 1985, the negotiating position of the three parties was incredibly far apart. The tribes argued that they had the primary rights to the fishery, arguing that the treaty rights were supreme; the state argued for an economic distribution of the fishery, which would benefit the commercial and sports fishers; and the United States wanted a fifty-fifty split similar to that reached in the *United States v. Washington* case.[142]

The State of Michigan's legal and political strategy to undermine Judge Fox's decision was a partial success. Although the state lost on nearly every key legal question, their delaying strategy forced the United States and the 1836 Treaty tribes into the long process of negotiating a final agreement, resulting in the 1985 Consent Decree.[143] Judge Enslen, who ordered the parties to negotiate a settlement if at all possible, noted that "the public interest in a peaceful, and practically enforceable resolution of this matter mandates as preferable a resolution by settlement rather than trial."[144] Judge Enslen himself, however, expressed skepticism that the parties could ever reach agreement, only to then express shock and deep satisfaction when they did.[145]

The 1985 Consent Decree

The consent decree reached on March 28, 1985, by the United States, the State of Michigan, the Grand Traverse Band, the Bay Mills Indian Community, and the Sault Ste. Marie Tribe of Chippewa Indians settled—for fifteen years—many of the major disputes over treaty fishing in the Great Lakes under the 1836 Treaty, while leaving many troubling issues unresolved.[146]

The agreement created an executive council, with representatives of each of the parties, to decide all major disputes between the parties, but did not vest that council with sufficient authority.[147] The agreement also allocated the fishery between Indians and non-Indians, and between tribes.[148] The parties created zones in Lakes Michigan, Huron, and Superior that created territories in which tribes would share the resources with others, and some territories in which a tribe had exclusive fishing rights.[149] The agreement finally created a cooperative regulatory scheme over the fishery. But the decree also contained structural incentives to overharvest the fishery.[150]

The cooperative character of the agreement is evidenced by Judge Enslen's 1992 comments during a federal court proceeding to decide a dispute involving the tribes. He stated:

> But through your acceptance of the 1985 Consent Decree, you committed to working together until the conflict was resolved, at least until the year 2000. That means I do not view these proceedings . . . as adversarial proceedings. We have a common goal, and that goal is the just implementation of the consent agreement.[151]

Grand Traverse Bay was a special case, however:

> The Grand Traverse Bay area was especially problematic. Fishing in this area was essential to the livelihood of GTB members; recreational fishing by non-Indians also was immensely popular. The Grand Traverse Bay Area Agreement was negotiated separately, and the GTB was the only tribe allowed to fish commercially in the waters around Leelanau County and the Grand Traverse Bay.[152]

The consent decree prohibited commercial fishing in the southern end of the bay, banned gill-netting in the middle of the Grand Traverse Bay, and limited the use of trap nets to the summer.[153] The consent decree required GTB fishers to stop gill-netting altogether after January 1, 1988, provided that the state supplied the fishers with replacement trap nets and technical assistance.[154]

From the point of view of the Grand Traverse Anishinaabe fishers, the consent decree was far from ideal. In fact, for some fishers, it was a disaster. The consent decree reserved the three grids surrounding the Leelanau Peninsula for the exclusive commercial use of the Grand Traverse Band, but the band agreed to stop fishing in two of the best gill-fishing grids in the bay.[155] The state agreed to develop and fund trap-net fishing operations as a replacement for the GTB fishers, but the state did not do its job.[156] Nevertheless, the state successfully petitioned Judge Enslen to close the grids to gill-netting in 1992.[157] As a result, the Grand Traverse Band sought to open the entire bay up to GTB fishers in a petition to Judge Enslen, a petition that the judge granted in 1997.[158]

The Perspectives of Grand Traverse Band Fishers on the 1985 Consent Decree

The 1985 Consent Decree was very unpopular with Grand Traverse fishers. First, they had to go far from home to fish.[159] James Raphael noted:

> Our reservation is here [Peshawbestown] because it is hidden from the wind. Now we got the state trying to say we cannot fish from here, which forces us into open water. I mean we were riding ten- to fifteen-foot seas just to catch some fish last fall going into winter. We were looking straight down into the water. Some of those waves were coming over the boat. They forced us out of here over there in open water.[160]

Moreover, Grand Traverse Band fishers could not fish with gill nets south of the 45th Parallel, where many of them say there is better fishing.[161] James Raphael argued:

> When they made this agreement in 1985, they blocked us off and made boundaries and lines. Wherever there was fish they made a line. They knew exactly what they were doing—the State of Michigan—trying to decide where to let us go and not to let us go. Even now, toward the end of this agreement, they have us boxed up right into nothing.[162]

Cindi John added that one of the best gill-netting areas was reserved for trap-netting, but the area was not so good for trap-netting:

> The grid up north, south of Charlevoix 616, should be opened up. It is a good gill-netting area. The bottom of it is not really suited for trap nets. It is a real flat ledge. Judge Enslen went through it and he said: "I am still not going to open the grid." . . . I thought he was going to open our waters and I left crying. I just thought—I could not believe that he would look at it that way but he sees things from a different viewpoint. That was my experience with Enslen.[163]

Before the consent decree, according to Yvonne Keshick from the Little Traverse Bay Bands of Odawa Indians, tribal fishers could move around the Great Lakes, following the fish:

> All the fishing people used to go to different places to fish. They would go to Lake Huron, Lake Superior, or Lake Michigan. Back then, you fished wherever you

felt like fishing. Then the lines started being drawn because of the controversy and the tribes allowed the government to divided and conquer.[164]

And yet, some tribal fishers argue that the consent decree was as good as the tribes could get from the state. According to Ron Paquin:

> It is not the best we are going to get but at least we can fish now. You can go out there and make a living. That is the best we can do. We are not going to get any better. Because if you prolong it and fight for more, you are going to be poorer than you are now. But at least we can go out and fish.[165]

Because of the relative arbitrariness of the grid lines, tribal fishers complain that they are forced to fish for inferior species.[166] Moreover, the tribal fishers complain that the fishing grids, coupled with the state interest in developing the lake-trout population, destroyed the whitefish fishery. According to James Raphael:

> This is supposed to be a good time to be fishing, but it is not. We used to have whitefish in here. They planted so many lake trout, they chased them and their predators away. They should be trying their damndest to restore the whitefish. I think they have in the past, but they are not putting a lot of effort into it. We should be trying. We should have a hatchery on the lake, with a pipe fish into the lake.[167]

Further, the state successfully persuaded the tribes to limit the amount of gill-net fishing, with the consent decree containing provisions encouraging the use of fish traps rather than gill nets.[168] The implementation of the provisions to train and equip tribal fishers to use fish traps was frustrating to tribal fishers. According to Ed John:

> They started a trap-net program working out of Omena. They got a boat from the feds. The boat's name was the *Lady Hilma*. I worked on that boat on a training program for about four years or five years. About three different crews went through the training program but nobody actually took over the vessel. It kept on being like a training program. I think the feds and the state funded it. I am not sure what was to take place after the program was over. It got to a point where the tribe no longer wanted to continue the program and it ended. The

end of fishing season came and we got these pink slips saying that the program was over. We did not know what to do. We went to a tribal council meeting of the Grand Traverse Band of Ottawa and Chippewa Indians. We addressed the tribal council and asked them about fishing the boat. There were three of us working on the boat at the time. They would allow us to fish it for a year. We had to get a lease agreement for the boat, and pay about $10,000 a year. But the crew could not lease it; the lease had to be in an individual's name. Then the effort went down the drain.[169]

Moreover, tribal fishers complained that a trap-net fishing operation was almost impossible to make profitable. Cindi John said:

In one of the all-time management highlights of the 1985 Consent Decree, they put together a group of biologists representing the state, tribe and federal governments, and told them that they were going to manage the [trap-net] project. All the usable data that they had and used to go to court was derived from us desperately trying to stay in the business and financing our own vessel. . . . We showed them that if you had a small trap-net vessel, it had to be built for its intended purpose. It had to be insurable. A boat builder will only build down to a certain size boat because of liability and all of the realities and nuts and bolts of it. But when we got the boat built, they did not have us work ten-foot trap nets off it. They had us work sixteen-, twenty-, and thirty-foot trap nets which, in essence, are the same size nets that you would work off a forty-five-foot vessel, except they made them skinny so that they would fit over the back of the little boat. So the gear did not change, but the boat size changed, and we worked in really unsafe conditions.

What we went through is documented. We could not remove gear from the water and we were held liable for it. At the same time, we showed them that you could go out and catch 100,000 pounds of fish with that vessel. But the true cost of the operation was the same as a large trap-net operation. . . .

I went in front of Judge Enslen on the small trap-boat issue. . . . We were in front of the judge and he looked at all the evidence. He started right off noting that we are not subsidized. He realized that if we had to buy all this equipment, we would lose $26,000 a year. Even if the equipment was bought for us and we were allowed to use it, he realized that we would lose $26,000 a year.[170]

Cindi John noted that a whole section of the Grand Traverse Bay was excluded from tribal fishing altogether because the implementation and planning of the trap-net operation was so poor:

> The tribes signed onto the 1985 Consent Decree without a database and thought, in good faith, that they would be provided with training in trap-net rigs. They did know what type of areas would be required for these rigs to sustain themselves. They should have come up with a plan that would have allowed our fishermen to use smaller boats with feasible gear. But this plan was not followed, particularly the way tribal fishers thought it would unfold—and a whole area of Grand Traverse Bay got shut down.[171]

The consent decree also codified the tribal regulatory structures that had been in place for as long as a decade or more in some places. Grand Traverse Band fishers like Cindi John have described the tribal regulatory scheme as being overly strict:

> We are really managed. Every month, we file a catch report. On a daily basis you tell where you fished, how much net you fished, species caught, the number of pounds of species caught, whether it was whole or gutted, and the price per pound. You tell where you launched. Then, to really make those figures credible, when you sell your fish, there is a wholesale report. There are three copies of the report. There is a copy that goes to the fishing person, a copy that goes to the tribes, and a copy that goes to the state. There are certain areas that you can use. Our code books define where you can fish, how you can fish, how deep you can fish, and when you can fish there and that was really dissected. Being a fishing person turns you into a mini-lawyer. We are enforced by the state and by our tribal conservation officers. Other tribes can enforce each other, as well as the federal officials and the Coast Guard. We have been boarded by all of them although not frequently. They boarded more frequently when we were gill netting than trap netting.[172]

Skip Duhamel adds:

> They think we are unregulated. We are the most highly regulated fishery. There is a fish council for every one of us. I mean, our own, and that is not county, the

state, and higher ups. That is tribal fishing. We have our own Fish and Wildlife. They call me up to find out if I am working on a weekend to find out whether or not they have to go to work or not. It is really quite funny. We do not get away with anything. As soon as they know I am here, they will be here every day checking and trying to figure out any way they can stop me.[173]

The Marina Cases: *Grand Traverse Band v. Michigan DNR*

In 1994, the Grand Traverse Band sued the Michigan Department of Natural Resources, the Township of Leland, and the Village of Northport. Leland and Northport had closed their public marinas to Grand Traverse Band commercial fishers. George ("Skip") Duhamel had begun to occasionally moor his large commercial fishing vessel at the public marinas in Leland and Northport. These two marinas were the only facilities close enough to the open waters in grids 615 and 714 for tribal fishers to maintain a viable commercial fishing operation in these grids. Local non-Indian opposition to tribal fishing made berthing there hazardous. According to Skip Duhamel:

> One particular time in Leland, they stole everything. I put five gangs in and they were all gone the next day. When we first started going over there, I was out by myself lifting nets a whole fleet of them, eight, ten of them came out on boats with intentions to sink me or do away with me because that is what they said on shore. We got to do away with him.[174]

The Michigan DNR contracted with the Northport public marinas in the 1960s to limit the commercial fishing boats in exchange for state financial assistance in constructing the marinas. The Leland marina made a similar agreement with the state in 1988. On July 2, 1993, Northport marina officials told Skip Duhamel to remove his vessel from the marina because their contract with the state DNR limited the number of mooring slips to be used for commercial purposes to a mere five. And those five were all being used by a tourist boat called the "Manitou."

Using what Judge Enslen characterized as "choice words," Duhamel refused to remove his vessel. He was cited for trespassing and disturbing the peace.[175] Northport and Leland marina officials informed the Grand Traverse Band that tribal commercial fishers would be cited for trespassing in the future should they continue to attempt to moor their boats there. Grand Traverse Band lawyers and leaders sought to negotiate a compromise, but the marina officials refused to budge.

Skip Duhamel testified that the only means of fishing safely in grids 615 and 714 in Lake Michigan was to use a large enough vessel and to have access to public marinas:

> Even if I had a trailer and truck large enough to haul a vessel this size, it would still be necessary to moor my vessel occasionally at public marinas to: tend nets set temporarily away from normal fishing areas in Grand Traverse Bay, to unload nets, off-load fish, and seek shelter from storms.[176]

James Mitchell testified that only large vessels had the capability for safe fishing in grids further out into Lake Michigan:

> To fish for chubs . . . it is necessary to use a large fishing tug which cannot be trailered and launched at public access launching ramps. Likewise, to fish for whitefish or other species using impoundment gear . . . it is necessary to use a large trap net boat which also cannot be trailered and launched at public access sites.[177]

Judge Enslen rejected all of the defenses and objections raised by the defendants. He wrote in the critical portion of the opinion:

> Whether or not there is some limit on the GTB's right of access based on interference with the municipalities' and MDNR's use of the improvements to the marinas, any such limit has not been exceeded here. The fishers maintain that they need to access the marinas only occasionally, for periods commensurate with what the municipalities and the MDNR consider "transient" use of up to two weeks. There are no more than a few tribal fishers in the community. The GTB's own marina will consist of only ten slips once completed. There is no evidence that all the fishers fish the same places at the same time; and, to the Court's knowledge, no more than three tribal vessels have ever attempted to moor at the same time at the same marina. The marinas each consist of over 100 slips for mooring, about half of which are reserved for transient use. The marinas are essentially vacant for nine months out of the year; only during the

summer months would the GTB fishers even have an opportunity to obtain a slip that might otherwise be occupied by a non-tribal vessel. No evidence has been offered to indicate why a tribal fisher could not be treated as any other transient vessel seeking a slip during the summer months. Nor even has it been demonstrated why an occasional tribal vessel could not be given preference during the peak season.[178]

Both Leland and Northport appealed to the Sixth Circuit Court of Appeals. The State of Michigan, agreeing to withdraw the contractual limitations on the number of commercial vessels at the public marinas as a result of the litigation, refused to participate in the appeal. The Sixth Circuit affirmed.[179]

The 2000 Consent Decree

In the year 2000—the year of expiration for the 1985 Consent Decree—the same concerns raised on all sides of the treaty fishing issue in the 1970s and 1980s seemed to arise again. Sports fishers once again threatened violence while making the same tired arguments about Indians depleting the fishery. Grand Traverse Band fishers worried that their concerns arising from the 1985 Consent Decree would not be addressed.

And, despite some small victories, the 2000 Consent Decree did not serve the Grand Traverse Band fishers well. After a year of negotiations, the five 1836 Treaty tribes, the United States, the State of Michigan, and several nonparty commercial and sports-fishing associations came to an agreement in August 2000.[180] The key points to the deal included:

- An equitable division between state and tribal fishermen of the species available for harvest. The tribal commercial fishery will generally concentrate on harvesting whitefish and will also harvest other species. The state licensed sport fishery will concentrate on harvesting recreational species and lake trout harvest will be shared approximately equally.
- The removal of more than 14 million feet of annual large-mesh tribal gill net effort. To accomplish this goal, many of the largest tribal gill net fishing operations will be converted to impoundment (trap net) operations. Conversion will be accomplished, in part, by the voluntary agreement of State commercial fishers to sell their trap net operations to the State. The

State will then provide these operations to tribal commercial fishers who chose to participate. This conversion will reduce by-catch of other species, including lake trout.

• All parties agree that lake trout rehabilitation is an important goal in the scheme of fishery management. The agreement provides specific management provisions intended to accomplish lake trout rehabilitation in order to re-establish indigenous naturally reproducing lake trout.

• The agreement creates the Technical Fisheries Committee, an entity composed of biologists for each party, for consultation and collaboration on biological issues under the agreement.

• The agreement adopts a joint tribal fishery management plan and creates a management body called the Chippewa Ottawa Resource Authority (CORA) to which the tribes have delegated certain management and regulatory authority.

• The agreement provides for regular reports of fishing activity, notice to all parties of any proposed state or tribal regulatory action affecting the fishery, and for the exchange of biological information regarding the fishery resource.

• The agreement creates a law enforcement committee to consult and collaborate on enforcement issues and to create annual work plans for state and tribal enforcement agencies within the 1836 waters.[181]

The agreement was a hard pill for the Grand Traverse Band tribal council to swallow. Ardith ("Dodie") Chambers, the first tribal chair and a councilor at the time of the deal, told the New York Times: "The Grand Traverse Band hesitantly, really hesitantly agreed to sign off on the deal. . . . All the state wants to do is take apart treaty rights, and so does the federal government."[182] For the Grand Traverse Band, the 2000 Consent Decree was not a great deal:

> The Grand Traverse Band has only a dozen fishermen left. Most will lose their livelihoods because they do not catch enough fish to qualify for trap-net boats from the state, and they will face new restrictions on the use of gill nets, Ms. Chambers said.
>
> The Grand Traverse Band agreed to the pact because it is engaged in a separate dispute with the state over its main livelihood, the Turtle Creek Casino, a few miles east of Traverse City. The tribe is so dependent on the casino that it felt compelled to accept the fishing deal.

> Unlike the other four northern Michigan tribes, the Grand Traverse Band
> is far from the trap-net fishing grounds being established.[183]

The agreement allowed Grand Traverse Band fishers to fish one mile further
south in the bay, but that was the extent of the advances made by the band in
this area.[184]

The key victory for the Grand Traverse Band and its treaty fishers was that
the ordeal of the negotiations was over.

"Until the Land Is Required for Settlement": The Inland Consent Decree

In April 2004, the United States filed a request to raise the question of inland
hunting, fishing, and treaty rights in *United States v. Michigan*.[185] Inland treaty
rights in the ceded territory are the focus of Article 13 of the 1836 Treaty. Judge
Fox set aside the question of inland treaty rights in the 1970s in order to focus
on the Great Lakes fishing case. Unlike the Great Lakes litigation, inland treaty
rights did not have the same commercial value to the State of Michigan and
to non-Indian commercial and sports fishers, and so there appeared to be less
financial impetus to challenge the exercise of inland treaty rights. Moreover,
the Great Lakes litigation did not involve the private property interests of
thousands of non-Indians, many of whom were hostile to tribal sovereignty and
American Indians. Throughout the 1980s and 1990s, there had been numerous
flare-ups, especially where local law enforcement had arrested treaty hunters
on ceded lands, or where treaty fishers had crossed private property in order
to reach federal and state lands within the ceded territory. The United States,
the state, and the tribes had long been able to avoid a major legal battle over
inland rights arising from one of these minor arrests or citations.

During the negotiations, four of the 1836 Treaty tribes cut a deal with the
United States on exercising treaty rights on federal lands in Michigan. On
November 3, 2006, the Grand Traverse Band and three of the 1836 Treaty tribes
signed a memorandum of understanding with the United States Fish and
Wildlife Service to formalize treaty gathering rights on federal forest lands.[186]
This helped to pave the way for the final deal on the 1836 Treaty inland rights.

In 2007, the five 1836 Treaty tribes concluded four years of negotiations
with the State of Michigan over inland treaty rights by preserving *for all time*
the right to hunt, fish, and gather on federal and state public lands within the

territory ceded in the treaty.[187] The agreement had no termination date, and so it preserves the treaty rights indefinitely. The five federally recognized 1836 Treaty tribes agreed to limits on walleye and steelhead fishing and a ban on gill-netting on inland waters, but also agreed to expansive deer hunting on state and federal lands, and extensive gathering rights. Tribes also preserved the right to use trap nets on inland waters in certain circumstances. Another key victory for the tribes was to preserve the tribal authority to regulate their own tribal-member hunting and fishing, even on public lands, and to issue licenses.[188]

The *Grand Rapids Press* editorial page lauded the agreement, focusing on the limits of tribal commercial fishing and hunting rights:

> The best part of the agreement is that it's of indefinite length. That means that, unlike the Great Lakes agreement, we won't have to go through the anguish and expense, 10 years hence, of negotiating it again. To begin with, there is to be no commercial hunting or fishing. Indians will not be allowed to kill deer or spear walleyes and sell them. That's big.[189]

In the state's press release, Jimmie Mitchell, the natural resources director for the Little River Band of Ottawa Indians, stated:

> Once we agreed to sit down and talk, it quickly became apparent that we might really be able to resolve our differences by agreement. . . . What we accomplished during this negotiation was a reaffirmation of what our respective governments agreed upon back in 1836 when the treaty was signed. This will allow our people to continue to derive subsistence based on age-old methodology in an expression of our cultural identity.[190]

CHAPTER SIX

The Story of the Development of Modern Tribal Law and Justice Systems

G rand Traverse Band's customs and traditions based on kinship have served as the foundation of the tribe's law and justice system since time immemorial, but this ancient structure has been modernized in recent decades. One of the foundations of the good governance model developed by the Grand Traverse Band of Ottawa and Chippewa Indians has been the structure of the tribal government as created in the tribal constitution. The constitution created a tribal council free from intrusive federal government interference, and allowed for the creation of a separate economic development corporation. The constitution preserved the independence of the tribal judiciary necessary for the administration of a fair and honorable rule of law. And the constitution provided for the development of the Grand Traverse Band Code.

Customary and Traditional Law and Justice

The first forms of law and order appeared long before the arrival of the Europeans, and usually entailed the resolution of disputes involving hunting, fishing, and gathering rights, privileges, and territories. There also was a sophisticated system for dealing with criminal acts, as well as negligent acts. The Anishinaabek often taught each other general rules of behavior for all people by relating stories linked to the landscape. The story of the Pukwudjinni at the Picture Rocks in the Upper Peninsula is a good example:[1]

Kwasind, the story goes, was a free-spirited Saginaw Chippewa, whose life consisted of a little hunting, fishing, and a great deal of visiting. Kwasind's visits took place annually, in the summer, as he canoed around Lake Superior, using a paddle made only of cedar. After leaving his home, he would skirt the coast, cross the Straits of Mackinac, hug the coast again, ascend the St. Mary's River, follow the Upper Peninsula westward, round the enormous lake, and return to his home. His last trip was largely completed, when the spirits appeared. "Kwasind had passed Michipicoten [in present-day Ontario, near Wawa], on the north shore, and was paddling east toward Cape Chaillon." Here was a large cliff, and Kwasind spotted a canoe approaching it. Kwasind urged his canoe forward to meet them, but they turned "their heads down so that he could not see their faces." Kwasind called to them, and he heard the first paddler say to the last, "You look more like a man than I do. You speak to him." They were memegwessiwug.

Angered, Kwasind shoved their canoe into the rocks, but the beings with their vessel simply disappeared into the cliff side. Kwasind heard them still, however:

"Well, well; so Kwasind thought he could smash our canoe."

"Hush! Don't you know Kwasind is a manitou and can hear us? Keep still."

Kwasind passed on his way, descending the St. Mary's River and approaching Lake George. There, on the north (Canadian) side, "are rocks called pukwudinin-niewug." Kwasind saw the beings of the same name, "little midgets," racing along the cliffs above him. He jeered at them, questioning their sacred power. "By the time he was passing along ten miles below, the little men, who had been getting more and more furious over his taunting, picked up stones to throw at him." When Kwasind batted away one of the missiles with his paddle, the cedar snapped. "His power must have been in his cedar paddle, for the next rock struck him on the head and killed him."

Kwasind, a man of too much independence, had apparently taken too many freedoms with the spirit world, forgetting his dependence upon it. Chippewas would remember his story as they saw the places where Kwasind was said to have passed.

Kwasind's story was told on the Upper Peninsula, and it has relevance for that place.[2]

Unlike so many tribes that had been removed by the federal government west, northern Michigan tribes like the Grand Traverse Band retain many of the stories that provide the backdrop for law and justice in Indian Country. These stories are based on the Anishinaabemowin language and upon the geographic characteristics of the Anishinaabek.[3]

Disputes involving hunting and fishing territories often were disputes between families. Given the seasonal character of Michigan Anishinaabe lives, with small, inland winter hunting camps, larger spring sugar camps, and still larger summer villages along the coast, different disputes would be resolved by different individuals depending on where the dispute originated. For example, a conflict over the winter hunting and trapping territory of a family, say, trespassing, would be resolved through discussion between the heads of households of the two families, with threats of violence perhaps, but rarely involving any physical conflict.[4] A dispute over sugaring grounds, with larger groups of extended family units coming together, would be resolved by the heads of households meeting and talking together. A dispute between villages would have to be resolved by the *ogemuk* of each village. A dispute between regional confederacies (i.e., bands, as in the Grand Traverse Band) would be resolved by the *ogemuk* of each band. And a dispute between *tribes* (e.g., the Odawa and the Ojibwe, or the Seneca and the Huron) would have to be resolved by treaty—or warfare.

On the most fundamental level, family property rights were the basic form of property rights.[5] Individuals had far less import in the property-rights algebra, except for *ogemuk*, who represented a family unit, a village, or a band, and were described as "owning" the property rights.[6] These family property rights made little sense to the individualistic Europeans, who often chided Odawa hunters for giving away all the meat they harvested.[7] Alexander Henry, a British fur trader who participated in the 1763 battle at Fort Michilimackinac, described Ottawa hunting rights as such:

> Arrived here [at a sugar grove near Lake Michigan], we turned our attention to sugar-making, the management of which . . . belongs to the women, the men cutting wood for the fires, and hunting and fishing. In this midst of this, we were joined by several lodges of Indians, most of whom were of the family to which I belonged, and had wintered near us. The lands belonged to this family, and it had therefore the exclusive right to hunt on them. This is according to the custom of the people; for each family has its own lands.[8]

Henry further wrote:

> The beaver dams—so persons conversant with the subject assured me—all have owners among the Indians, and are handed down from father to son. The sugar camps . . . have all an owner, and no Indian family would think of making sugar at a place where it had no right. Even the cranberry patches, or places in the swamp and bush where that berry is plucked, are family property; and the same with many other things.[9]

Ruth Landes argued that territorial disputes—or even territories themselves—did not arise unless there was a shortage of some resources, or if there was an outside actor creating a large market for the resource.[10] It is possible that there was no need to delineate hunting and fishing territories prior to the arrival of the Europeans,[11] but there is no way in the printed record to determine this. Moreover, trade routes "could be used only by the family who pioneered them and who maintained a gift-exchange and kinship ties which assured safe passage for traders and a supply of goods when they reached their destination."[12] Even family members used a trade route only with the permission of the *ogema*.[13] Trespassers could be fined, charged some sort of toll, or even executed.[14] A tribal treaty fisher from St. Ignace, Ronald Paquin, recalled a story about an early fight over fishing territories:

> Years ago, the fishing that was going on here by Gros Cap was done by those of Indian and French extraction. This is way back in the 1800s. An Ottawa Indian who made a chief gave the white commercial fishermen a place called Point aux Chenes. There is a nice reef there. We fish it every fall when we fish whitefish. From Point aux Chenes to Millecoquins Lake is one of the oldest known reservation areas in history. Every time they did around there they find things. Anyway, there was one hell of a battle when the Ottawa who was made a chief gave the white people permission to fish the Indian grounds out there which they had been fishing for years. That was the first battle over fishing they say. I do not know if it was fist fighting or ramming boats or whatever, but that was the first battle.[15]

This form of property rights was a form of survival. Resources in the region were sufficient for the Michigan Anishinaabek, but the fabric of property rights ensured that the Anishinaabek utilized the correct amount of resources, and at the proper time of the year, so as to preserve the resources for the future.[16] The Anishinaabe calendar system of marking the months through describing the actions to be taken during that time, such as harvesting berries or fishing for sucker, demonstrate how this operated.[17]

As for individual rights, James McClurken wrote that "the first rule in Ottawa society was respect for the individual. No one person could determine the fate of another."[18] But all members of the community shared their wealth, labor, and food.[19] A person acquired prestige, respect, and even wealth by the act of gifting:

> The value of trading and gift giving was not only in acquiring goods for oneself, but in the social act of giving. By giving, individuals and families gained prestige and respect. A rich person did not have any more goods than his kinsmen; he simply gave more of what he had. The exchange of gifts was governed by a set of rules which bound giver and receiver. Each gift required some form of return and extended obligations of reciprocity across family lines to other tribes as well. The emphasis on sharing was so strong in Ottawa society that almost no interaction could be carried on without it.[20]

The act of violence by one person against another, as well as the act of stealing or even hoarding important resources, was a source of enormous danger to the small Ottawa communities.[21] Every person had an important role to play in the day-to-day activities of the community, such as producing food and shelter, and the loss of one person or one person's production capacity could be devastating. Ottawa communities would exile, or even execute, persons who violated the trust of the people through the act of murder or other crimes. Attempting to acquire too much personal or family power could result in exile as well, which often was voluntary.

Anishinaabe people dealt with acts of violence, especially accidents, not through retaliation but through remediation. One incident involving the accidental death of a small child through the misuse of a firearm by another child in 1846 is instructive. Peter Dougherty wrote that the family of the deceased child received a large gift of "guns and traps and blankets" from the other family.[22] This also demonstrates the importance of hunting and trapping to the Grand Traverse Anishinaabek.

Anishinaabe customs and traditions of domestic rules of marriage and divorce often differ from the norms of today. One Anishinaabek practice exemplifies the relative autonomy that Anishinaabekwewag (Anishinaabe women) enjoyed during this period. About 70 percent of all the food consumed in Anishinaabe villages was produced by women,[23] a fact that gave women individual authority. According to James McClurken:

> Because the work that Odawa women did in their traditional society was so important, they were afforded a great deal of personal freedom. For example, before the missionaries arrived at Wawgawnawkezee [L'Arbre Croche] in 1829, marriages were made when a groom moved into a woman's house. A woman could divorce a man simply by placing his belongings outside the door of the house.[24]

The ease of ending intimate relationships may have led outsiders to infer that the Anishinaabek practiced polygamy. In fact, polygamy was not typical for the Michigan Anishinaabek. Certain respected and wealthy *ogemuk* acquired political power within a local tribal community by taking additional wives.[25] These *ogemuk* could only do so if they had the economic power to take care of all of these families, and it was this economic power that demonstrated the political power of the *ogemuk*, not to mention the sheer numbers of supporters one could acquire by taking care of additional families.

Tribal leadership in a particular village involved four different individuals (*ogemuk*), according to James McClurken:

> In the traditional Odawa village, there were four *Ogemuk*, each with a special job to fulfill. *Meaosad*, or head chief, was the most respected man in the village. *Meaosad* was traditionally a middle-aged man with two or three wives and many children and grandchildren. As the head of a prominent family, he could call on his kinspeople to provide food and gifts for feasts as well as to support his opinions in council. Sometimes, *Meaosad* had distinguished himself in war and could call on his fellow warriors to support him.
>
> The *Wendikawad Ogema*, or deputy chief, was a younger man than *Meaosad* who showed promise as a leader. Often, the *Wendikawad Ogema* was a son or son-in-law of *Meaosad*. When *Meaosad* could no longer lead, the *Wendikawad Ogema* filled his position. Then there was *Dewewege*, the leader who beat the drum, who was responsible for opening ceremonies, and *Mejinowe*, the official voice of the village, who was so skilled in oration that when a formal council was held, either between Odawa villages or with non-Anishinaabe people, *Mejinowe* spoke the words of the *Ogemuk* and thus represented the people.[26]

Tribal leadership structures had a difficult time surviving during the period beginning in the treaty times. Much tribal customary law and tradition is encoded in the social ways of the living and future ways of the people of the Grand Traverse Band.

Interregnum

The customs and traditions of the Grand Traverse Band often fell by the wayside after the intervention and dominance by non-Indian governments and people from the treaty period (1795 to 1855) to the present day.[27] While traditional governance structures such as the recognition by an Anishinaabek community of a particular leader (*ogema*) (e.g., Ben Peshawbe) persisted, the overall internal social structure of the Grand Traverse Ottawa often fell apart. As times became harder and harder, with many more non-Indians present in or near Indian communities, it was more difficult to reach a consensus within a particular community over a course of action.[28] Perhaps just as important to overall Anishinaabe social structures, the lack of plenty—even bordering on starvation and penury for Indian people—all but foreclosed the ability of individuals and groups to continue the practice of gifting, or sharing, food and other resources.[29] Similarly, the various bands of Ottawas and Chippewas in Michigan also began to splinter. For example, during some treaty negotiations, Little Traverse Odawa *ogemuk* preferred to cede land in exchange for annuities, while Grand Traverse *ogemuk* did not.[30] This factionalization of Anishinaabek governance worked to the advantage of the Americans in many ways, but the Grand Traverse Band would persevere in another form.

The post-1836 Treaty Grand Traverse Band group demonstrates the transition of the community from a tribal group to a nation. The individual *ogemuk* who traveled to Washington—Aishquagonabe, Aghosa, and Oshawun Epenaysee—represented villages. Aishquagonabe and his nephew Aghosa were Ojibwe, the leaders of their respective villages located on the eastern shore of the Grand Traverse Bay. They were the leaders of their village because they were the heads of the major families in those villages. The rest of the villages were Ottawa and located mostly in what is now Leelanau County, or the western side of the Grand Traverse Bay. These villages collectively selected Oshawun Epenaysee, a prominent family and community leader, to represent them all in the treaty council. At the council, surely Aishquagonabe, who had taken scalps in the War of 1812, was the most influential Grand Traverse *ogema*, and likely the most influential Lower Peninsula *ogema*. His nephew and Oshawun Epenaysee would have followed his lead, but they had individual responsibilities to the communities that appointed them as representatives, and so they would not be required to follow Aishquagonabe.

This form of governmental structure remained intact through and beyond the next major treaty council, which negotiated the 1855 Treaty of Detroit. In that treaty council, Aghosa for a second time, Onawmoneese, and Peshawbe represented the Grand Traverse Bay communities. Several other lesser Grand Traverse Bay Anishinaabe leaders participated and signed the treaty as well. In a replay of the 1836 treaty council, the Lower Peninsula and Upper Peninsula Anishinaabe again selected separate speakers, preferring to negotiate as separate alliances. The American treaty commissioners—George Manypenny, the commissioner of Indian Affairs; and Henry Gilbert, Michigan Indian agent—did not have the wherewithal of Henry Schoolcraft, but still succeeded in forcing the various Anishinaabe bands to execute a treaty favoring the United States and its non-Indian constituents.

The terms of the treaty were disastrous to the Michigan Anishinaabek and forced some significant, unplanned, and yet incremental changes to tribal government structures. The key result of the treaty was to dispossess the Anishinaabek of their lands even as federal agents attempted to implement the terms of the treaty. This forced the Anishinaabe villages that existed on the perimeters of the various reservations to become the primary land base of the various bands. This consolidation helped to transform village government from one based on family structures to more of a municipal government, although that process took at least five or six decades.

By the 1870s, the United States had misinterpreted the 1855 Treaty language to mean that the Lower Peninsula bands that signed the treaty had voluntarily agreed to disband and abandon their tribal relations. Interestingly, the United States continued to recognize the Upper Peninsula bands. The treaty provision at issue appeared first in the 1836 Treaty, which identified the Indians who sat in the treaty council as a united Ottawa and Chippewa "nation." Obviously, this was not the case, in that there was a clear division between the Lower and Upper Peninsula tribal communities. The 1855 Treaty formally eliminated the fictional "nation," at the request of the tribal negotiators. Federal officials not present at the treaty council interpreted the provision to mean that the treaty signatories had agreed to self-terminate. Thus, administrative termination was born.

And so from the 1870s to the passage of the 1934 Indian Reorganization Act (IRA), the Lower Peninsula band governments focused on reconstituting the federal-tribal relationship begun in the 1836 Treaty and terminated in the 1870s. Meanwhile, in one instance, the band governments sued the United States to recover funds allocated under the 1855 Treaty for the tribes but never paid. The combination of these efforts formalized a government structure based on regional territories rather than family relationships. The tribal efforts in the 1930s and 1940s pressing for the right to reorganize under the IRA, and the decades-long Indian Claims Commission claims ending in the 1970s all but perfected the transformation of family-based village units to modern governments. Finally, in 1980 and in 1994, the United States recognized three Lower Peninsula Ottawa bands who signed the 1836 and 1855 treaties.[31]

These federally recognized Indian tribes—American Indian tribal nations— retain much of their character as family-based village groups, especially in that all of them require some sort of blood lineage in order to qualify as citizens. And perhaps because of this close relationship, many Anishinaabe customs and traditions—including the language and culture—remain intact, even if narrowly so. But in virtually all other respects, these Indian tribes are nations.

The Dispute over the Grand Traverse Band Constitution (1980–1988)

The Grand Traverse Band's petition for federal recognition, filed on its behalf by Leelanau Indians, Inc., contained important documentation about the tribe's history and ongoing attempts to restore its federal recognition, but it also included documents pertaining to how the tribe would begin governing itself after federal recognition. One important document included in the petition was a draft tribal constitution.

Newly recognized Indian tribes must "organize" under the terms of the Indian Reorganization Act (IRA), which includes the requirement that the tribe adopt foundation governing documents such as a constitution. This first constitution, under federal law, must be approved by the secretary of the Interior before the tribal community can vote to ratify it.[32]

The history of tribal constitutions for the Michigan Indian tribes who were federally recognized in 1934, when the IRA was passed, is spotty. The tribes in the Upper Peninsula adopted a form of what would later be derisively called a "model IRA constitution."[33] This tribal constitution included several basic provisions, following a loose structure that created a tribal council, election procedures for the tribal council, and amendment procedures for the constitution itself. What these constitutions also included was a provision that major decisions of the tribal council involving land or legal counsel had to be made with the concurrence of the secretary of the Interior. This was endemic in tribal constitutions ratified in the 1930s and beyond.[34]

Worse still, for the Saginaw Chippewa Indian Tribe, was the secretary's interference in that tribe's membership criteria. Tribal appellate judge Frank Pommersheim documented this incredible story in a tribal court opinion deciding a membership case in 2005.[35] He wrote about how the tribal leaders excitedly drafted an indigenous tribal constitution as soon as Congress passed the IRA, but were forced to discard it when the Bureau of Indian Affairs officers told them they had to vote on whether to adopt the IRA at all in the first place. This initial referendum included a broad voting electorate, according to the bureau's instructions, from the tribal communities on the Isabella Reservation as well as outlying Indian communities near Saginaw, Port Huron, and in the vicinity. In the bureau's view, the larger the number of possible voters, the more likely the tribe would choose to ratify the IRA. And so the tribe ratified the IRA easily.

But when the tribe returned with its draft constitution, the bureau again forced the tribe to discard much of it. They wanted the Saginaw Chippewa constitution to conform to the same general guidelines that the Upper Peninsula tribal constitutions followed—the same guidelines used nationwide. Moreover, the federal government was concerned that the membership provisions that the tribe proposed would include too many people, increasing the number of people eligible for additional federal services. And so the local BIA agents required the tribe to adopt membership criteria *excluding* many of the same people that the federal government wanted to *include* in the IRA ratification vote. The schizophrenic membership criteria imposed by the government contributed directly to the horrific membership disputes that plague the Saginaw Chippewa Indian Tribe to this day.

And, much as in the story of the Saginaw Chippewa, the Department of the Interior objected to the Grand Traverse Band's membership criteria. Since the Grand Traverse Band was the only Michigan Ottawa tribe to have achieved federal recognition by the 1980s, and since the relationships between the people of the Michigan Ottawa tribes was so close, the original membership criteria proposed by the drafters of the tribal constitution allowed for the people of the other Ottawa communities to become members of the Grand Traverse Band. This would not do for the federal government, then running under the strictures of the Reagan administration—which, like the Depression-era Department of the Interior, was driven by a desire to keep tribal membership low as a means of reducing federal appropriations.[36] According to former chairman Joseph C. (Buddy) Raphael:

> What happened to the Grand Traverse Band—basically, in a nutshell—we petitioned the federal government, and they said "yes" to 297 people, never realizing they were saying yes to thousands. . . . Once they realized their mistake, they readily backtracked and tried to confine us. They were somewhat successful. We went through years of negotiation to achieve our membership status as it stands today.[37]

The primary drafters of the Grand Traverse Band constitution—Michael Petoskey and William Rastetter—entered into long and tedious negotiations with the federal government over the membership criteria, as well as other sticking points. The government pointed out that the petition for federal recognition asserted that there were only 297 members of the Grand Traverse Band.[38] That was a number the Bureau of Indian Affairs could accept. But that list of tribal members was never intended to be exclusive. It included mostly people from

Leelanau and Grand Traverse counties, generally excluding the hundreds of Grand Traverse Band members who lived in urban areas like Detroit, Grand Rapids, and elsewhere. It even excluded many people who lived in other parts of the six-county service area, and it excluded tribal members who lived with family in other parts of Michigan's Indian Country. And, especially important, the list often excluded people who were eligible for membership in one or more other Michigan tribes, especially the other Michigan Ottawa tribes that did not yet enjoy federal recognition.

The dispute with the federal government over the membership criteria reached a peak when the Grand Traverse Band, represented by Bill Rastetter, filed a complaint in federal court over the government's reluctance to accept the tribe's membership criteria.[39] After the tribe filed the lawsuit, the assistant Interior solicitor wrote a letter to chairman Buddy Raphael asserting that the government would reconsider the decision to recognize the Grand Traverse Band if they continued to insist upon a larger membership base.[40] In other words, the government threatened to once again victimize the tribe with administrative termination.

The lawsuit, while never concluded with a court order, did its job. The government and the tribe compromised on key elements in the membership criteria. The tribe would limit membership to Indians of one-quarter blood quantum, so long as at least one-eighth of the Indian blood derived from Grand Traverse Band ancestors listed on the Durant Rolls of the 1900s.[41] The tribe still prevailed in many of its concerns by writing into the constitution an adoption provision that would allow the tribe to grant membership to most of the people the government wanted kept out,[42] primarily members of the community that would later become the Little Traverse Bay Bands of Odawa Indians. Then-chairman Raphael's letter to the tribal membership explained the painful compromise:

> A major point of contention throughout this exercise was membership criteria adopted by the Tribe. For years now, we have enrolled people based on tracing back to several books of the Durant Rolls and Field Notes. The Bureau [of Indian Affairs] contended that we should limit the books and notes we referenced to what they defined as the "Historic Grand Traverse Bands." They contended that some of the "Traverse Notes" related to what was termed the Little Traverse Band.
>
> After a good deal of disagreement, we compromised on the issue. We agreed with limiting the notes and books to be referenced if the Bureau would agree to

allow members that reside in the five-county service area to stay enrolled, whether or not they traced to the notes the Bureau felt were applicable. In addition, we demanded that the Bureau go on record recognizing the present day existence of the Little Traverse Band, and that they further agree, in writing, to assist the Little Traverse Band to organize as a present day Tribal entity.[43]

Then-chairman Raphael's letter to the membership also noted the disagreement about whether the Grand Traverse Band should limit its membership to quarter-blood Indians:

> Some have contended that we should not hold with the one-quarter blood requirement. It should be understood that in the beginning negotiations regarding the Constitution the blood quantum discussed was just for the village of Peshawbestown. Also, the first blood quantum discussed was to limit membership to half-blood Grand Traverse Band. As we went along, it was agreed to go to one-quarter blood Grand Traverse Band and to include other Ottawa and Chippewa in the region. Now we are at a point where quarter blood with tracing to GTB is the rule, should the Constitution be adopted. We feel this has opened the door sufficiently, and still allows for the majority of Indian people seeking entry to ally with the Grand Traverse Band.
>
> Our goal is to retain the Indian blood line and establish a viable Native community made up of Indian people. To go further in opening the door would diminish the heritage.[44]

In general, the Grand Traverse Band constitution included many of the same standard provisions found in the other Michigan tribal constitutions dating back to the 1930s, but the tribal negotiators secured several critical provisions. First, the tribal constitution created a separate branch of government, an independent tribal judiciary.[45] Other Michigan tribes had tribal courts, but they were courts created by the tribal councils—and subject to their complete defeasance by simple legislation.[46] The Grand Traverse Band's tribal court was the first in Michigan to be completely independent, meaning that the tribal council could not, under the constitution, control the court through legislation.[47] Under many of the tribal constitutions adopted by the secretary of the Interior before the 1980s, important tribal-council decisions had to be approved by the secretary of the Interior, an archaic policy dating back to the nineteenth century when the federal government maintained authoritarian control over Indian Country.[48]

The Grand Traverse Band's constitution eliminated those burdensome and paternalistic provisions, except as amendments to the constitution itself.

However, the federal-government negotiators insisted on a provision in the tribal constitution incorporating one aspect of federal control—secretarial approval of attorney contracts.[49] One section in the United States Code, Title 25, Section 81, required that any agreement between a tribe and an attorney was subject to the approval of the secretary of the Interior. The government had often used that provision historically to deny tribes the right to sue the United States to vindicate tribal trust rights and other rights.[50] But tribal negotiators were able to secure a proviso stating that the secretarial approval of tribal attorney contracts would become invalid if Section 81 were amended to end this practice. And so, in 2000, after Congress finally did away with the measure, this provision in the tribal constitution became functionally inoperative.

In 1987, the secretary finally authorized an election to determine whether the Grand Traverse Band would ratify its draft constitution. In December, by a vote of 376 in favor to 47 against, out of 635 eligible voters, the tribal electorate approved the tribal constitution. The assistant secretary for Indian Affairs, Ross O. Swimmer, approved the constitution on March 29, 1988.

A Brief History of the Grand Traverse Band's Leadership

After federal recognition in 1980, the leadership of the Grand Traverse Band was in flux. Leelanau Indians, Inc. had been the driving force behind the petition for federal recognition and also served as the focus of the band's nominal governance structure during that period, but the corporation was not the entity recognized as an Indian tribe. And so the very first federally recognized tribal government for the band came into being on April 26, 1980, at a meeting called by the president of Leelanau Indians, Inc. (LII), Ardith (Dodie) Harris. At that meeting, the participants voted to create an interim tribal council. Days later, on April 30, the interim tribal council elected Dodie Harris as the chair, Darlene Chippewa as the vice-chair, and George Bennett as the secretary/treasurer.[51] The interim tribal council enacted its first resolution, accepting the task of handling the newly recognized Indian tribe's responsibilities, including the drafting of a tribal constitution, for sixty days.[52]

The task placed before the interim tribal council was all but impossible. On May 10, 1980, the Grand Traverse Band was dead broke. The minutes from that day's meeting read:

The Chairperson informed the Council that, at this point in time, the Band is penniless. Donations from the Council members were given to the Secretary/Treasurer in the amount of $13.00, of which $3.50 was returned to the LII coffee fund. Balance of the donation to be used for postage.[53]

The Grand Traverse Band, in its first months as a federally recognized Indian tribe, did not even possess the minimum amount of funds ($100) to open a checking account.[54]

The process of transitioning the Grand Traverse Band's leadership from Leelanau Indians, Inc. was also complicated and fractious. In the fall of 1979, LII had received a grant of $211,000 from the United States Department of Housing and Urban Development to fund tribal housing projects. But the government pulled the grant from LII in April 1980, deciding that LII was not a tribal entity eligible to receive the grant. Moreover, the government concluded that the Grand Traverse Band, the political successor to LII, was not eligible either, because the band's name did not appear on lists of federally recognized tribes generated by the Departments of Interior and Treasury until March 25, 1980, near the end of the 1979 fiscal year. Fortunately, federal Judge Benjamin Gibson of the Western District of Michigan rejected the government's legal theory in *Leelanau Indians, Inc. v. United States Department of Housing and Urban Development*, a case brought by Michigan Indian Legal Services and two of their attorneys, Barry Levine and Bill Rastetter.[55] Judge Gibson wrote:

> The current practice of looking only at the lists clearly does not comply with the congressional intention of expanding Indian eligibility, and is in actuality a step in the other direction.
>
> What is equally clear is that plaintiffs represent a legitimate Indian tribe. In the March 25, 1980 Federal Register the Department of Interior, Bureau of Indian Affairs published a "Determination for Federal Acknowledgment of the Grand Traverse Band of Ottawa and Chippewa Indians as an Indian Tribe." ... The determination is a recognition of the fact that the Grand Traverse Band has existed as a tribe continuously since as early as 1675.[56]

More complicated questions arose a few years later when the band sought to acquire the lands held in trust by Leelanau County. The county had held over 147 acres of land in trust for the benefit of the Peshawbestown Indians since 1970, but would not grant the land to the United States Department of the Interior for the benefit of the tribe.[57] This is the land where the heart of the Grand Traverse Band's governmental complex sits. But by then, the old leadership of Leelanau Indians, Inc. had claimed to be the proper beneficiary of the Leelanau County trust land, and so in 1983 the Grand Traverse Band sued in a case captioned *Grand Traverse Band of Ottawa and Chippewa Indians v. Leelanau Indians, Inc. and Leelanau County.* In 1985, the federal court concluded the case by finding that the Grand Traverse Band, not Leelanau Indians, Inc., was the proper beneficiary.[58] In late 1985, the county settled the case by granting the land to the federal government in trust for the band.[59]

But still Leelanau County fought the band, and later asserted the right to object to the federal government's acquisition of the trust lands in Peshawbestown in 1987.[60] The county also brought suit against the band and the federal government in *Leelanau County v. Grand Traverse Band of Ottawa and Chippewa Indians* over the construction of a tribal house within the challenged lands.[61] Finally, the county instructed the Cherryland Rural Electric Cooperative Association not to hook up power to the tribal housing construction site, and zoned all tribal lands as "governmental," eliminating the opportunity for the band to use the lands for residential or economic development purposes.[62] Eventually, the band and the county settled the lawsuit, and the lands held in trust by Leelanau County went into trust with the secretary of the Interior.

By 1990, the Grand Traverse Band and Leelanau County had resolved many of their differences. That year, the band and the county entered into a precedent-setting agreement in which the law-enforcement personnel of each jurisdiction would agree to assist each other—a mutual-aid agreement.[63] The agreement authorized Grand Traverse Band law-enforcement personnel to engage in "fresh pursuit" of suspects beyond tribal lands. In 1997, the band and the county expanded the cooperation by entering into a cross-deputization agreement, in which tribal and county officers both had authority to enforce state and tribal laws on or off reservation lands.[64] The agreement has been a large success for both the band and the county, and has been cited as an example of how tribal law-enforcement cooperative agreements should work.[65]

The Grand Traverse Band Tribal Judiciary

The Grand Traverse Band tribal court began operations in the late 1980s, with Michael D. Petoskey serving as the court's first chief judge.[66] The tribal court was the first tribal court in Michigan to be included in the tribal constitution as a separate and independent branch of government, much like the federal judiciary.[67] During the early decades of the tribal court, the court has heard and decided numerous complex and important issues on behalf of the band, including questions of tribal sovereign immunity, tribal membership, political corruption, tribal election disputes, and many, many other questions. The tribal court also has a robust criminal docket, and an award-winning Peacemaker Court.

A significant part of the Grand Traverse Band's history is captured in cases decided by the tribal court since 1990, when the court's docket began to increase steadily. In 2001, former chairwoman Ardith (Dodie) Chambers testified before the United States Senate Committee on Indian Affairs to demonstrate the independence, authority, integrity, and competence of the tribal judiciary.[68] She highlighted two tribal court cases, *In re McSauby* and *DeVerney v. Grand Traverse Band of Ottawa and Chippewa Indians*, showing that the tribal court had ruled against the tribal government in some key cases. The first case, *In re McSauby*, involved the referral of John McSauby, an elected official of the tribal council, to the tribal court for removal for ethics violations.[69] Over the objection of the tribal government, the tribal court first held that McSauby's attorney was entitled to attorney fees, paid for by the tribal government, on the grounds that the question of how and when a tribal council member could be removed was so important and complex that a defending council member should be entitled to adequate legal representation.[70] On the merits, the tribal court agreed to order the removal of Mr. McSauby, on the grounds that he had admitted to using his authority as a tribal council member to push through the sale of his personally owned land to the band, a violation of provisions in the tribal constitution prohibiting misconduct and self-dealing.[71]

The second case, *DeVerney*, involved a challenge to a decision by the band's tribal-membership department.[72] The case involved a complicated mix of sovereign immunity, due process, administrative law, and tribal constitutional interpretation. The issue involved the administrative disenrollment of several members of the band in 1996, when the tribal membership office learned that the members were also enrolled members of the Sault Ste. Marie Tribe of Chippewa Indians,[73] a violation of the dual enrollment prohibition in the tribal constitution.[74] The question was whether the membership office could unilaterally terminate a tribal member's membership, or whether the tribe had to hold a hearing first. The tribal court, and then the tribal appellate court held that the tribe first had to provide due process to the members before they were disenrolled.[75]

Councilwoman Chambers also testified to Congress about the band's Peace-maker Court, which won an award in 1999 from the Harvard Project on American Indian Economic Development at the John F. Kennedy School of Government.[76] The Peacemaker Court—Mnaweejeendwin—incorporates nonadversarial and traditional dispute resolution techniques, rather than Western-style, adversarial courtroom procedures and rules.[77] The Mnaweejeendwin is designed to help juvenile offenders avoid jail and to learn and understand the consequences of their actions, and to help victims of crime reach an agreement where offenders make amends to them. Peacemaking involves talking and reaching consensus on how these goals might be achieved. Western-style justice is all but rejected. According to former chief judge Petoskey:

> There is an Indian saying, that the watch is the white man's handcuff. . . . Peacemaking is not time limited. If it takes time, it takes time. Everyone has an opportunity to say what they want to say. They take whatever time necessary to develop a consensus. . . .
>
> The way we typically do things in an adversarial court is really counter productive. . . . We are saying all the negative things about people instead of working together toward common ground. Things people say about each other can be very hurtful and lasting.[78]

The Mnaweejeendwin avoids those problems. Instead of a judge looking down at the parties to a dispute, issuing orders and punishments that may or may not reflect the wishes of the parties, the Mnaweejeendwin forces the parties—with the help of their families and other community members—to face and discuss Litigation before the Grand Traverse Band tribal court is very similar in process, rules, and statutes to litigation before state and federal courts—with a key dif-ference. Former chief judge of the tribal court JoAnne Gasco speaks about how the written pleadings of a case between tribal members usually is merely the tip of the iceberg of the dispute.[79] The tribal court judges will ask the parties to go all the way back to the beginning, maybe as far back as generations, to ascertain and understand the origins of the dispute. Conversely, a state or federal court will do nothing more than look at the pleadings and the arguments made in court. Parties to a state or federal court case know going in that the findings of fact made by the judge or jury will not be a terribly close approximation of the truth, and even the winners walk away with a bad taste in their mouths. Tribal-court parties might feel the same way, but tribal-court judges at the Grand

Traverse Band are taught to look beyond the pleadings in order to better craft remedies suitable to the parties.

The Grand Traverse Band's Tribal Economy

Part of self-determination in the modern era for Indian tribes, including the Grand Traverse Band, is the development of a functioning and sustainable tribal economy. As noted above, in 1980 the tribal government was penniless, but in the past decade, the Grand Traverse Band has generated hundreds of millions of dollars in economic revenue that has helped the band's membership and the surrounding communities.

The story of the development of the Grand Traverse Band economy is remarkable, given the incredible disadvantages the band has faced since its origins. Former tribal chair Ardith (Dodie) Chambers testified in 2002 during the Turtle Creek trial that there were only about ten homes and about twenty people in Peshawbestown when she was growing up during the 1950s.[80] Her family did not have electricity until 1959 and did not have running water or indoor bathrooms until the early 1970s.[81] Those early homes were insulated by newspaper and cardboard, and heated by wood stoves, contributing to a terrible series of fires.[82] Many of the Great Society programs of the late 1960s and early 1970s were unavailable to Grand Traverse Band Indians.[83] Before federal recognition in 1980, the members of the Grand Traverse Band received from the federal government "*no services* except welfare."[84]

In the early years of the Grand Traverse Band, the community was in "extremely tough shape."[85] Barry Burtt, the tribal manager beginning in 1983, testified in the Turtle Creek trial, "Things were very, very . . . desperate at the Grand Traverse Band."[86] Housing conditions in those early years were "deplorable," and several individuals were virtually homeless.[87] The community had a 61 percent unemployment rate.[88] In 1983, the band petitioned the regional office of the United States Department of Housing and Urban Development for emergency money to build homes for the Peshawbestown Indians. The government promised $1 million in emergency funds, but the band was technically ineligible to use the money because it did not have the land in trust, due to conflicts with Leelanau County.[89]

A tribal economy is impossible without tribal lands, and the band's land base has always been small. In 1980, the tribal land base was a few acres of land in Peshawbestown, Michigan. The secretary of the Interior did not declare a tribal reservation until 1984, and that initial reservation was only about twelve acres.[90] The band was forced to engage in litigation to secure the acquisition of tribal lands held in trust by Leelanau County in the mid-1980s.[91] Because of that litigation, and because of the conflict over the tribal constitution, the secretary of the Interior refused to take any more land into trust for the band until 1989, when it finally agreed to take into trust land located in Williamsburg Township—land that would eventually be home to the Turtle Creek Casino and Hotel.[92]

Tribal economic development is also impossible without an adequate legal structure. So in 1998, the Grand Traverse Band's tribal council chartered the Grand Traverse Band Economic Development Corporation under federal law.[93] The band had previously chartered the Economic Development Authority under tribal law. The federally chartered corporation—sometimes called a Section 17 corporation[94]—owns the band's major economic development enterprises, including the Turtle Creek Casino and Hotel, the Leelanau Sands Casino and Resort, and the Grand Traverse Resort and Spa.

The separation of the band's businesses from the tribal government creates special advantages to the tribe under federal Indian law. First, the business assets of the band will not be mixed with the critical tribal-government assets, including the children's trust fund and the tribal economic development fund.[95] So, if an outsider acquires a court judgment against the businesses of the tribe, the critical governmental funds of the tribe will be secure from these claims, protecting the future of the tribe. Second, the Grand Traverse Band petitioned for and received private letter rulings from the Internal Revenue Service recognizing federal income-tax advantages related to the trust funds established by the band's Revenue Allocation Ordinance.[96]

CHAPTER SEVEN

The Story of the Grand Traverse Band's Gaming Operations

T|he Grand Traverse Band opened its first gaming hall in 1984, and its gaming operations —the Leelanau Sands Casino and the Turtle Creek Casino—remain the greatest sources of the revenue for the tribal government.

The Origins of Gaming in Peshawbestown

The Grand Traverse Band opened the first high-stakes Indian bingo hall in the State of Michigan in 1984, when the tribe opened the Super Bingo Palace and the Leelanau Sands Casino. In 1985, the Leelanau Sands Casino moved to a larger location and added table games.

Although it may have seemed to outsiders that Indian tribes originated gaming operations as a means of exploiting the immunities from state taxation and regulation articulated in federal Indian law, and that perhaps Indians were just trying to get rich quick, nothing could be farther from reality. Consider that in 1984, the Grand Traverse Band tribal council enacted a gaming ordinance—not for profit, but for the purpose of regulating "games of Indian Bingo and/or other lawful gambling activities within the reservation ... for the purposes of promoting tribal self-government and self-sufficiency through tribal economic development in order to support the health, education and welfare of the Grand Traverse Band and its members."[1]

The ordinance tracked statements of federal Indian law and policy made by President Ronald Reagan, the United States Department of the Interior, and Congress in 1982 and 1983. Like President Richard Nixon before him, President Reagan sought to encourage Indian tribes to engage in creative means of generating governmental revenue. In his 1983 federal Indian policy statement, he said, "It is important to the concept of self-government that tribes reduce their dependence on Federal funds by providing a greater percentage of the cost of their self-government."[2] This was part and parcel of the President's goal of reducing the size of government by eliminating the need for federal appropriations. Ironically, it was the President's conservative, anti-federal government politics that fueled the explosion in Indian gaming that has occurred over the last few decades.

Shortly after President Reagan issued his policy statement, the secretary of the Interior issued a statement opposing any federal legislation that would expose Indian gaming operations to state regulation. In particular, the statement noted:

A number of Indian tribes have begun to engage in bingo and similar gambling operations on their reservations for the very purpose enunciated in the President's Message. Given the often limited resources which tribes have for revenue-producing activities, it is believed that this kind of revenue-producing possibility should be protected and enhanced.[3]

The Department of the Interior's statement also mirrored the general statements that Congress had made in regard to the value of tribal economic development. In 1982, Congress had enacted the Tribal Tax Status Act.[4] It was the latest in a long line of piecemeal congressional acts, dating all the way back to the Indian Reorganization Act, that offered a recognition of the fact that the large majority of Indian tribes would not be able to fund tribal governmental services through the imposition of taxes, as federal, state, and local governments could.[5] The 1982 Act restated Congress's view that Indian tribes should be encouraged to engage in economic development activities for the purpose of reducing their dependence on congressional appropriations. At various times, Congress had encouraged individual Indians to form small businesses, or had encouraged Indian tribes to form federal economic development corporations, or had created preferences in federal contracting for Indian tribes and individual Indian-owned businesses.

The Department of the Interior, the Indian Health Service, and the Small Business Administration had quietly been offering construction funds, sanitation services, and loan guarantees to Indian tribes for the purpose of constructing high-stakes bingo halls to tribes in New York, Florida, and California since at least the late 1970s. Some Indian tribes may have engaged in high-stakes bingo or other forms of gaming since the late 1960s. The 1983 statements from President Reagan and the Department of the Interior allowed the subtle encouragement of Indian gaming to grow into overt support.

The reason high-stakes bingo became an important objective for many Indian tribes was that under foundational principles of federal Indian law, state laws and regulations—even criminal laws—did not apply to on-reservation tribal activity. The Supreme Court had stated in 1832 that state law has "no force" in Indian Country.[6] Congress could, if it chose, extend state jurisdiction into Indian Country, as it had for some states with the enactment of Public Law 280,[7] but Congress had never authorized the State of Michigan to enforce criminal laws in Michigan's Indian land.[8] The State of Michigan had strictly limited (and still does limit) the possible jackpots of bingo within its borders. Moreover, bingo could be conducted only in certain circumstances, such as for charity or church activities. Those statutes did not apply to bingo on the reservation. There were a few federal court cases out of Florida, California, Connecticut, and Wisconsin that confirmed this reading of the law.[9]

So, following the lead of tribes in other states, the Grand Traverse Band began to offer bingo at stakes far higher than was allowed under state jurisdiction. While state and local law-enforcement officials threatened to shut down the bingo halls, it was clear, *on paper*, that they had no jurisdiction or authority to do so.

Bingo was a success, but the revenues would be nothing compared to those generated by true Vegas-style casino gaming—poker, blackjack, craps, keno, and slot machines. Visitors to the bingo hall would experience a quiet and orderly gaming experience, owned and operated by tribal members.[10] Interviewed by Kathleen Stocking, a local writer, in 1986, Chairman Joseph C. "Buddy" Raphael noted:

> If allowed to continue, we could become less dependent on federal dollars. . . . We run a clean operation. It's a cash business. You have to have strict accountability. We've offered to open up our books to the courts. The Mafia can't come in here. Entry into any controlling aspect of this business is Indian.
>
> People have a common misperception about gambling—you open the doors, the money flows in. People wouldn't gamble if they couldn't win. Sometimes we lose money. This is not an easy business to be in.[11]

Shortly after introducing bingo to the reservation, the Grand Traverse Band began to introduce casino gaming. The lines of people waiting to get into the casino in Peshawbestown when it opened at 5 P.M. began to grow longer and longer.[12]

The Twilight Zone: *United States v. Bay Mills Indian Community et al.*

Indian bingo, if at all, would be subject to state regulation or prohibition, a legal fact that allowed the Grand Traverse Band to exercise its sovereignty as an Indian nation as a shield from state government interference. But that shield might have no impact if the federal government chose to interfere. And since federal statutes flatly prohibited casino-style gaming in Indian Country, there might be a problem. The State of Michigan had no jurisdiction to enforce gaming laws in Indian Country, but the United States Department of Justice through the United States Attorney's Office in Grand Rapids did.

As five federally recognized tribes in Michigan began to extend their casino gaming operations in 1984 and 1985, the United States Attorney for the Western District of Michigan filed suit in federal court against the tribes, seeking an injunction that would shut down the casino gaming operations.[13] The case was styled *United States v. Bay Mills Indian Community, et al.* and assigned to Judge Douglas W. Hillman.[14] The case involved Bay Mills, the Grand Traverse Band, Hannahville Indian Community, Keweenaw Bay Indian Community, and the Sault Ste. Marie Tribe of Chippewa Indians.

It is important to remember the context of that lawsuit. Tribal gaming operations were still microscopic compared to Vegas or Atlantic City casinos. During the lawsuit or shortly after the dismissal of the suit in 1989, the casino operated by Bay Mills actually shut down for a time because the market for gaming was not profitable for them.[15] None of the seven tribes were getting filthy rich. They had powerful arguments about exercising tribal sovereignty for the solitary purpose of providing desperately needed tribal governmental services to Indian people.[16] Second, the federal statute banning casino gaming in Indian Country said nothing about gaming operations conducted by Indian *tribes*, but instead seemed more concerned about non-Indian organized-crime elements setting up shop in Indian Country.[17] Third, different agencies within the federal government had been helping tribes develop their gaming operations—including Vegas-style gaming—for several years. This schizophrenic federal government policy on Indian gaming would eventually go a long way towards undermining the United States' case in the *Bay Mills Indian Community* litigation. Finally, Indian gaming had been on Congress's legislative agenda since 1983.[18] If any governmental entity had the capacity to speak with finality on the question of Indian gaming nationally, it would be Congress, empowered by the Constitution's mandate—the Indian Commerce Clause.[19]

Despite these factors, which tended to lean in favor of the tribes, the years between 1985 and 1993, when the seven tribes finally received approval for their gaming compacts, were difficult and uncertain years. Like the treaty fishing wars, some tribal members were willing to go to jail for Indian gaming, such as Fred Dakota, chairman of the Keweenaw Bay Indian Community.[20] But unlike fishing, which was a means of basic subsistence for Indian people, gaming was something else—it was a vice. And potentially, it was very big money. So in 1987, when *U.S. News and World Report* quoted the assistant United States attorney in charge of the *Bay Mills* litigation, Daniel M. LaVille, as saying, "[Indian casino gaming] exists in a legal twilight zone,"[21] no one was surprised.

Meanwhile, Congress endlessly debated how or if the federal government would choose to regulate Indian gaming operations. Each year, the Department of the Interior would support light regulation of Indian gaming, following by angry protestations from the Department of Justice about lawlessness in Indian Country if Congress did not flatly prohibit tribal gaming.[22] Each year, state governments seeking to protect their own governmental lottery revenues, as well as their constituent gambling industries in horse and dog racing, sports books, and even card rooms, pressured Congress to limit or ban Indian gaming.[23] Congress weighed proposals to ban Indian bingo or to allow Indian bingo to go unregulated, but the proposals gaining traction involved limited state and federal regulation of Indian bingo. No one knew what Congress would do about Indian casino-style gaming, but tribal lobbyists suspected that if Congress acted on casino-style gaming, it would ban or strictly limit it. As a result, most tribes opposed any congressional action.[24] In retrospect, that was unfortunate, but not devastating.

In early 1986, the State of California asked the United States Supreme Court to decide its civil and criminal authority to regulate the high-stakes bingo hall of the Cabazon Band of Mission Indians. The case was called *California v. Cabazon Band of Mission Indians*.[25] The Ninth Circuit Court of Appeals had ruled that California and its political subdivisions had no authority to regulate the Cabazon bingo operation.[26] Usually, the Supreme Court waits to decide a complex question of law until there is a split in lower-court authority on the matter, but federal Indian law is an exception. As of 1986, there had been no split in authority, but several state attorneys general had written an amicus brief asking the Court to hear the case[27]—and so it did. That decision did not bode well for tribal interests. Historically, the Court reverses a large majority of the lower-court cases it decides to hear. More often than not, the Court accepts a case for the express purpose of correcting the lower court's decision.

Many tribal observers assumed that it would be the end of Indian gaming altogether. Tribes that hoped Congress would act to preserve Indian gaming watched as the state-government negotiators seeking a ban or strict limits stopped participating in the negotiations over Indian gaming. The anti-tribal gaming interests also believed the Court would rule in favor of California, so they chose to wait until the Court rendered its decision.[28] If the Court did rule in favor of California, the anti-tribal gaming interests would hold all of the bargaining power in Congress. Then they would be able to dictate terms on national legislation involving Indian gaming.

Judge Hillman put the *Bay Mills* case on hold pending the Supreme Court's decision. As a technical, legal matter, the *Cabazon Band* case would not necessarily control the outcome of the *Bay Mills* case. First, California is a Public Law 280 state, meaning that Congress had authorized the State of California to exercise some aspects of criminal and civil jurisdiction in Indian Country. Michigan was not a Public Law 280 state, an advantage for the Michigan tribes. Second, the *Cabazon Band* case involved nothing except high-stakes bingo, while the *Bay Mills* case involved allegations that the Michigan tribes were violating federal law on casino-style gaming. While the cases were very different, Judge Hillman was correct in waiting for the Supreme Court's decision, which could provide important guidance on all questions of Indian gaming.

The Grand Traverse Band signed on to an important amicus brief in the case, along with dozens of other tribes.[29] In 1987, the Supreme Court shocked Indian Country by ruling 6–3 in favor of the Cabazon Band.[30] While a great deal of the Court's reasoning focused on the Public Law 280 question, the Court noted that the federal government had long been supportive of Indian gaming. The Court quoted President Reagan's 1983 statement on Indian policy and relied upon the fact that several federal agencies had been overly supportive of Indian gaming for years. The Court gave its stamp of approval to the legal theory that smaller tribes with little or no land base or natural resources required creative means of raising governmental revenue, a critical boon to the small tribes in Michigan like the Grand Traverse Band. Perhaps most importantly, the Court noted that the State of California's arguments about the threat of lawlessness in Indian Country relating to the spread of gambling and the ever-present specter of organized crime rang hollow, given that the State of California itself had endorsed numerous forms of gaming (horse and dog tracks, a state lottery, and poker and card rooms) without succumbing to the criminal element.

After a further round of briefing following *Cabazon Band*, Judge Hillman denied the United States request for an injunction in August 1988.[31] Since the United States had only asked for an injunction against Indian casino-style

gaming, as opposing to seeking grand jury indictments against gaming operators, the government's legal theory was fundamentally flawed. An injunction
is an extraordinary remedy, difficult to acquire from a court, and generally not
allowable in a criminal context. An injunction forces a party to stop its activity,
and nothing more. Judge Hillman implicitly reminded the government that if
a federal crime such as murder or kidnapping had occurred, the government's
remedy would not be a federal court order demanding that the murderer or
kidnapper stop its activity, but a criminal prosecution.

The government's error was compounded for Judge Hillman because the
remedy of an injunction is also an equitable remedy, meaning that the party
seeking an injunction must come to the court with clean hands. And, while the
government's hands were not exactly dirty, the government was badly conflicted.
As the Supreme Court noted in *Cabazon Band*, other arms of the United States
had long been supportive of Indian gaming, even implicitly supportive of
casino-style gaming. It was unfair for the Department of Justice to seek to stop
a tribal activity that other federal agencies had supported.

Judge Hillman's decision in *Bay Mills Indian Community* was soon followed
by Congress's enactment in October 1988 of an omnibus statutory scheme to
regulate Indian gaming—the Indian Gaming Regulatory Act.[32] As a result of the
passage of the gaming act, the United States Attorney declined to appeal Judge
Hillman's decision to the Sixth Circuit Court of Appeals.

The Indian Gaming Regulatory Act and the Gaming Compact Negotiations

Congress went to work right away on national legislation following *Cabazon
Band*. Instead of states and other anti-tribal interests dictating terms, tribes
and states were equal players at the bargaining table. Congress identified three
classes of gaming: traditional tribal games, bingo, and everything else (i.e.,
casino-style gaming).[33] Tribes would regulate traditional games exclusively,
while sharing some regulation of bingo with the National Indian Gaming
Commission. As to bingo, Congress intended to simply codify the *Cabazon Band*
decision excluding state jurisdiction over Indian bingo, applying the decision
nationwide. As to casino-style gaming, the most lucrative and most vulnerable
form of Indian gaming, Congress created a complex compromise in the form of
a negotiated compact between tribes and state governors.[34] If tribes wanted to
operate high-stakes bingo or traditional games, they would not need a compact.

In a small provision of the statute, Congress authorized the tribes in the State of Michigan and a few other states to continue their ongoing casino-style table games, such as poker, blackjack, and craps.[35] This was known as the "grandfather" provision.

Once Congress passed the act and President Reagan signed it into law, the Michigan Indian tribes began the long, arduous process of negotiating a gaming compact for the purpose of authorizing casino-style gaming, especially slot-machine gaming. The act required Indian tribes who wanted to engage in the more lucrative style of gaming to negotiate a compact with the governor of the State of Michigan, James Blanchard. The first eighteen months of gaming-compact negotiations for the Michigan tribes went nowhere. Eventually, the seven federally recognized tribes sued the State of Michigan under a provision in the gaming act that required state governments to negotiate a compact in good faith.[36]

Interestingly, Congress anticipated the scenario where a state refused to negotiate on fair terms with the tribes, so the gaming act included provisions that would help tribes solve the problem of governors who refused to negotiate in good faith. Congress never intended to give states an absolute veto over casino-style gaming, but instead offered states the right to participate in the regulation and scope of gaming through the compact process. The tribes' remedy in this instance was a federal court lawsuit, where the federal judge would be asked to determine if the governor had refused to negotiate in good faith. If the court determined that the governor had not negotiated in good faith, then the tribe could petition the secretary of the Interior to begin a complicated round of compact negotiation and mediation.

In June 1990, five tribes sued the State of Michigan in federal court, alleging that Governor Blanchard (and later, Governor John Engler) failed to negotiate in good faith.[37] The five tribes were the Grand Traverse Band, Bay Mills Indian Community, Hannahville Indian Community, Keweenaw Bay Indian Community, Sault Ste. Marie Tribe of Chippewa Indians, and Lac Vieux Desert Band of Lake Superior Chippewa Indians (which had acquired federal recognition in 1988, separating from Keweenaw Bay). The Saginaw Chippewa Indian Tribe, the other federally recognized tribe, did not participate. The case was captioned *Sault Ste. Marie Tribe of Chippewa Indians et al. v. State of Michigan*, or alternatively, *Tribes v. State of Michigan*.

The Development of the Leelanau Sands Casino amid Uncertainty

By 1990, the Grand Traverse Band's gaming profits reached $1 million a year.

The period of uncertainty involving Michigan casino-style gaming did not end when Congress passed the Indian Gaming Regulatory Act, or when the United States Attorney declined to seek an appeal of the *United States v. Bay Mills Indian Community et al.* litigation as a result. Michigan tribes continued gaming despite the fact that they had no official gaming compact with the State of Michigan, and while *Tribes v. State of Michigan* wound its way through the courts.

The uncertainty created a form of economic hardship for the Grand Traverse Band in the early 1990s. Because much of the tribe's land was held in trust by the federal government, or was the subject of a request from the tribe to take the land into trust, the tribe had no land to use as collateral for the purpose of taking on debt. So the tribe had no real opportunity to borrow money to be used to expand the tribe's minimal gaming operations. Many gaming tribes are in this position if they have a small land base.

The passage of the gaming act provided certainty as to the future stability of the bingo operation, guaranteeing for the foreseeable future that bingo, at least, would be protected. Gaming tribes that have a stable source of gaming revenue, even as modest as the bingo revenues, can use that revenue stream as collateral. But a revenue stream is never as steady or stable as land, so banks that would lend to the tribe using bingo revenue as collateral tended to be more insecure. That translated to higher interest rates and other costs.

And yet in 1991, the Grand Traverse Band completed construction on the new location of the Leelanau Sands Casino. The tribe financed the development using private loans supplemented by federal economic development grants and the tribe's own revenues.[38]

Tribes v. Engler and the 1993 Gaming Compact

The enactment of the Indian Gaming Regulatory Act in 1988 settled many of the legal uncertainties arising out of the development of Indian gaming in the 1970s and 1980s. One of the key provisions of the act was the gaming-compact provision for casino-style games, referred to in the act as Class III games. This provision was a major compromise for the states, who wanted little or no Class III gaming, and for tribes, who wanted no state regulation of Class III gaming.

The gaming-compact provision required tribes and states to negotiate over a series of limited terms: what kind of games, how they would be played, who would be the primary governmental regulator, and a few other things. Linked to this compromise was a powerful provision that banned states outright from forcing tribes to accept state taxation of Class III games in the compact provisions.

The six tribes that sued the State of Michigan in *Tribes v. State of Michigan* had chosen to rely upon a promise made by Congress that if a state governor refused to negotiate a Class III gaming compact, the tribes could sue in federal court, starting a process that would allow the tribes to acquire a gaming compact even if the governor did not consent.

But there was a fatal flaw in the process—the Eleventh Amendment.

The Eleventh Amendment to the United States Constitution states that state governments are immune from suit from citizens of another state absent their consent.[39] The concept of sovereign immunity is not hard to understand. All states and the federal government retain immunity from suit in federal or state court unless those governments consent to the lawsuit. Indian tribes also retain immunity from suit in federal, state, and tribal courts, unless they waive their immunity.[40]

But when Congress enacted the gaming act's provisions in 1988, the drafters were not very concerned about the Eleventh Amendment. The United States Supreme Court had ruled that Congress had the power to abrogate the sovereign immunity of state governments, assuming it was acting in accordance with the Constitution when it did so. Still, in 1989, the Supreme Court waffled on the question in a case called *Pennsylvania v. Union Gas Co.*,[41] where the Court ruled 5–4 that Congress did have the power to abrogate state sovereign immunity using its power to regulate commerce. The problem arose when one of the justices in the majority of that case raised serious doubts about the conclusion. In 1991, the Supreme Court held that the Eleventh Amendment barred suits by Indian tribes against states.[42] The only hope for tribes was the provision in the gaming act in which Congress authorized tribal suits against states.

But in *Tribes v. State of Michigan*, Judge Benjamin F. Gibson held that the Eleventh Amendment foreclosed the tribes' suit against the State of Michigan.[43] The Sixth Circuit dismissed the tribes' appeal on procedural grounds.[44] But Judge Gibson allowed the tribes to amend their complaint to take advantage of a legal fiction that might allow a suit compelling the governor to negotiate—suing Governor Engler himself, instead of the state.[45] In early 1993, Judge

Gibson scheduled oral argument over the question of whether Governor Engler also was immune from suit, but the tribes and the state reached a settlement before the case was argued.

The settlement, joined in the late stages by the Saginaw Chippewa Indian Tribe, came in the form of three documents.[46] First, the Stipulation for Entry of Consent Judgment informed the court that the parties had reached an agreement. Second, the Consent Judgment itself was the document that Judge Gibson ultimately signed, ending the litigation. The third document was a Class III gaming compact, with the terms for each of the seven tribes to be identical.

Other than perhaps the treaties themselves, these documents are the most litigated documents in Michigan tribal history. Many of the provisions are noncontroversial, such as the provisions describing the scope of Class III gaming allowed under the compacts. Interestingly, Governor Engler chose to wipe his hands clean of Indian gaming, insisting that the tribes regulate their own gaming operations. As a result, each of the gaming facilities owned by the seven tribes has a statement somewhere on the grounds disclaiming state regulation of the casino. The Grand Traverse Band's notice reads:

NOTICE

THIS FACILITY IS REGULATED BY ONE OR MORE OF THE FOLLOWING: THE NATIONAL INDIAN GAMING COMMISSION, BUREAU OF INDIAN AFFAIRS OF THE U.S. DEPART-MENT OF THE INTERIOR AND THE GOVERNMENT OF THE GRAND TRAVERSE BAND.

THIS FACILITY IS NOT REGULATED BY THE STATE OF MICHIGAN.

The more controversial provisions of the consent decree included provisions that required the gaming tribes to share their revenues with the State of Michigan and with local units of government.[47] The tribes agreed to send 8 percent of their slot-machine net win (i.e., profit) to the State of Michigan. Moreover, the tribes agreed to distribute 2 percent of their net win to local units of government. The tribes retained the right to decide which local units of government would receive the 2 percent.

Since the gaming act prohibited any state taxation of tribal gaming revenues,[48] and since the revenue-sharing provisions looked a lot like state taxation, the consent decree stated that the tribes would receive a monopoly on casino-style gaming in the entire State of Michigan. In other words, in exchange for the revenue-sharing payments, the state would not authorize any others (including other tribes) to operate casino-style gaming that might compete with the tribal casinos. This brought the revenue-sharing provisions out of the realm of state taxation, since the tribes received a benefit for making the payments.

Another provision that Governor Engler insisted upon in the gaming compacts themselves was Section 9, which dealt with off-reservation gaming. The gaming act prohibited Indian gaming in lands acquired after the passage of the act, October 1988, unless one of several exceptions was met.[49] Moreover, the gaming act prohibited Indian gaming outside of Indian Country. In theory, however, what that meant was that an Indian tribe could ask the secretary of the Interior to take land into trust away from its reservation (say, in an urban area with a bigger market for gaming) and begin gaming on that land, assuming it met one of the exceptions. Governor Engler believed that the Michigan tribes would seek to commence gaming in markets like Detroit, Grand Rapids, and elsewhere under these provisions, so he negotiated for a provision that did not ban off-reservation gaming under the compacts, but required the tribes to share revenue from off-reservation gaming with each other. He believed that the tribes would veto each other's attempts to game off-reservation because of this additional revenue-sharing provision.

The Detroit Casinos and the Death of Tribal Exclusivity

Despite Governor Engler's belief that the Michigan gaming tribes would not cooperate on off-reservation gaming, the tribes immediately began to form business partnerships with each other for the purpose of expanding the tribal gaming market into Detroit. In 1994, the Grand Traverse Band teamed up with the Lac Vieux Desert Band of Lake Superior Chippewa Indians to acquire an option on the historical Hudson Building in Detroit. Other tribes made other alliances and proposals to game in Detroit as well. The tribes proposed to ask the secretary of the Interior to take the land into trust, seeking to take advantage of a provision in the gaming act that allowed tribes to expand their gaming operations off the reservation if they met two requirements. First, the secretary of the Interior would have to make a determination that the gaming operation would be in the best interest of the tribes. Second, the governor of the state would have to concur in that assessment. This was called the "two-part determination."[50]

The tribes convinced the secretary of the Interior that the Detroit gaming operation would benefit both tribes, even considering the fact that the tribes would be forced under the gaming compacts to share their revenue with the five other tribes. It then turned to Governor Engler. And the politics began.

Governor Engler had long opposed any gaming as a public matter, but in retrospect, it appears that he was out to make the best monetary deals he could for purposes of generating revenue for the State of Michigan. In the tribal-gaming-compact fight, he finally agreed to sign the compacts and settle the litigation when the tribes agreed to part with 10 percent of their profits. In the Detroit arena, with several tribal proposals floating around, Governor Engler thought he could do better. Eventually, he backed a state constitutional amendment that allowed for three non-Indian casinos to be licensed in the City of Detroit, with a massive 30 percent tax rate on each casino. The amendment passed in 1996 as the Michigan Gaming Control and Revenue Act.[51]

Of course, Governor Engler's new deal meant that the seven tribes who had signed the 1993 gaming compacts no longer had a monopoly on casino-style gaming in Michigan. The seven tribes brought an action in federal court against Governor Engler under the consent decree, seeking a judgment that they no longer had to pay 8 percent of their net win to the State of Michigan. In 1997, Judge Gibson interpreted the consent decree to mean that the gaming monopoly that the tribes negotiated for in 1993 would not expire until the Michigan Gaming Control Board actually issued the Detroit casino licenses, and the Sixth Circuit affirmed the judgment.[52]

It did not take long for the State of Michigan to create the legal justification for the seven 1993 compacting tribes to stop making payments to the state. On February 18, 1999, the State of Michigan entered into four Class III gaming compacts with newly recognized Michigan tribes—the Nottawaseppi Huron Band of Potawatomi Indians, Little Traverse Bay Bands of Odawa Indians, the Little River Band of Ottawa Indians, and the Pokagon Band of Potawatomi Indians. Four months later, the state also issued three gaming licenses for Detroit casinos. Either event would be sufficient to trigger the legal justification for ending the 8 percent payments to the state, according to Judge Gibson. As such, the tribes stopped the revenue-sharing payments to the state.

This time, it was Governor Engler bringing suit in federal court to enforce the revenue-sharing provisions of the 1993 compacts. By that time, the *Tribes v. Engler* docket had been transferred to Judge Douglas W. Hillman, the same judge as in the *United States v. Bay Mills Indian Community* case. Judge Hillman ruled that the effective date of the four new gaming compacts (February 19, 1999) was the proper ending date for the 8 percent payments, an outcome affirmed by the Sixth Circuit.[53]

Grand Traverse Band v. United States Attorney: 1996–2004

On June 14, 1996, the Grand Traverse Band opened the Turtle Creek Casino in Whitewater Township, just east of Acme, Michigan, and the Grand Traverse Bay. On that day, the tribe filed a lawsuit in federal court in Grand Rapids seeking an order that the operation of the casino was legal and in accordance with the Indian Gaming Regulatory Act. The United States government, the defendant in the case, sought to prove that the operation of the casino was illegal, as did the State of Michigan, which intervened in the lawsuit.

The tribe purchased the land upon which Turtle Creek was located in 1989, shortly after the passage of the gaming act by Congress, and placed the land into trust. The purpose for the land was to provide a location from which the tribe could provide services to tribal members living in and around Grand Traverse, Antrim, and Charlevoix counties, and for economic development. Tribal leaders believed the location was on or near the Grand Traverse Reservation boundaries created in the 1836 Treaty of Washington. For several years, the location had served as a satellite office for the tribal government, providing services to local tribal members, but the tribe had always kept open the possibility of using the location for economic development. Eventually, the tribe opened satellite offices in Traverse City and outside of Charlevoix, rendering the Whitewater Township office somewhat redundant.

The Whitewater Township parcel's 1989 purchase date was important under the Indian Gaming Regulatory Act because the act generally prohibited gaming on lands acquired after October 1988, when it became operative.[54] But there were several exceptions to this general rule, intending to benefit tribes with small land bases and those tribes only recently extended federal recognition. The Grand Traverse Band believed that the parcel met an exception that would become known as the "restored lands/restored tribes" exception. That exception stated that the general ban will not apply to "lands . . . taken into trust as part of . . . the restoration of lands for an Indian tribe that is restored to Federal recognition."[55] The major weakness in this theory was that no court had ever decided a case interpreting the "restored lands/restored tribes" exception, so it was an unknown. Moreover, the tribe would have to hire expert witnesses to prove that the tribe was a "restored tribe," and especially, to prove that the lands upon which Turtle Creek rested were "restored lands," whatever that meant. The fact that the theory was untested in federal court and would require the tribe to invest a large amount of resources to conduct the historical research counseled against asserting the theory unless as a last resort.

Fortunately, a federal court judge in Grand Rapids, Judge David W. McKeague, issued a ruling in a gaming case involving the Keweenaw Bay Indian Community that provided the tested legal theory the Grand Traverse Band could use to open a casino at the Whitewater Township location. The case, *Keweenaw Bay Indian Community v. United States*,[56] stood for the proposition that the State of Michigan agreed in the 1993 gaming compacts to allow any of the compacting tribes to commence gaming on any lands then part of the tribe's reservation. The Grand Traverse Band, similarly, believed that the Whitewater Township parcel, purchased and placed into trust in 1989, was part of the Grand Traverse Band's reservation lands when the compacts were signed in 1993. Because the second legal theory actually had the stamp of approval from a federal court, the Grand Traverse Band believed that it was the stronger legal theory.

Using this second legal theory, the Grand Traverse Band was able to avoid a preliminary ruling from the federal court (Judge Hillman once again) shutting down the casino.[57] Judge Hillman agreed to wait until the Sixth Circuit decided the *Keweenaw Bay* case before ruling on the motions by the United States and the State of Michigan seeking to shut down Turtle Creek. And in 1998, the Sixth Circuit reversed Judge McKeague's ruling on the second legal theory,[58] forcing the Grand Traverse Band to rely upon the first theory, the unknown.

In 1999, in a major preliminary ruling, Judge Hillman decided that the Turtle Creek Casino could continue operating, but asked the National Indian Gaming Commission to issue an opinion on whether the casino was authorized by the Indian Gaming Regulatory Act.[59] He tentatively accepted the tribe's theory on the "restored lands/restored tribes" exception, relying upon the preliminary expert report prepared by Dr. James M. McClurken.

Judge Hillman believed that the Whitewater Township parcel met criteria he read into the statute relating to the question of whether the land was "restored" as understood in the gaming act. First, the land met "geographic" criteria, meaning that the land was located well within the traditional territory of the Grand Traverse Band. While there was some question as to whether the parcel was located within the 1836 reservation boundaries, it was still part of the tribe's historical lands. Second, the land met "temporal" criteria, meaning the tribe had purchased the land for economic development purposes within a few short years of receiving reaffirmation of its federal recognition. In fact, while the United States had extended federal recognition to the tribe in 1980, because of a dispute over the tribe's constitution the United States had refused to take much land into trust for the tribe until 1988. As such, the United States took the Whitewater Township parcel into trust within a year or so of the tribe's first land purchases, around the same time the government took into trust several parcels that now constitute the bulk of the Grand Traverse Reservation. This land, Judge Hillman concluded, was intended to be part of the restoration of the lands of the Grand Traverse Reservation. Third, Judge Hillman thought it very important that the Whitewater Township parcel was probably located within the exterior boundaries of the 1836 reservation.

Judge Hillman also concluded that the Grand Traverse Band met the definition of a "restored tribe" for purposes of the gaming act. He noted that the plain meaning of the term "restored" was "brought back or put back into a former position or condition." Since the Grand Traverse Band once had been federally recognized, at least until the 1870s, then administratively terminated, and then extended federal recognition in 1980, that the Grand Traverse Band's federal recognition had been "restored."

According to the terms of Judge Hillman's order, the parties would have to ask for an opinion from the National Indian Gaming Commission on how to interpret the "restored lands/restored tribes" exception, and whether the specific facts of the Grand Traverse Band fit the exception.[60] Once again, the tribe, the United States, and the State of Michigan submitted mountains of papers and evidence on the question, this time to the general counsel of the National Indian Gaming Commission, Kevin K. Washburn.[61]

It was the first time that a federal court had asked the commission to opine on the "restored lands/restored tribes" exception, but the Solicitor's Office in the Department of the Interior had issued opinions called "Indian Lands Opinions" in the cases of the Little Traverse Bay Bands of Odawa Indians and the Pokagon Band of Potawatomi Indians.[62]

General Counsel Washburn adopted Judge Hillman's general framework for determining whether the Whitewater Township parcel constituted "restored lands" under the Indian Gaming Regulatory Act.[63] He relied upon Dr. Mc-Clurken's exhaustive ethnohistory of the eastern shore of Grand Traverse Bay that demonstrated a significant presence of Grand Traverse Band people from before treaty times, through the period of administrative termination, and on through to the present day. He also found that the tribe had purchased the land and put it into trust with the United States during the first major push the tribe made to restore as much land as possible to tribal ownership and control in the Grand Traverse Bay region. He concluded, as Judge Hillman presupposed, that the Turtle Creek Casino rested on lands that constituted restored lands, as that term was used in the gaming act. He also agreed with Judge Hillman that the Grand Traverse Band was a tribe that had been restored to federal recognition.

Interestingly, after conducting the necessary historical research, both Dr. McClurken and the expert witness hired by the United States, Helen Hornback Tanner, once the tribal expert in the *United States v. Michigan* treaty-rights litigation, concluded that the Turtle Creek site rested 1.5 miles outside of the exterior boundaries of the 1836 reservation. Though the tribe had long asserted that the site was within the reservation, it conceded this newly discovered fact. Ultimately, it did not matter. The nexus of the casino site to the historical and traditional territories of the Grand Traverse Band remained significant.

General Counsel Washburn released the opinion letter in August 2001. Shortly thereafter, the United States Department of Justice, which had been prosecuting the case, accepted the opinion and asked to be dismissed from the litigation. This left only the State of Michigan, which continued to oppose the Turtle Creek Casino. The Grand Traverse Band sought, and received, an expedited trial schedule for January 2002 before Judge Hillman, sitting without a jury.

At the trial, Riyaz Kanji, John Petoskey, Phil Katzen, Wenona Singel, and Bill Rastetter represented the tribe, with important contributions from Grand Traverse Band member and then-college student Zeke Fletcher. Former Grand Traverse Band tribal council vice-chairman Eva Petoskey testified as to the 1989 decision of the tribal council to purchase the land and put it into trust for economic development purposes. Grand Traverse Band councilor Ardith "Dodie" Chambers and former tribal manager Barry Burtt testified as to the horrific state of affairs that existed on the reservation when the United States granted federal recognition to the tribe in 1980. Chairman Robert Kewaygoshkum testified about the importance of the gaming revenues generated at Turtle Creek to the operations of the tribal government. Finally, Dr. McClurken testified that although the Turtle Creek site rested outside of the 1836 Treaty reservation borders, the site still remained at the heart of the Grand Traverse Band's traditional territory.

On April 22, 2002, Judge Hillman agreed with the Grand Traverse Band on every issue.[64] He held that the Turtle Creek Casino and the Grand Traverse Band met the "restored lands/restored tribes" exception. In his findings of fact, Judge Hillman wrote:

> The Turtle Creek site is located within the lands ceded by the Band to the United States by the Treaty of 1836, and from 1861 until its purchase by the Band on April 20, 1989, it was privately owned. Although 1.5 miles outside the 1836 treaty reservation, evidence suggests that the site was located within the contemplated reservation, which was not designated for four years after the treaty was signed.
>
> The land, located on the east shore of Grand Traverse Bay, is at the heart of the region that comprised the core of the Band's aboriginal territory and was historically important to the economy and culture of the Band. According to archaeological investigations, the east shore of Grand Traverse Bay has been occupied by indigenous peoples for thousands of years. The Band itself has occupied the region continuously from at least 100 years before treaty times until the present. The site is at the heart of a region providing a range of important natural resources for food, shelter, tools and medicine. The region also was traversed by a network of trails extending along the shore of Grand Traverse Bay and connecting to major routes to Saginaw and Cadillac that in turn connected with trails spreading across the continent. In the late nineteenth century, Band members continued to reside on the east shore of Grand Traverse Bay and sought title to land in order to remain in the region.
>
> Similarly, in the twentieth century, Band members continued to live on the east shore and maintained an economic, spiritual and cultural connection to the area. Acquisition of the Turtle Creek site was important for the Band to maintain a connection to the east shore region and to provide services and economic development to its members located on the east shore....
>
> In fiscal year 2001, Turtle Creek provided approximately 89% of the Band's gaming revenue. The casino now employs approximately 500 persons, approximately half of whom are tribal members. Revenues from the Turtle Creek Casino also fund approximately 270 additional tribal government positions, which administer a variety of governmental programs, including health care,

elder care, child care, youth services, education, housing, economic development and law enforcement. The casino also provides some of the best employment opportunities in the region, and all of its employees are eligible for health insurance benefits, disability benefits and 401(k) benefit plans. The casino also provides revenues to regional governmental entities and provides significant side benefits to the local tourist economy.[65]

After a delay attributed to the retirement of one of the State of Michigan's trial attorneys, the state appealed to the Sixth Circuit on the narrow issue of whether the Grand Traverse Band was a "restored tribe" under the Indian Gaming Regulatory Act. The state argued that when Congress referred to "restored tribes," it meant only those tribes that Congress had terminated during the 1950s and 1960s during the so-called Termination Era and then later "restored." But the tribe was able to show that Congress used the term "restored" loosely. In fact, it had used the term "restored" when reaffirming the federal recognition of the Pokagon Band of Potawatomi Indians, a tribe that, like the Grand Traverse Band, had been administratively terminated. In May 2004, the Sixth Circuit affirmed Judge Hillman's decision.[66] The State of Michigan declined to seek Supreme Court review and, finally, after nearly eight years of litigation, the Turtle Creek Casino stood free and clear of legal challenges.

The Future of Grand Traverse Band Gaming

Indian gaming revenues nationwide continue to rise. In 2005, total national revenues of all Indian gaming operations reached $22.6 billion, a 16 percent increase from 2004 and a 35 percent increase from 2003.[67] However, much of this gain took place in California and other regions outside of Michigan. Indian gaming revenues in the Midwest region, which includes Michigan, Wisconsin, and Minnesota, rose more slowly.

Indian gaming revenues in Michigan topped $1 billion among the nine gaming tribes by 2003,[68] but those revenues have stagnated since then. There are eighteen Indian gaming facilities now, three casinos in downtown Detroit, and two other possible Indian casinos currently under construction (Nottawaseppi Huron Band of Potawatomi Indians and the Gun Lake Band of Pottawatomi Indians).

The gaming industry in general, and the Grand Traverse Band's primary market in particular, is very competitive. The tribe faces competition from two existing Indian gaming facilities, each approximately 65 miles from the current facilities. The tribe also faces regional competition from existing Indian gaming facilities located within 140 miles of Traverse City, Michigan, and faces further competition from gaming facilities elsewhere in Michigan, including in Detroit and in the Upper Peninsula. Many of the tribe's competitors in the region are undergoing or planning expansions at this time. In addition, other Indian tribes are considering the construction of gaming facilities.

Moreover, the 1993 gaming compact was scheduled to expire in 2013, although the parties may extend the deadline through 2018. At least one year prior to the expiration of the compact, and thereafter at least one year prior to the expiration of each subsequent five-year period, either the state or the tribe may serve written notice on the other of its right to renegotiate the compact. In the event that either party gives written notice of its right to renegotiate the compact, the tribe, pursuant to the procedures of the gaming act, may request that the state enter into negotiations for a successor compact. If the tribe and the state are unable to negotiate a new compact, the current compact remains in full force and effect pending exhaustion of the judicial and administrative remedies set forth in the gaming act.

At various times, lawsuits have been filed challenging the validity of the gaming compacts entered into between the State of Michigan and tribes in Michigan. To date, these lawsuits have not been successful, and the compact is in full force and effect. There is no litigation presently pending challenging the validity of the tribe's compact.

State legislators and a citizen group called Taxpayers of Michigan against Casinos (TOMAC) brought suits in both federal and state court asserting that the governor did not have authority to bind the state in the 1997 compacts executed by the Nottawaseppi Huron Band of Potawatomi Indians, Little Traverse Bay Bands of Odawa Indians, Little River Band of Ottawa Indians, and Pokagon Band of Potawatomi Indians. These lawsuits asserted that such compacts were unconstitutional under state law. The federal suit was dismissed for procedural reasons.[69] In 2004, the Michigan Supreme Court ultimately upheld the validity of the 1997 compacts.[70]

TOMAC and other citizen groups, Citizens Exposing Truth about Casinos (CETAC) and Michigan Gambling Opposition (MichGO), have been more successful in significantly slowing down the expansion of Indian gaming by relying upon the National Environmental Policy Act, but not in stopping those tribes.[71]

In 2003, the Grand Traverse Band purchased the Grand Traverse Resort and Spa, located a few miles down the road from the Turtle Creek Casino. After considerable deliberation, the Grand Traverse Band opted to not pursue gaming at the resort. Instead, in 2007, the Grand Traverse Band began a major expansion of the Turtle Creek Casino that would include a hotel. In June 2007, the Grand Traverse Band opened the revamped Turtle Creek Casino & Hotel, one of the first eco-friendly casinos in the world.[72]

Carcieri v. Salazar and the Band's Future Land Base

In 2009, the United States Supreme Court handed down its decision in *Carcieri v. Salazar*,[1] a case involving the authority of the secretary of the Interior to acquire land in trust for the Narragansett Tribe in Rhode Island. Unfortunately, the Court's decision indirectly implicated the authority of the secretary to take land into trust for a host of Michigan Indian tribes, including the Grand Traverse Band. The Court held that the secretary may not take land into trust for Indian tribes that were not "under federal jurisdiction" at the time Congress enacted the Indian Reorganization Act—1934. The Grand Traverse Band, along with seven other Michigan tribes, and perhaps upwards of a hundred other Indian tribes nationally, did not enjoy federal recognition in 1934.

The Grand Traverse Band had been following the case since at least 2003, when the State of Rhode Island under its governor Donald Carcieri appealed a trial court decision to the federal First Circuit Court of Appeals. The band has been a contributor to the Tribal Supreme Court Project, a group formed by numerous Indian tribes and administered by the Native American Rights Fund and the National Congress of American Indians. The First Circuit hears very few Indian law cases, and so the band authorized its attorneys to participate in the case as *amicus curiae* to present the views of the Grand Traverse Band.

The ultimate question revolved around Section 5 of the Indian Reorganization

Act.[2] Section 5 authorizes the secretary of the Interior to acquire land in trust for the benefit of Indians and Indian tribes. The sticky part is the definition of "Indian" provided by the act. The act defines the term "Indian" to "include all persons of Indian descent who are members of any recognized Indian tribe *now under Federal jurisdiction.*"[3] Rhode Island argued that the Narragansett Tribe was not an eligible tribe in 1934, as it was not federally recognized in 1934. Like the Grand Traverse Band, the Department of the Interior refused to allow the Narragansett Tribe to reorganize under the act in the 1930s. The Narragansett Tribe, after filing land claims in the 1970s, was able to persuade the Department of the Interior to extend federal recognition to it in 1983 under the same process used by the Grand Traverse Band.[4] The Narragansetts had previously settled their land claims via an act of Congress in 1978,[5] but were forced to agree to state jurisdiction over their reservation lands as a result.

The federal government (then represented by Interior Secretary Gale Norton) argued, along with the Tribal Supreme Court Project and various Indian tribes (including the Grand Traverse Band), that the definition of "now" meant at the time of the secretary's decision to take land into trust, not at the time of the enactment of the Indian Reorganization Act. In fact, the Department of the Interior's interpretation of Section 5 had held steady for over seventy years, and in too many instances to count, it had taken land into trust for Indian tribes not federally recognized in 1934.

The First Circuit heard the case twice—once in a normal three-judge panel,[6] and then later in an unusual *en banc* panel consisting of the entire six-judge Circuit.[7] Before the First Circuit, the state was unable to persuade a single judge that "now" meant at the time of the enactment.[8] Two of the six judges did rule in favor of the state, but only on grounds that the Rhode Island Indian Claims Settlement Act foreclosed secretarial authority under Section 5.[9]

Over the objections of the federal government, the Supreme Court decided to hear the state's appeal, and reversed the First Circuit with an opinion by Justice Thomas. The *Carcieri* Court held, in essence, that "now" means "now"—as in 1934. Interestingly, the Court seemed to say that "federal recognition," as is now understood, is irrelevant to whether a tribe was "under federal jurisdiction" in 1934. Whether a tribe was under federal jurisdiction has *never* been litigated, and all of the parties assumed that federal recognition stood in for federal jurisdiction. But because the decision applied only to the Narragansett Tribe, which Justice Thomas asserted was under *state* jurisdiction in 1934, Indian tribes and the federal government cannot be sure what "under federal jurisdiction" means.

The *Carcieri* decision was accompanied by several concurring and dissenting opinions, all of which mentioned the Grand Traverse Band in some manner. The band's history of being administratively terminated by the Department of the Interior in the 1870s, only to be administratively recognized by the department in 1980, confounded the majority's version of history. Justice Breyer, who agreed that the Narragansett Tribe was not under federal supervision in 1934, nevertheless disagreed with Justice Thomas's majority opinion that "now" means 1934. He relied upon the very fact that the department once terminated then recognized the Grand Traverse Band as evidence that there "is no time limit on recognition."[10] Similarly, in Justice Stevens's dissent, the Grand Traverse Band's recognition and the fact that the Department of the Interior had acquired land in trust for the band served to demonstrate a "well-trodden path" of "administrative practice" supporting the taking of land into trust for Indian tribes not recognized in 1934.[11]

In fact, the history of the Grand Traverse Band—a treaty tribe illegally terminated by the Department of the Interior before 1934, then recognized after 1934—formed a key part of the foundation of Indian Country's response to the State of Rhode Island's attack on the federal government's position. An amicus brief signed by several American Indian law experts (including this author) focused heavily on the history of the Grand Traverse Band to demonstrate that the department should be allowed to correct past mistakes.[12]

Several months after the *Carcieri* decision, the chairman of the Grand Traverse Band, Derek Bailey, appeared as a witness in an important hearing before the Senate Committee on Indian Affairs regarding delays in the Department of the Interior's process for administering the fee to trust process.[13] Chairman Bailey testified that even before *Carcieri*, the Department of the Interior's process for determining whether to take land into trust was broken.[14] The department had returned four trust acquisition applications from the band in 2007 for being "stale" due to the department's own failure to process them, despite the fact that the lands in question were not for gaming and were generally located in Peshawbestown.[15] And the department had not made a decision on eight other trust applications from the band totaling over 260 acres, some of which had been pending for more than fifteen years.[16]

A few months before Chairman Bailey's testimony, the band had delivered to the Department of the Interior a submission detailing the reasons why the band was "under federal jurisdiction" in 1934 in accordance with the *Carcieri* decision.[17] The band's submission, titled "Submission on *Carcieri*'s 'Under Federal Jurisdiction' Requirement in Connection with Pending Fee-To-Trust Applications," detailed the band's history as a treaty tribe.

As such, at virtually the same time as Chairman Bailey's testimony, the Department of the Interior, now operated by the Obama administration, did acquire some lands into trust for the band—about 78 acres in Antrim County, Michigan, for housing development.[18]

Once again, the Grand Traverse Band served as a precedent-setting tribe, proving as a practical matter the outside contours of American Indian law.

Notes

INTRODUCTION

1. Henry Schoolcraft, who named many of the counties in Michigan after Indian words and words he thought sounded Indian, created the name for Leelanau County. Interestingly, his wife Jane, who was Ojibwe, often contributed poems and stories to her husband's magazine, *The Literary Traveler*, under the pen name "Leelinau." *See* Jeremy Mumford, *Mixed-Race Identity in a Nineteenth-Century Family: The Schoolcrafts of Sault Ste. Marie, 1824–1827*, 25 MICHIGAN HISTORICAL REVIEW, Spring 1999, at 1, 9.
2. 471 F. Supp. 192 (W.D. Mich. 1979).
3. 369 F.3d 920 (6th Cir. 2004).
4. 129 S. Ct. 1058 (2009).

CHAPTER ONE. THE STORY OF THE 1836 TREATY OF WASHINGTON

1. Benjamin Ramirez-shkwegnaabi, *The Dynamics of American Indian Diplomacy in the Great Lakes Region*, 27 AMERICAN INDIAN CULTURE AND RESEARCH JOURNAL 53, 53 (2003).
2. *See* Richard White, *Ethnohistorical Report on the Grand Traverse Ottawas*, unpublished manuscript, at i (1979).
3. *See* EDWARD BENTON-BENAI, THE MISHOMIS BOOK: THE VOICE OF THE OJIBWAY 94–102 (1975); JAMES M. MCCLURKEN, GAH-BAEH-JHAGWAH-BUK: THE WAY IT HAPPENED, A VISUAL CULTURE HISTORY OF THE LITTLE TRAVERSE BAY BANDS OF ODAWA INDIANS 3 (1991).
4. *See* VINE DELORIA JR., RED EARTH, WHITE LIES 62–63 (1997) (citing WERNER MULLER, AMERICA: THE NEW WORLD OR THE OLD? (1989)).
5. *See* RUTH CRAKER, THE FIRST PROTESTANT MISSION IN THE GRAND TRAVERSE REGION 4–5 (1932) (Rivercrest House 1979). *See also* Louise Erdrich & Michael Dorris, *Manitoulin Island*, ANTÆUS, No. 64/65, at 381 (Spring–Autumn 1990).
6. *See* MCCLURKEN, GAH-BAEH-JHAGWAH-BUK, *supra* note 3, at 3.
7. *See* CRAKER, *supra* note 5, at 2.
8. *See* CRAKER, *supra* note 5, at 25.
9. Ramirez-shkwegnaabi, *supra* note 1, at 56.
10. *See* White, *Ethnohistorical Report on the Grand Traverse Ottawas*, *supra* note 2, at ii.
11. Leelanau Indians, Inc. v. U.S. Dept. of Housing & Urban Dev., 502 F. Supp. 741, 743 (W.D. Mich. 1980); Leelanau Transit Co. v. Grand Traverse Band of Ottawa and Chippewa Indians, No. 92-240, 1994 U.S. Dist. LEXIS 2220, at 2 (W.D. Mich., Feb. 1, 1994).
12. *See* "Humans May Have Hunted Mastadons," National Public Radio (Nov. 27, 2007), *transcript available at* http://turtletalk.wordpress.com/2007/11/28/underwater-evidence-that-michigan-indians-may-have-hunted-mastadons/.

13. *See* John Low, *Keepers of the Fire: The Pokagon Potawatomi Nation*, slides 14–15 (2006), http://www.pokagon.com/presentation/SMCppt_20080112.pdf (quoting Frank Bush, from the film *Keepers of the Fire*, WNIT Public Television (1993)).

14. *See* Low, *supra* note 13.

15. *See* Gregory E. Dowd, *The Meaning of Article 13 of the Treaty of Washington, March 28, 1836*, at 2, Expert Report prepared for the Chippewa Ottawa Resource Authority *in* United States v. Michigan, No. 2:73 CV 26 (W.D. Mich., Oct. 11, 2004); James M. McClurken, *The Ottawa, in* PEOPLE OF THE THREE FIRES: THE OTTAWA, POTAWATOMI, AND OJIBWAY OF MICHIGAN 1, 2 (1986).

16. *See* MCCLURKEN, GAH-BAEH-JHAGWAH-BUK, *supra* note 3, at 3; Dowd, *supra* note 15, at 63.

17. *See* MCCLURKEN, GAH-BAEH-JHAGWAH-BUK, *supra* note 3, at 3; McClurken, *The Ottawa, supra* note 15, at 5.

18. *See* Dowd, *supra* note 15, at 14; McClurken, *The Ottawa, supra* note 15, at 13.

19. *See* CRAKER, *supra* note 5, at 22–23; MCCLURKEN, GAH-BAEH-JHAGWAH-BUK, *supra* note 3, at 3; HELEN HORNBACK TANNER, ATLAS OF GREAT LAKES INDIAN HISTORY 30–35 (1987); White, *Ethnohistorical Report on the Grand Traverse Ottawas, supra* note 2, at 2–3.

20. *See* McClurken, *The Ottawa, supra* note 15, at 13; Leroy V. Eid, *The Ojibwa-Iroquois War: The War the Five Nations Did Not Win*, 26 ETHNOHISTORY 297, 317 (1979).

21. *See* CRAKER, *supra* note 5, at 6; Dowd, *supra* note 15, at 14; McClurken, *The Ottawa, supra* note 15, at 13.

22. *See* Eid, *supra* note 20, at 321 (citing ANDREW J. BLACKBIRD, HISTORY OF THE OTTAWA AND CHIPPEWA INDIANS OF MICHIGAN 81 (1887)).

23. *See* MCCLURKEN, GAH-BAEH-JHAGWAH-BUK, *supra* note 3, at 3.

24. *See* MCCLURKEN, GAH-BAEH-JHAGWAH-BUK, *supra* note 3, at 3; James M. McClurken, *Augustin Hamlin, Jr.: Ottawa Identity and the Politics of Persistence, in* BEING AND BECOMING INDIAN: BIOGRAPHICAL STUDIES OF NORTH AMERICAN FRONTIERS 82, 85–86 (James A. Clifton, ed. 1989); Dowd, *supra* note 15, at 14.

25. *See* Dowd, *supra* note 15, at 14; A. E. Parkins, *The Indians of the Great Lakes Region and Their Environment*, 6 GEOGRAPHICAL REVIEW 504, 506–07 (1918).

26. *See* CRAKER, *supra* note 5, at 23–25.

27. McClurken, *The Ottawa, supra* note 15, at 14; *see also* MCCLURKEN, GAH-BAEH-JHAGWAH-BUK, *supra* note 3, at 3–4 (noting that the Ottawas sold surplus food to the forts).

28. *See* MCCLURKEN, GAH-BAEH-JHAGWAH-BUK, *supra* note 3, at 18–19; Dowd, *supra* note 15, at 15–16; McClurken, *The Ottawa, supra* note 15, at 14–15. *See also* Melissa A. Pflüg, *"Pimiadaziwin": Contemporary Rituals in Odawa Community*, 20 AMERICAN INDIAN QUARTERLY 489, 492–95 (1996) (detailing modern examples and importance of "gifting").

29. *See* MCCLURKEN, GAH-BAEH-JHAGWAH-BUK, *supra* note 3, at 4.

30. *See* McClurken, *The Ottawa, supra* note 15, at 15.

31. *See* MCCLURKEN, GAH-BAEH-JHAGWAH-BUK, *supra* note 3, at 4; Dowd, *supra* note 15, at 16.

32. *See* MCCLURKEN, GAH-BAEH-JHAGWAH-BUK, *supra* note 3, at 4.

33. *See* MCCLURKEN, GAH-BAEH-JHAGWAH-BUK, *supra* note 3, at 4; White, *Ethnohistorical Report on the Grand Traverse Ottawas, supra* note 2, at 4. *See also* McClurken, *The Ottawa, supra* note 15, at 17 (describing the development of Ottawa villages).

34. *See* CRAKER, *supra* note 5, at 8–9.

35. *See* MCCLURKEN, GAH-BAEH-JHAGWAH-BUK, *supra* note 3, at 4–5.

36. *See* CRAKER, *supra* note 5, at 27.

37. *See* MCCLURKEN, GAH-BAEH-JHAGWAH-BUK, *supra* note 3, at 19, 25.

38. *See* Dowd, *supra* note 15, at 16; McClurken, *The Ottawa*, *supra* note 15, at 16.

39. *See* TANNER, ATLAS OF GREAT LAKES INDIAN HISTORY, *supra* note 19, at 58–59.

40. *See* White, *Ethnohistorical Report on the Grand Traverse Ottawas*, *supra* note 2, at 5 (citing BLACKBIRD, *supra* note 22, at 15).

41. *See* CRAKER, *supra* note 5, at 7–8. *Cf.* White, *Ethnohistorical Report on the Grand Traverse Ottawas*, *supra* note 2, at 4 (describing the Mush-co-desh or Prairie People); James A. Clifton, *Michigan's Indians: Tribe, Nation, Estate, Racial, Ethnic or Special Interest Group?*, 20 MICHIGAN HISTORICAL REVIEW, Fall 1994, at 93, 94–95 (describing the Mascouten people as assimilating into the Kickapoo Tribe before 1812).

42. *See* White, *Ethnohistorical Report on the Grand Traverse Ottawas*, *supra* note 2, at 5 (citing Peter Dougherty, *Diaries*, 30 JOURNAL OF THE PRESBYTERIAN HISTORICAL SOCIETY 95, 109 (June 1952)).

43. *See* White, *Ethnohistorical Report on the Grand Traverse Ottawas*, *supra* note 2, at 10.

44. *See generally* Reginald Horsman, *British Indian Policy in the Northwest, 1807–1812*, 45 MISSISSIPPI VALLEY HISTORICAL REVIEW 51 (1958).

45. *See* McClurken, *The Ottawa*, *supra* note 15, at 16, 17.

46. *See* McClurken, *The Ottawa*, *supra* note 15, at 18–19.

47. *See* McClurken, *The Ottawa*, *supra* note 15, at 19–20.

48. *See* Dowd, *supra* note 15, at 16–17.

49. *See* McClurken, *The Ottawa*, *supra* note 15, at 17. For details on the Ottawa war party that participated in the War of 1812, see MCCLURKEN, GAH-BAEH-JHAGWAH-BUK, *supra* note 3, at 5–6.

50. *See* McClurken, *The Ottawa*, *supra* note 15, at 19.

51. *See* McClurken, *The Ottawa*, *supra* note 15, at 19–21.

52. *See, e.g.*, U. P. HEDRICK, THE LAND OF THE CROOKED TREE 27 (1948) (detailing bad fortunes of Ottawas from Michilimackinac who sided with the British); George M. Blackburn, *George Johnston: Indian Agent and Copper Hunter*, 54 MICHIGAN HISTORY 108, 110–11 (1970) (detailing retribution heaped on the Johnston family by the Americans after they sided with the British).

53. *See* Clark F. Norton, *Michigan Statehood: 1835, 1836, or 1837*, 36 MICHIGAN HISTORY 321 (1952).

54. *See* Dowd, *supra* note 15, at 3; Robert H. Keller, *An Economic History of Indian Treaties in the Great Lakes Region*, AMERICAN INDIAN JOURNAL, Feb. 1978, at 2, 9; McClurken, *The Ottawa*, *supra* note 15, at 11.

55. *See* Parkins, *supra* note 25, at 506 (noting travel as far as 500 leagues, or 1,500 miles).

56. *See* Dowd, *supra* note 15, at 26.

57. *See* Dowd, *supra* note 15, at 26.

58. Dowd, *supra* note 15, at 79.

59. *See* TANNER, ATLAS OF GREAT LAKES INDIAN HISTORY, *supra* note 19, at 132 ("The Ottawa canoe trips across Lake Michigan brought them in contact with Ojibwa of the Bay de Noc region, some of whom came to Michigan villages. In the 1830s, the Ottawa and Ojibwa frequented traditional fishing sites on the islands and shorelines at river mouths, near shoals and offshore islets."); McClurken, *The Ottawa*, *supra* note 15, at 11.

60. Dowd, *supra* note 15, at 79 (citations omitted).

61. THOMAS L. MCKENNEY, SKETCHES OF A TOUR TO THE LAKES, OF THE CHARACTER AND CUSTOMS OF THE CHIPPEWAY INDIANS 199–200 (1827) (Ross & Haines 1994), *quoted in* Dowd, *supra* note 15, at 80.

62. *See* Dowd, *supra* note 15, at 80–81.

63. *See* Patrick Russell Lebeau, Rethinking Michigan Indian History 179 (2005).

64. *See* Dowd, *supra* note 15, at 148 (describing the Lower Peninsula Indians as "corn-fed folk"). *See also* Wilbert B. Hinsdale, *Indian Corn Culture in Michigan*, 8 Papers of the Michigan Academy of Science, Arts, and Letters 31 (1928).

65. *See* White, *Ethnohistorical Report on the Grand Traverse Ottawas, supra* note 2, at 2.

66. *See* McClurken, *The Ottawa, supra* note 15, at 11.

67. *See* McClurken, *The Ottawa, supra* note 15, at 11.

68. *See* McClurken, *The Ottawa, supra* note 15, at 3; White, *Ethnohistorical Report on the Grand Traverse Ottawas, supra* note 2, at 2, 6.

69. Blackbird, *supra* note 22, at 11.

70. *See* Hinsdale, *supra* note 64, at 33 (citing M. L. Leach, Grand Traverse Region: A History (1883)).

71. McClurken, *The Ottawa, supra* note 15, at 3–4; *see also* Dowd, *supra* note 15, at 5 (describing the importance of corn to the Anishinaabek).

72. McClurken, *The Ottawa, supra* note 15, at 4.

73. *See* Dowd, *supra* note 15, at 83–84.

74. *See* Dowd, *supra* note 15, at 84; Hinsdale, *supra* note 64, at 37. *See also* McClurken, *Augustin Hamlin, supra* note 24, at 104 ("By the mid-1840s, many Ottawa lived in log houses. They had much increased the size of their fields, and agricultural surpluses were sold to support an ever more sedentary life.").

75. For a description of the importance of the seasons and some of the ceremonies that accompanied them, see McClurken, *The Ottawa, supra* note 15, at 10–11. *See also* Dowd, *supra* note 15, at 3–4.

76. *See* Dowd, *supra* note 15, at 11–12.

77. James M. McClurken, *We Wish to Be Civilized: Ottawa-American Political Contests on the Michigan Frontier*, at 53–54 (Ph.D. dissertation, Michigan State University 1988), *quoted in* Dowd, *supra* note 15, at 9.

78. *See* Craker, *supra* note 5, at 12; Dowd, *supra* note 15, at 8; White, *Ethnohistorical Report on the Grand Traverse Ottawas, supra* note 2, at 6.

79. *See* Craker, *supra* note 5, at 19–20.

80. *See* Keller, *supra* note 54, at 11; White, *Ethnohistorical Report on the Grand Traverse Ottawas, supra* note 2, at 6.

81. *See* McClurken, *The Ottawa, supra* note 15, at 4.

82. *See* Craker, *supra* note 5, at 18–19; McClurken, *The Ottawa, supra* note 15, at 5.

83. *See* McClurken, *The Ottawa, supra* note 15, at 5; Parkins, *supra* note 25, at 506.

84. *See* McClurken, *The Ottawa, supra* note 15, at 5.

85. *See* Dowd, *supra* note 15, at 7.

86. *See* Charles E. Cleland, *The Inland Shore Fishery of the Northern Great Lakes: Its Development and Importance in Prehistory*, 47 American Antiquity 761, 765, 772 (1982); Dowd, *supra* note 15, at 45.

87. Keller, *supra* note 54, at 12.

88. *See* Dowd, *supra* note 15, at 56.

89. *See* Craker, *supra* note 5, at 19.

90. *See* Dowd, *supra* note 15, at 56–57.

91. *See* Dowd, *supra* note 15, at 46–55.

92. *See* Dowd, *supra* note 15, at 55.

93. *See* Dowd, *supra* note 15, at 56 & n. 105 (collecting studies).

94. *See* Dowd, *supra* note 15, at 58–59.

95. Johann Georg Kohl, Kitchi-Gami: Life Among the Lake Superior Ojibway 326–27 (Ralf Neufang and Ulrike Böcker, trans.) (Minnesota Historical Society Press 1985), *quoted in* Dowd, *supra* note 15, at 57.

96. *See* McClurken, *The Ottawa, supra* note 15, at 12.

97. *See* McClurken, *The Ottawa, supra* note 15, at 25.

98. *See generally* Dowd, *supra* note 15, at 120–21, 128–34.

99. *See* White, *Ethnohistorical Report on the Grand Traverse Ottawas, supra* note 2, at 6.

100. *See* Dowd, *supra* note 15, at 25.

101. *See* Dowd, *supra* note 15, at 25.

102. *See* Dowd, *supra* note 15, at 63–67; *see also id.* at 68–69 (retelling Andrew Blackbird's story about his mother's harvest of maple sugar, which could reach 80–100 pounds a season).

103. *See* Dowd, *supra* note 15, at 34.

104. *See* Dowd, *supra* note 15, at 59, 61–62.

105. *See* Dowd, *supra* note 15, at 120–21 (discussing the cyclical character of the fur trade).

106. *See* Dowd, *supra* note 15, at 122.

107. McClurken, *Augustin Hamlin, supra* note 24, at 104.

108. *See* Dowd, *supra* note 15, at 121.

109. *See* Craker, *supra* note 5, at 65; White, *Ethnohistorical Report on the Grand Traverse Ottawas, supra* note 2, at 5.

110. *Cf.* Dowd, *supra* note 15, at 2 (noting that Ottawa villages were more likely to be permanent than Chippewa villages).

111. *See* Craker, *supra* note 5, at 20–21.

112. *See* Tanner, Atlas of Great Lakes Indian History, *supra* note 19, at 133; White, *Ethnohistorical Report on the Grand Traverse Ottawas, supra* note 2, at 8–9.

113. Craker, *supra* note 5, at 30; *see also* Graham MacDonald, *Introduction, in* Frederic Baraga's Short History of the North American Indians 5–6 (2004) (noting that Father Baraga lived at Little Traverse Bay for two years starting in 1831).

114. *See* Dowd, *supra* note 15, at 2.

115. Dowd, *supra* note 15, at 2.

116. *See generally* McClurken, Gah-Baeh-Jhagwah-BukK, *supra* note 3, at 73, 125.

117. McClurken, *The Ottawa, supra* note 15, at 5; *see also* McClurken, Gah-Baeh-Jhagwah-Buk, *supra* note 3, at 73.

118. *E.g.,* Emerson F. Greenman, *Chieftainship among Michigan Indians,* 24 Michigan history 361, 369 (1940).

119. Some assert there were "civil" and "war" *ogemuk,* but this distinction is probably irrelevant. *See* Greenman, *Chieftainship, supra* note 118, at 362–63.

120. *See* White, *Ethnohistorical Report on the Grand Traverse Ottawas, supra* note 2, at 7–8.

121. Ramirez-shkwegnaabi, *supra* note 1, at 56 (quoting William W. Warren, History of the Ojibway People 348 (1957)).

122. *See* Ramirez-shkwegnaabi, *supra* note 1, at 57.

123. Ramirez-shkwegnaabi, *supra* note 1, at 57–58.

124. McClurken, Gah-Baeh-Jhagwah-Buk, *supra* note 3, at 73.

125. *See* McClurken, Gah-Baeh-Jhagwah-Buk, *supra* note 3, at 73.

126. *See* Dowd, *supra* note 15, at 138. *Cf.* McClurken, Gah-Baeh-Jhagwah-Buk, *supra* note 3, at

74 (noting that the L'Arbre Croche Ottawas refused to attend the 1821 treaty negotiations).

127. Mih-neh-weh-na, *quoted in* WILLIAM W. WARREN, HISTORY OF THE OJIBWAY PEOPLE 137 (1885) (Minnesota Historical Society 2009).

128. *See* Colin G. Calloway, *The End of an Era: British-Indian Relations in the Great Lakes after the War of 1812*, 12 MICHIGAN HISTORICAL REVIEW, Fall 1986, 1, 18.

129. According to Keller, "Lewis Cass, for example, had purchased 500 acres near Detroit for $12 thousand in 1816; he sold the same property for $450 thousand in 1836." Keller, *supra* note 54, at 7 (citing ALEC R. GILPIN, THE TERRITORY OF MICHIGAN, 1805–1837, at 172 (1970)).

130. Keller, *supra* note 54, at 8 (citing 2 AMERICAN STATE PAPERS: INDIAN AFFAIRS 136–39 (1815–1827)).

131. TANNER, ATLAS OF GREAT LAKES INDIAN HISTORY, *supra* note 19, at 160.

132. *See* Keller, *supra* note 54, at 8 ("The Indians thought that they were only selling the right to mine or cut timber, with the tribe retaining occupancy rights.").

133. *See* Susan E. Gray, *Article 13 in the Treaty of Washington and Land Use in the Session, 1836 to the Present* 9–10, Expert Report prepared for the Chippewa Ottawa Resource Authority *in* United States v. Michigan, No. 2:73 CV 26 (W.D. Mich., Oct. 19, 2004).

134. *See* McClurken, *Augustin Hamlin*, *supra* note 24, at 90.

135. *See* Dowd, *supra* note 15, at 160.

136. *See* Keller, *supra* note 54, at 7; Helen Hornback Tanner, *Mapping the Grand Traverse Indian Country: The Contributions of Peter Dougherty*, 31 MICHIGAN HISTORICAL REVIEW 45, 64 (2005) (noting Schoolcraft's interest in Grand River Valley lands).

137. *See* ROBERT DOHERTY, DISPUTED WATERS: NATIVE AMERICANS AND THE GREAT LAKES FISHERY 9 (1990).

138. Tanner, *Mapping the Grand Traverse Indian Country*, *supra* note 136, at 59, 60.

139. *See* Dowd, *supra* note 15, at 137–49.

140. By 1826, Henry Schoolcraft was displeased to note that relatively few Americans had moved to Michigan, because of the short growing season. *See* Dowd, *supra* note 15, at 146.

141. *See* Dowd, *supra* note 15, at 143.

142. Gray, *Expert Report*, *supra* note 133, at 20. *See also* McClurken, *Augustin Hamlin*, *supra* note 24, at 91 ("The Ogamuk attending the council at L'Arbre Croche in May 1835 ... proposed disposing only of the Manitou Islands in Lake Michigan, and Upper Peninsula lands shared with the Chippewa."). Gregory Dowd noted the possibility that the Upper Peninsula lands might have been the same lands that the Michigan Anishinaabek had acquired during conflicts with the Haudenosaunee, and specifically perhaps the lands upon which the Anishinaabek had defeated the Haudenosaunee in the 1650s. *See* Dowd, *supra* note 15, at 168–69. Schoolcraft, it appears, did not believe the L'Arbre Croche had a good-faith claim to these lands. *See id.*

143. *See* McCLURKEN, GAH-BAEH-JHAGWAH-BUK, *supra* note 3, at 74; Dowd, *supra* note 15, at 162–66; McClurken, *The Ottawa*, *supra* note 15, at 28. Emerson Greenman misinterpreted the charge from the L'Arbre Croche community to have been equivalent to the ascension of Hamelin to "chief" of all the Ottawa communities. *See* Greenman, *Chieftainship*, *supra* note 118, at 363–64. Hamelin may also have "exaggerated" his authority. *See* McClurken, *Augustin Hamlin*, *supra* note 24, at 83.

144. *See* McClurken, *Augustin Hamlin*, *supra* note 24, at 91–92.

145. *See* McCLURKEN, GAH-BAEH-JHAGWAH-BUK, *supra* note 3, at 74; McClurken, *Augustin Hamlin*, *supra* note 24, at 91.

146. *See* Dowd, *supra* note 15, at 152–53.

147. *See* McClurken, *Augustin Hamlin*, *supra* note 24, at 93 ("The Grand River Ottawa opposed sale

on any terms and threatened to kill an Ogema who cooperated with Americans.").

148. *See* Dowd, *supra* note 15, at 154.

149. *See* McClurken, *The Ottawa*, *supra* note 15, at 28. *See also* McClurken, *Augustin Hamlin*, *supra* note 24, at 93.

150. *See* Dowd, *supra* note 15, at 144–45.

151. *See* McClurken, *The Ottawa*, *supra* note 15, at 28.

152. *See* Dowd, *supra* note 15, at 154–55; Douglas Dunham, *Rix Robinson and the Indian Land Cession of 1836*, 36 MICHIGAN HISTORY 374, 375 (1952).

153. *See* Jeremy Mumford, *Mixed-Race Identity in a Nineteenth-Century Family: The Schoolcrafts of Sault Ste. Marie, 1824–1827*, 25 MICHIGAN HISTORICAL REVIEW 1, 1 (1999).

154. Tanner, *Mapping the Grand Traverse Indian Country*, *supra* note 136, at 60. *See also* ROBERT DALE PARKER, THE SOUND THE STARS MAKE RUSHING THROUGH THE SKY: THE WRITINGS OF JANE JOHNSTON SCHOOLCRAFT 1–28 (2007); Mumford, *supra* note 153, at 1.

155. Margaret Noori, *The Complex World of Jane Johnston Schoolcraft*, 47 MICHIGAN QUARTERLY REVIEW, Winter 2008, at 141 (reviewing PARKER, *supra* note 154).

156. *See generally* Blackburn, *George Johnston: Indian Agent and Copper Hunter*, *supra* note 52.

157. *See* Dowd, *supra* note 15, at 171; Gray, *Expert Report*, *supra* note 133, at 19.

158. *See* Dowd, *supra* note 15, at 171–72; McClurken, *The Ottawa*, *supra* note 15, at 28–29.

159. *See* Dowd, *supra* note 15, at 180; Dunham, *supra* note 152, at 376–77; Tanner, *Mapping the Grand Traverse Indian Country*, *supra* note 136, at 60.

160. *See* McClurken, *The Ottawa*, *supra* note 15, at 28–29.

161. *See* Dunham, *supra* note 152, at 376.

162. *See* Dunham, *supra* note 152, at 385.

163. *See* Dowd, *supra* note 15, at 150–52, 156.

164. *See* FRANCIS PAUL PRUCHA, AMERICAN INDIAN TREATIES: THE HISTORY OF A POLITICAL ANOMALY 118 (1994).

165. *See* Dowd, *supra* note 15, at 126.

166. *See* Dowd, *supra* note 15, at 130.

167. *See* Dowd, *supra* note 15, at 156–57.

168. *See generally* Alfred Cave, *Abuse of Power: Andrew Jackson and the Indian Removal Act of 1830*, 65 THE HISTORIAN 1330 (2003); ANTHONY F. C. WALLACE, THE LONG, BITTER TRAIL: ANDREW JACKSON AND THE INDIANS (1993).

169. *See* Dowd, *supra* note 15, at 183–84.

170. *See* Dowd, *supra* note 15, at 185–86.

171. *See* Dowd, *supra* note 15, at 192, 333.

172. *See* Dowd, *supra* note 15, at 194.

173. CRAKER, *supra* note 5, at 68.

174. CRAKER, *supra* note 5, at 68. Aghosa, also known as Addison, likely was the grandfather of Robert Aghosa, who graduated from Haskell Indian School. *See* Greenman, *Chieftainship*, *supra* note 118, at 366.

175. *See* CRAKER, *supra* note 5, at 33; MCCLURKEN, GAH-BAEH-JHAGWAH-BUK, *supra* note 3, at 5–6.

176. The name "Leelanau" is not an Indian word, but instead is a variant of a pseudonym used by Schoolcraft's wife, Jane Johnston Schoolcraft, who wrote fiction, poetry, letters, and Indian stories under the name "Leelinau." PARKER, *supra* note 154, at 67; Mumford, *supra* note 153, at 9–11. *See also* LeBeau, *supra* note 63, at 185.

177. Tanner, *Mapping the Grand Traverse Indian Country*, *supra* note 136, at 61.

178. *See* Dowd, *supra* note 15, at 178.

179. *See* Dowd, *supra* note 15, at 176–78.

180. *See* Dowd, *supra* note 15, at 182.

181. *See* Susan E. Gray, *Limits and Possibilities: White-Indian Relations in Western Michigan in the Era of Removal*, 20 MICHIGAN HISTORICAL REVIEW, Fall 1994, at 71, 78.

182. *See* Tanner, *Mapping the Grand Traverse Indian Country*, *supra* note 136, at 61–62.

183. *See* Ramirez-shkwegnaabi, *supra* note 1, at 58–59 (noting that hundreds and even thousands of Anishinaabek attended the treaty councils at Glaize River in 1792, at Chicago in 1821, and elsewhere).

184. *See* Tanner, *Mapping the Grand Traverse Indian Country*, *supra* note 136, at 59.

185. *See* McClurken, *The Ottawa*, *supra* note 15, at 29.

186. *See* Ramirez-shkwegnaabi, *supra* note 1, at 68; White, *Ethnohistorical Report on the Grand Traverse Ottawas*, *supra* note 2, at 19.

187. *See* George M. Blackburn, *Foredoomed to Failure: The Manistee Indian Station*, 53 MICHIGAN HISTORY 37, 38 (1969).

188. John Hulbert, "Records of a Treaty Concluded with the Ottawa & Chippewa Nations at Washington, D.C., March 28, 1836" (quoting Henry R. Schoolcraft), *quoted in* Tanner, *Mapping the Grand Traverse Indian Country*, *supra* note 136, at 61.

189. Dowd, *supra* note 15, at 204.

190. *See* Dowd, *supra* note 15, at 204–05.

191. *See* Dowd, *supra* note 15, at 205.

192. Dowd, *supra* note 15, at 205 (quotations and citation omitted).

193. *See* Treaty of Washington, March 28, 1836, arts. 2–3, 7 Stat. 491, 491–92; Tanner, *Mapping the Grand Traverse Indian Country*, *supra* note 136, at 62.

194. Tanner, *Mapping the Grand Traverse Indian Country*, *supra* note 136, at 62.

195. Tanner, *Mapping the Grand Traverse Indian Country*, *supra* note 136, at 67 n. 47.

196. *See* Dowd, *supra* note 15, at 197.

197. *See* Dowd, *supra* note 15, at 202–04.

198. *See* Dowd, *supra* note 15, at 197 n. 134.

199. *See* Dowd, *supra* note 15, at 206.

200. Gray, *Expert Report*, *supra* note 133, at 7.

201. *See* Gray, *Expert Report*, *supra* note 133, at 37 ("Schoolcraft's final formulation of Article 13 'until the lands are required for settlement' was unprecedented.").

202. *See generally* Gray, *Expert Report*, *supra* note 133.

203. Gray, *Expert Report*, *supra* note 133, at 25; *see also id.* at 30 ("Like other nineteenth-century Americans, Schoolcraft saw farming, lumbering, and mining as distinct economic activities, and associated only the first with settlement.").

204. Gray, *Expert Report*, *supra* note 133, at 26.

205. Gray, *Expert Report*, *supra* note 133, at 45.

206. *See* Gray, *Expert Report*, *supra* note 133, at 46.

207. *See* Gray, *Expert Report*, *supra* note 133, at 125.

208. *See* Gray, *Expert Report*, *supra* note 133, at 46–47.

209. *See* Gray, *Expert Report*, *supra* note 133, at 125.

210. Dowd, *supra* note 15, at 209 (quoting Henry Schoolcraft to T. Hartley Crawford, Michilimackinac (Sept. 30, 1839)).

211. *See* McClurken, *The Ottawa*, *supra* note 15, at 29.

212. *See* MᶜCLURKEN, GAH-BAEH-JHAGWAH-BUK, *supra* note 3, at 75; Dowd, *supra* note 15, at 220–24; McClurken, *The Ottawa, supra* note 15, at 29.

213. *See* McClurken, *The Ottawa, supra* note 15, at 29; Tanner, *Mapping the Grand Traverse Indian Country, supra* note 136, at 63.

214. *See* Dowd, *supra* note 15, at 225–26.

215. Tanner, *Mapping the Grand Traverse Indian Country, supra* note 136, at 63–64. *See also* MᶜCLURKEN, GAH-BAEH-JHAGWAH-BUK, *supra* note 3, at 75; Dowd, *supra* note 15, at 232–34.

216. *See* Tanner, *Mapping the Grand Traverse Indian Country, supra* note 136, at 64.

217. *Cf.* Dowd, *supra* note 15, at 229–31.

218. *See* McClurken, *The Ottawa, supra* note 15, at 29.

219. *See* Tanner, *Mapping the Grand Traverse Indian Country, supra* note 136, at 65.

220. *See* Dowd, *supra* note 15, at 237.

221. *See* Dowd, *supra* note 15, at 236.

222. Helen Tanner notes that the Manistee Reservation was surveyed, but never occupied by Indians. *See* Tanner, *Mapping the Grand Traverse Indian Country, supra* note 136, at 74. *See generally* Blackburn, *Foredoomed to Failure, supra* note 187.

223. For an extended recounting of the story of Peter Dougherty from his diaries, see CRAKER, *supra* note 5, at 38–89.

224. *See* Dougherty, *Diaries, supra* note 42.

225. *See* Treaty of Washington, art. 4, clauses 2 & 3, 7 Stat. at 492:

> 2nd. Five thousand dollars per annum, for the purpose of education, teachers, schoolhouses, and books in their own language, to be continued twenty years, and as long thereafter as Congress may appropriate for the object. 3rd. Three thousand dollars for missions, subject to the conditions mentioned in the second clause of this article.

226. *See* Tanner, *Mapping the Grand Traverse Indian Country, supra* note 136, at 66; Virgil J. Vogel, *The Missionary as Acculturation Agent: Peter Dougherty and the Indians of Grand Traverse*, 51 MICHIGAN HISTORY 185, 186–87 (1967).

227. Tanner, *Mapping the Grand Traverse Indian Country, supra* note 136, at 66; *see also* CRAKER, *supra* note 5, at 42 ("Mr. Johnston recommends the Grand Traverse as the most promising point. He says two or three villages have concentrated on the shore north of the bay, some 50 or 60 miles from the lake.... He says no traders are among them, and he thinks that they will not have to remove in a number of years.") (quoting Dougherty's diary).

228. Vogel, *supra* note 226, at 188 (quoting Dougherty, *Diaries, supra* note 42, at 112); *see also* CRAKER, *supra* note 5, at 42–43 (same).

229. *See* CRAKER, *supra* note 5, at 46; Vogel, *supra* note 226, at 188.

230. Tanner, *Mapping the Grand Traverse Indian Country, supra* note 136, at 66.

231. Tanner, *Mapping the Grand Traverse Indian Country, supra* note 136, at 66–67.

232. *See* Tanner, *Mapping the Grand Traverse Indian Country, supra* note 136, at 67; *see also* Vogel, *supra* note 226, at 189 ("[At Grand River] Dougherty met Rev. William Montague Ferry, a former missionary at Mackinac, who advised him that Grand Traverse was the most promising place for mission work, but doubted that much could be done for the Indians."); *see also* Blackburn, *Foredoomed to Failure, supra* note 187, at 39, 50.

233. *See* Dowd, *supra* note 15, at 145.

234. *See* CRAKER, *supra* note 5, at 51–52.

235. *See* CRAKER, *supra* note 5, at 53–54.

236. *See* CRAKER, *supra* note 5, at 59; Tanner, *Mapping the Grand Traverse Indian Country, supra* note 136, at 68–69; Vogel, *supra* note 226, at 190–91.

237. *See* BLACKBIRD, *supra* note 22. *See also* ODAWA LANGUAGE AND LEGENDS: ANDREW J. BLACKBIRD AND RAYMOND KIOGIMA (Constance Cappel, ed. 2006).

238. *See* CRAKER, *supra* note 5, at 56; Tanner, *Mapping the Grand Traverse Indian Country, supra* note 136, at 76; Vogel, *supra* note 226, at 193; White, *Ethnohistorical Report on the Grand Traverse Ottawas, supra* note 2, at 9.

239. *See* BLACKBIRD, *supra* note 22, at 56; White, *Ethnohistorical Report on the Grand Traverse Ottawas, supra* note 2, at 9.

240. *See* George M. Blackburn, *George Johnston and the Sioux-Chippewa Boundary Survey*, 51 MICHIGAN HISTORY 313, 322 (1967); Blackburn, *George Johnston: Indian Agent and Copper Hunter, supra* note 52, at 115.

241. *See* Tanner, *Mapping the Grand Traverse Indian Country, supra* note 136, at 70.

242. *See* CRAKER, *supra* note 5, at 55–56; Vogel, *supra* note 226, at 192–93; White, *Ethnohistorical Report on the Grand Traverse Ottawas, supra* note 2, at 14.

243. White, *Ethnohistorical Report on the Grand Traverse Ottawas, supra* note 2, at 10.

244. CRAKER, *supra* note 5, at 64.

245. CRAKER, *supra* note 5, at 67.

246. McClurken, *The Ottawa, supra* note 15, at 29. Susan Gray added that Ottawa communities in southwestern Michigan did the same. *See* Gray, *Limits and Possibilities, supra* note 181, at 79 (discussing Ottawa "colonies" in Allegan County and elsewhere).

247. Gray, *Limits and Possibilities, supra* note 181, at 83.

248. George N. Smith, while at the Old Wing Colony in Allegan County, noted a similar frustration. *See* Gray, *Limits and Possibilities, supra* note 181, at 84.

249. *See* Tanner, *Mapping the Grand Traverse Indian Country, supra* note 136, at 53, 55, 70–71.

250. Tanner, *Mapping the Grand Traverse Indian Country, supra* note 136, at 71 (quoting Peter Dougherty to Henry Schoolcraft, September 1839).

251. *See* Tanner, *Mapping the Grand Traverse Indian Country, supra* note 136, at 71–72 (quoting Henry Schoolcraft to T. Hartley Crawford, May 18, 1840).

252. Tanner, *Mapping the Grand Traverse Indian Country, supra* note 136, at 72.

253. J. W. Whitcomb to T. Hartley Crawford, August 10, 1840, *quoted in* Tanner, *Mapping the Grand Traverse Indian Country, supra* note 136, at 72.

254. *See* Tanner, *Mapping the Grand Traverse Indian Country, supra* note 136, at 73.

255. *See* Dowd, *supra* note 15, at 240–41. The Odawa complaints against Schoolcraft focused on his refusal to forward more of the federal annuity money directly to the Indian communities, which he kept for various spurious administrative expenses. *See id.*; McClurken, *Augustin Hamlin, supra* note 24, at 99.

256. *See* Tanner, *Mapping the Grand Traverse Indian Country, supra* note 136, at 76 (citing CHARLES C. ROYCE, INDIAN LAND CESSIONS IN THE UNITED STATES, plate 136, "Michigan 1" (1899)).

257. *See* White, *Ethnohistorical Report on the Grand Traverse Ottawas, supra* note 2, at 12.

258. Vogel, *supra* note 226, at 195 (quoting J. B. GARRITT, HISTORICAL SKETCH OF THE MISSIONS AMONG THE NORTH AMERICAN INDIANS 6 (1881)); *see also* White, *Ethnohistorical Report on the Grand Traverse Ottawas, supra* note 2, at 12–13.

259. *See* White, *Ethnohistorical Report on the Grand Traverse Ottawas, supra* note 2, at 13.

260. White, *Ethnohistorical Report on the Grand Traverse Ottawas, supra* note 2, at 14.

261. *See* Dowd, *supra* note 15, at 242.

CHAPTER TWO. THE STORY OF THE 1855 TREATY OF DETROIT

1. Richard White, *Ethnohistorical Report on the Grand Traverse Ottawas*, unpublished manuscript, at 13 (1979).

2. Robert H. Keller, *An Economic History of Indian Treaties in the Great Lakes Region*, AMERICAN INDIAN JOURNAL, Feb. 1978, at 2, 8 (*quoting* Commissioner of Indian Affairs, Annual Report 342 (1840)).

3. *See* H.W.S. Cleveland, *The Grand Traverse Region of Michigan*, 26 ATLANTIC MONTHLY, August 1870, at 191, 191–95.

4. *See* JAMES M. MCCLURKEN, GAH-BAEH-JHAGWAH-BUK: THE WAY IT HAPPENED, A VISUAL CULTURE HISTORY OF THE LITTLE TRAVERSE BAY BANDS OF ODAWA INDIANS 75–76 (1991).

5. *See* Gregory E. Dowd, *The Meaning of Article 13 of the Treaty of Washington, March 28, 1836*, at 242, Expert Report prepared for the Chippewa Ottawa Resource Authority *in* United States v. Michigan, No. 2:73 CV 26 (W.D. Mich., Oct. 11, 2004). *See also* George N. Fuller, *The Settlement of Michigan*, 2 MISSISSIPPI VALLEY HISTORICAL REVIEW 25, 36–38 (1915) (noting that the Michigan Territory, with its rampant land speculation, first felt the effects of what would become known as the "Panic of 1837" as early as 1833).

6. *See* Dowd, *supra* note 5, at 337.

7. Helen Tanner places the date at 1841, *see* HELEN HORNBACK TANNER, ATLAS OF GREAT LAKES INDIAN HISTORY 166 (1987), while Robert Keller relies upon official federal correspondence from Commissioner of Indian Affairs George Manypenny to place the date at 1854, *see* Keller, *supra* note 2, at 9. Keller's date is probably more accurate as a practical manner than Tanner's because the Grand Traverse Anishinaabek believed until at least that time that removal was a serious and acute threat to them. However, in 1841, Robert Stuart, a former trader who opposed removal, replaced Schoolcraft as Michigan Indian agent. *See* James M. McClurken, *The Ottawa*, *in* PEOPLE OF THE THREE FIRES: THE OTTAWA, POTAWATOMI, AND OJIBWAY OF MICHIGAN 1, 31 (1986).

8. *See* McClurken, *The Ottawa*, *supra* note 7, at 30–31.

9. *See* Dowd, *supra* note 5, at 330–32.

10. McClurken, *The Ottawa*, *supra* note 7, at 31.

11. *See* Keller, *supra* note 2, at 9 (citing letters written by Henry Schoolcraft in 1838 and 1841).

12. Keller, *supra* note 2, at 8.

13. *See* MCCLURKEN, GAH-BAEH-JHAGWAH-BUK, *supra* note 4, at 76.

14. James M. McClurken, *Augustin Hamlin, Jr.: Ottawa Identity and the Politics of Persistence*, *in* BEING AND BECOMING INDIAN: BIOGRAPHICAL STUDIES OF NORTH AMERICAN FRONTIERS 82, 98 (James A. Clifton, ed. 1989).

15. Dowd, *supra* note 5, at 337; Elizabeth Neumeyer, *Michigan Indians Battle against Removal*, 55 MICHIGAN HISTORY 275, 283 (1971).

16. Dowd, *supra* note 5, at 346 (quoting Aishquagonabe and Aghosa to Henry Schoolcraft (Jan. 5, 1841)).

17. Dowd, *supra* note 5, at 338; Neumeyer, *supra* note 15, at 383.

18. *See* Neumeyer, *supra* note 15, at 383.

19. *See* Colin G. Calloway, *The End of an Era: British-Indian Relations in the Great Lakes after the War of 1812*, 12 MICHIGAN HISTORICAL REVIEW, Fall 1986, at 1, 4.

20. *See* Calloway, *supra* note 19, at 6.

21. Keller, *supra* note 2, at 9.

22. *See* JAMES A. CLIFTON, THE PRAIRIE PEOPLE: CONTINUITY AND CHANGE IN POTAWATOMI

INDIAN CULTURE, 1665–1965, at 299–300 (1977).

23. *See* WILLIAM E. UNRAU AND H. CRAIG MINER, TRIBAL DISPOSSESSION AND THE OTTAWA INDIAN UNIVERSITY FRAUD 29–58 (1985).

24. *See* CLIFTON, *supra* note 22, at 299–300; Helen Hornback Tanner, *Mapping the Grand Traverse Indian Country: The Contributions of Peter Dougherty*, 31 MICHIGAN HISTORICAL REVIEW 76 (2005).

25. *See* Tanner, *Mapping the Grand Traverse Indian Country, supra* note 24, at 77–78 (noting a "considerable exodus" from the northern portion of the Lower Peninsula).

26. *See* RUTH CRAKER, THE FIRST PROTESTANT MISSION IN THE GRAND TRAVERSE REGION 33 (1932) (Rivercrest House 1979); Dowd, *supra* note 5, at 335–36; White, *Ethnohistorical Report on the Grand Traverse Ottawas, supra* note 1, at 11–12.

27. *See* McCLURKEN, GAH-BAEH-JHAGWAH-BUK, *supra* note 4, at 76.

28. *See* Dowd, *supra* note 5, at 335 ("greatly weakened the federal drive for removal").

29. *See* Calloway, *supra* note 19, at 6; Tanner, *Mapping the Grand Traverse Indian Country, supra* note 24, at 45, 80. *But see* Fuller, *supra* note 5, at 31 (asserting the British stopped giving presents in 1839).

30. Keller, *supra* note 2, at 19.

31. Schoolcraft's downfall began when, due to his increasing unpopularity with the Ottawas, his brother-in-law William Johnston, along with Augustin Hamlin, formally accused Schoolcraft of illegal actions involving treaty funds. *See* McClurken, *Augustin Hamlin, supra* note 14, at 99.

32. *See* Tanner, *Mapping the Grand Traverse Indian Country, supra* note 24, at 79.

33. *See* CRAKER, *supra* note 26, at 71; Dowd, *supra* note 5, at 344. *See also* McCLURKEN, GAH-BAEH-JHAGWAH-BUK, *supra* note 4, at 76 (noting similar land purchases at L'Arbre Croche in 1839).

34. *See* Dowd, *supra* note 5, at 346; Tanner, *Mapping the Grand Traverse Indian Country, supra* note 24, at 80–81.

35. Tanner, *Mapping the Grand Traverse Indian Country, supra* note 24, at 81.

36. *See* Tanner, *Mapping the Grand Traverse Indian Country, supra* note 24, at 81; *see also* Dowd, *supra* note 5, at 344 (noting that the Grand Traverse Anishinaabek were worried about the future of their improvements to the land as early as 1841). According to Helen Tanner, "Cherry trees that Dougherty planted are credited with starting the agricultural enterprise that eventually made Traverse City the 'National Cherry Capital.'" Tanner, *Mapping the Grand Traverse Indian Country, supra* note 24, at 87. *See also* A. E. Parkins, *The Indians of the Great Lakes Region and Their Environment*, 6 GEOGRAPHICAL REVIEW 504, 506–07 (1918) (noting apple orchards and vineyards cultivated by the Ottawas).

37. *See* CRAKER, *supra* note 26, at 69; Tanner, *Mapping the Grand Traverse Indian Country, supra* note 24, at 81.

38. MICHIGAN CONSTITUTION (1850), art. 7. *See also* CRAKER, *supra* note 26, at 71; Tanner, *Mapping the Grand Traverse Indian Country, supra* note 24, at 85; Virgil J. Vogel, *The Missionary as Acculturation Agent: Peter Dougherty and the Indians of Grand Traverse*, 51 MICHIGAN HISTORY 185, 198 (1967); White, *Ethnohistorical Report on the Grand Traverse Ottawas, supra* note 1, at 60–61.

39. *See* Dowd, *supra* note 5, at 243. In 1835, Michigan legislators had debated including American Indians in the category of those eligible to vote in the first Michigan constitution, but declined to do so. *See* DEBORAH A. ROSEN, AMERICAN INDIANS AND STATE LAW: SOVEREIGNTY, RACE, AND CITIZENSHIP, 1790–1880, at 131–33 (2007).

40. *See generally* PAUL W. GATES, HISTORY OF PUBLIC LAND LAW DEVELOPMENT 219–47 (1979).

41. *See* GATES, *supra* note 40, at 219.
42. *See* Dowd, *supra* note 5, at 238–39.
43. *See* Dowd, *supra* note 5, at 244–45, 287–88.
44. *See* Dowd, *supra* note 5, at 244.
45. *See* MCCLURKEN, GAH-BAEH-JHAGWAH-BUK, *supra* note 4, at 76.
46. *See* MCCLURKEN, GAH-BAEH-JHAGWAH-BUK, *supra* note 4, at 76; McClurken, *The Ottawa*, *supra* note 7, at 31.
47. MICHIGAN CONSTITUTION (1850), art. 7. For a legislative history of this provision, see ROSEN, *supra* note 39, at 133–36.
48. White, *Ethnohistorical Report on the Grand Traverse Ottawas, supra* note 1, at 61. *See, e.g.,* Dowd, *supra* note 5, at 353 (describing how Bingham Township election officials refused to allow Grand Traverse Band members to vote in 1866).
49. *See* Dowd, *supra* note 5, at 245–52 (detailing federal support for these rights); *id.* at 248–49 (noting the federal government's refusal to provide the support in 1837).
50. *See* Dowd, *supra* note 5, at 264.
51. *See* Dowd, *supra* note 5, at 267.
52. *See* Dowd, *supra* note 5, at 266.
53. *See* Dowd, *supra* note 5, at 274–75. Robert Stuart, Schoolcraft's successor, also defined "settlement" in this manner. *See id.* at 275–76. Gregory Dowd also documents that federal public-lands law and policy was consistent with this view. *See id.* at 276–90.
54. *See* Dowd, *supra* note 5, at 348–49.
55. *See* Dowd, *supra* note 5, at 350.
56. *See* Dowd, *supra* note 5, at 351.
57. *See* Dowd, *supra* note 5, at 252–53.
58. White, *Ethnohistorical Report on the Grand Traverse Ottawas, supra* note 1, at 14 (quoting Commissioner on Indian Affairs, Annual Report 33 (1855)).
59. Keller, *supra* note 2, at 9–10 (quoting Dwight Goss, *The Indians of the Grand River Valley*, 30 MICHIGAN PIONEER AND HISTORICAL COLLECTIONS 184–85 (1900)).
60. *See* MCCLURKEN, GAH-BAEH-JHAGWAH-BUK, *supra* note 4, at 77.
61. Tanner, *Mapping the Grand Traverse Indian Country, supra* note 24, at 88 (quoting William Johnston to Orlando Brown, June 1, 1850).
62. Tanner, *Mapping the Grand Traverse Indian Country, supra* note 24, at 88.
63. *See* Tanner, *Mapping the Grand Traverse Indian Country, supra* note 24, at 88 (citing George Manypenny to R. McClelland, August 30, 1852).
64. *See* Tanner, *Mapping the Grand Traverse Indian Country, supra* note 24, at 88–89 (quoting Henry C. Gilbert to George Manypenny, March 6, 1854).
65. *See* White, *Ethnohistorical Report on the Grand Traverse Ottawas, supra* note 1, at 16.
66. *See* CRAKER, *supra* note 26, at 73.
67. Ruth Craker wrote:

> Many times the Indians came to Mr. Dougherty to ask him a question, or to give him an interesting bit of information about something. He invariably replied in the Indian tongue, "O-ma-nah," meaning it is so. The Indians were amused at his answer, and they gave him the nickname of O-me-nah. The Indians thought that this term would be an appropriate name for the settlement at the Mission, and so they named it O-me-nah. This is the origin of the name Omena.

CRAKER, *supra* note 26, at 86; *see also* JULIA TERRY DICKINSON, THE STORY OF LEELANAU 10, 27 (1951); VIRGIL J. VOGEL, INDIAN NAMES IN MICHIGAN 185 (1986). Virgil Vogel asserts that Omena may be a corrupted version of *o minan*, which he translates as "he gives to him." *See id.*

68. *See* CRAKER, *supra* note 26, at 71; Tanner, *Mapping the Grand Traverse Indian Country, supra* note 24, at 86. Helen Tanner and Virgil Vogel assert that Aghosatown, or New Mission, was founded in 1852. *See* TANNER, ATLAS OF GREAT LAKES INDIAN HISTORY, *supra* note 7, at 179; Vogel, *supra* note 38, at 198.

69. *See* Tanner, *Mapping the Grand Traverse Indian Country, supra* note 24, at 85–86.

70. *See* Tanner, *Mapping the Grand Traverse Indian Country, supra* note 24, at 87.

71. *See* Bruce Rubenstein, *To Destroy a Culture: Indian Education in Michigan, 1855–1900*, 60 MICHIGAN HISTORY, Summer 1976, at 137, 145, 147.

72. *See* White, *Ethnohistorical Report on the Grand Traverse Ottawas, supra* note 1, at 16; DICKINSON, *supra* note 67, at 10–11 ("Peshabestown"). Helen Tanner asserts that Eagletown, later Peshawbestown, was founded in 1856. *See* TANNER, ATLAS OF GREAT LAKES INDIAN HISTORY, *supra* note 7, at 179. She also asserts that Peshawbe was living in one of the villages at the base of Old Mission Peninsula in 1842. *See* Tanner, *Mapping the Grand Traverse Indian Country, supra* note 24, at 87.

73. *See* Rubenstein, *To Destroy a Culture, supra* note 71, at 139.

74. *See* VOGEL, *supra* note 67, at 45.

75. *See* J. Fraser Cocks III, *George N. Smith: Reformer on the Frontier*, 52 MICHIGAN HISTORY 37 (1968).

76. *See* Cocks, *supra* note 75, at 47–49 (noting date as 1849); Susan E. Gray, *Limits and Possibilities: White-Indian Relations in Western Michigan in the Era of Removal*, 20 MICHIGAN HISTORICAL REVIEW, Fall 1994, at 71, 91 (noting the date as 1848). Julia Terry Dickinson asserted that George Smith moved alone to Northport and found Waukazoo and his people already there, but this is very likely erroneous. *See* DICKINSON, *supra* note 67, at 9.

77. *See* TANNER, ATLAS OF GREAT LAKES INDIAN HISTORY, *supra* note 7, at 179; Tanner, *Mapping the Grand Traverse Indian Country, supra* note 24, at 84, 87; White, *Ethnohistorical Report on the Grand Traverse Ottawas, supra* note 1, at 15–16.

78. White, *Ethnohistorical Report on the Grand Traverse Ottawas, supra* note 1, at 17.

79. FREDERICK BARAGA, CHIPPEWA INDIANS AS RECORDED BY REVEREND FREDERICK BARAGA IN 1847, at 21 (1976), *quoted in* White, *Ethnohistorical Report on the Grand Traverse Ottawas, supra* note 1, at 25.

80. *See* White, *Ethnohistorical Report on the Grand Traverse Ottawas, supra* note 1, at 26.

81. *See* White, *Ethnohistorical Report on the Grand Traverse Ottawas, supra* note 1, at 19.

82. *See* White, *Ethnohistorical Report on the Grand Traverse Ottawas, supra* note 1, at 35.

83. *See* MCCLURKEN, GAH-BAEH-JHAGWAH-BUK, *supra* note 4, at 77. They included Kayquaytosay, Shawbwawsung, Louis Micksawby, Maydwayawshe, Metayomeig, and Menawquot. *See* Treaty of Detroit, 11 Stat. 621, 625 (July 31, 1855).

84. *See* White, *Ethnohistorical Report on the Grand Traverse Ottawas, supra* note 1, at 36.

85. According to Richard White, Asagon was not an *ogema*, but "instead was selected for his skill as a negotiator." White, *Ethnohistorical Report on the Grand Traverse Ottawas, supra* note 1, at 36.

86. *See* White, *Ethnohistorical Report on the Grand Traverse Ottawas, supra* note 1, at 37.

87. White, *Ethnohistorical Report on the Grand Traverse Ottawas, supra* note 1, at 36.

88. *See* White, *Ethnohistorical Report on the Grand Traverse Ottawas, supra* note 1, at 37 ("Actual

Ottawa participation in the treaty was somewhat complex. They selected delegates on the basis of bands, signed the treaty according to regional confederation, and negotiated the treaty as a tribe"; "[Grand Traverse] delegates played only a minor role, allowing As-sa-gon, as Speaker for the Ottawas, to do their negotiating").

89. Benjamin Ramirez-shkwegnaabi, *The Dynamics of American Indian Diplomacy in the Great Lakes Region*, 27 AMERICAN INDIAN CULTURE AND RESEARCH JOURNAL 53, 67 (2003). *See generally* White, *Ethnohistorical Report on the Grand Traverse Ottawas, supra* note 1, chapter 2.

90. Ramirez-shkwegnaabi, *supra* note 89, at 68.

91. *See* White, *Ethnohistorical Report on the Grand Traverse Ottawas, supra* note 1, at 38.

92. White, *Ethnohistorical Report on the Grand Traverse Ottawas, supra* note 1, at 26.

93. During the nineteenth century, a "memorial" was a document of claims made against the federal government or others that was presented to Congress for its review in hopes of legislation that would settle the claims. *Cf.* LINDSAY G. ROBERTSON, CONQUEST BY LAW: HOW THE DISCOVERY OF AMERICA DISPOSSESSED INDIGENOUS PEOPLES OF THEIR LANDS 15–43 (2005).

94. *See* Tanner, *Mapping the Grand Traverse Indian Country, supra* note 24, at 89.

95. *See* White, *Ethnohistorical Report on the Grand Traverse Ottawas, supra* note 1, at 26–27.

96. *See* White, *Ethnohistorical Report on the Grand Traverse Ottawas, supra* note 1, at 35.

97. *See* White, *Ethnohistorical Report on the Grand Traverse Ottawas, supra* note 1, at 36.

98. *See* White, *Ethnohistorical Report on the Grand Traverse Ottawas, supra* note 1, at 36. *See also* Brief of Law Professors Specializing in Federal Indian Law as *Amicus Curiae*, at 33–34, Carcieri v. Kempthorne, 129 S. Ct. 1058 (No. 07-526), http://www.narf.org/sct/carcieri/merits/law_professors.pdf.

99. White, *Ethnohistorical Report on the Grand Traverse Ottawas, supra* note 1, at 25.

100. White, *Ethnohistorical Report on the Grand Traverse Ottawas, supra* note 1, at 29.

101. *See* White, *Ethnohistorical Report on the Grand Traverse Ottawas, supra* note 1, at 29.

102. *See* Ramirez-shkwegnaabi, *supra* note 89, at 68.

103. Ramirez-shkwegnaabi, *supra* note 89, at 68–69 (quoting the treaty journal).

104. *See* White, *Ethnohistorical Report on the Grand Traverse Ottawas, supra* note 1, at 38.

105. *See* Ramirez-shkwegnaabi, *supra* note 89, at 69.

106. Ramirez-shkwegnaabi, *supra* note 89, at 69–70 (quoting the treaty journal); White, *Ethnohistorical Report on the Grand Traverse Ottawas, supra* note 1, at 38.

107. White, *Ethnohistorical Report on the Grand Traverse Ottawas, supra* note 1, at 30.

108. Commissioner of Indian Affairs, Annual Report 4 (1853), *quoted in* White, *Ethnohistorical Report on the Grand Traverse Ottawas, supra* note 1, at 31.

109. Henry Gilbert, Mackinac Indian Agent, to George Manypenny, Commissioner on Indian Affairs (March 6, 1854), *quoted in* White, *Ethnohistorical Report on the Grand Traverse Ottawas, supra* note 1, at 31–32.

110. *See* 1 FRANCIS PAUL PRUCHA, THE GREAT FATHER: THE UNITED STATES GOVERNMENT AND THE AMERICAN INDIANS 327 (1984).

111. *See* White, *Ethnohistorical Report on the Grand Traverse Ottawas, supra* note 1, at 35.

112. *See* White, *Ethnohistorical Report on the Grand Traverse Ottawas, supra* note 1, at 40.

113. *See* Treaty of Detroit, art. I, 11 Stat. 621, 622–23 (July 31, 1855); White, *Ethnohistorical Report on the Grand Traverse Ottawas, supra* note 1, at 33.

114. McClurken, *The Ottawa, supra* note 7, at 34.

115. White, *Ethnohistorical Report on the Grand Traverse Ottawas, supra* note 1, at 41.

116. White, *Ethnohistorical Report on the Grand Traverse Ottawas, supra* note 1, at 41–42.

117. White, *Ethnohistorical Report on the Grand Traverse Ottawas, supra* note 1, at 34 (quoting Henry C. Gilbert).
118. White, *Ethnohistorical Report on the Grand Traverse Ottawas, supra* note 1, at 35.
119. *See* White, *Ethnohistorical Report on the Grand Traverse Ottawas, supra* note 1, at 42–43.
120. *See* Treaty of Detroit, art. III, 11 Stat. 621, 624 (July 31, 1855); White, *Ethnohistorical Report on the Grand Traverse Ottawas, supra* note 1, at 45.
121. *See* ANDREW J. BLACKBIRD, HISTORY OF THE OTTAWA AND CHIPPEWA INDIANS OF MICHIGAN 52–53 (1887).
122. *See* White, *Ethnohistorical Report on the Grand Traverse Ottawas, supra* note 1, at 44–45.
123. White, *Ethnohistorical Report on the Grand Traverse Ottawas, supra* note 1, at 48.
124. White, *Ethnohistorical Report on the Grand Traverse Ottawas, supra* note 1, at 50.
125. *See* White, *Ethnohistorical Report on the Grand Traverse Ottawas, supra* note 1, at 66–68.
126. *See* White, *Ethnohistorical Report on the Grand Traverse Ottawas, supra* note 1, at 69.
127. *See* McCLURKEN, GAH-BAEH-JHAGWAH-BUK, *supra* note 4, at 78.
128. *See* White, *Ethnohistorical Report on the Grand Traverse Ottawas, supra* note 1, at 71.
129. *See* White, *Ethnohistorical Report on the Grand Traverse Ottawas, supra* note 1, at 122.
130. *See* White, *Ethnohistorical Report on the Grand Traverse Ottawas, supra* note 1, at 122–23.
131. *See* White, *Ethnohistorical Report on the Grand Traverse Ottawas, supra* note 1, at 123.
132. *See* McCLURKEN, GAH-BAEH-JHAGWAH-BUK, *supra* note 4, at 25–26; ELIZABETH WOOD, COUNCIL TREES OF THE OTTAWAS 3 (1937).
133. *See* WOOD, *supra* note 132, at 5–6.
134. *See* White, *Ethnohistorical Report on the Grand Traverse Ottawas, supra* note 1, at 124–25.
135. *See* White, *Ethnohistorical Report on the Grand Traverse Ottawas, supra* note 1, at 126.
136. *See* White, *Ethnohistorical Report on the Grand Traverse Ottawas, supra* note 1, at 126–27.
137. White, *Ethnohistorical Report on the Grand Traverse Ottawas, supra* note 1, at 128.
138. *See* Eugene T. Petersen, *Wildlife Conservation in Michigan,* 44 MICHIGAN HISTORY 129, 130–34 (1960); White, *Ethnohistorical Report on the Grand Traverse Ottawas, supra* note 1, at 128–29.
139. *See* White, *Ethnohistorical Report on the Grand Traverse Ottawas, supra* note 1, at 129–30.
140. *See* White, *Ethnohistorical Report on the Grand Traverse Ottawas, supra* note 1, at 130–31.
141. Hon. C. S. Linkletter, "Township History of Almira in Benzie County," 31 MICHIGAN PIONEER AND HISTORICAL COLLECTIONS 113 (1902), *quoted in* Susan E. Gray, *Article 13 in the Treaty of Washington and Land Use in the Session, 1836 to the Present,* at 32, Expert Report prepared for the Chippewa Ottawa Resource Authority *in* United States v. Michigan, No. 2:73 CV 26 (W.D. Mich., Oct. 19, 2004).
142. Letter from E. J. Brooks to Commissioner of the General Land Office (Dec. 27, 1877), *reprinted in* White, *Ethnohistorical Report on the Grand Traverse Ottawas, supra* note 1, at 132.
143. *See* White, *Ethnohistorical Report on the Grand Traverse Ottawas, supra* note 1, at 132.
144. *See* White, *Ethnohistorical Report on the Grand Traverse Ottawas, supra* note 1, at 132–33.
145. *See* White, *Ethnohistorical Report on the Grand Traverse Ottawas, supra* note 1, at 133.
146. *See* White, *Ethnohistorical Report on the Grand Traverse Ottawas, supra* note 1, at 134.
147. *See* White, *Ethnohistorical Report on the Grand Traverse Ottawas, supra* note 1, at 135.
148. White, *Ethnohistorical Report on the Grand Traverse Ottawas, supra* note 1, at 135 (*quoting* GRAND TRAVERSE HERALD, Dec. 22, 1881).
149. GRAND TRAVERSE HERALD, July 18, 1889, *quoted in* White, *Ethnohistorical Report on the Grand Traverse Ottawas, supra* note 1, at 136.
150. *See* Report of the Commissioner on Indian Affairs, at 113 (1885), *cited in* White, *Ethnohistorical*

Report on the Grand Traverse Ottawas, supra note 1, at 134.

151. *See* White, *Ethnohistorical Report on the Grand Traverse Ottawas, supra* note 1, at 136.

152. *See* White, *Ethnohistorical Report on the Grand Traverse Ottawas, supra* note 1, at 136 (*citing* the Durant Rolls and a Letter from August Ance to the Commissioner of Indian Affairs (July 3, 1909)).

CHAPTER THREE. THE STORY OF THE DISPOSSESSION OF THE GRAND TRAVERSE BAND LAND BASE

1. *See* Gregory E. Dowd, *The Meaning of Article 13 of the Treaty of Washington, March 28, 1836,* at 97–98, Expert Report prepared for the Chippewa Ottawa Resource Authority *in* United States v. Michigan, No. 2:73 CV 26 (W.D. Mich., Oct. 11, 2004); *see also* Dowd, *supra,* at 103–04 (*quoting* Peter Dougherty to War Department, Office of Indian Affairs, Grand Traverse Bay (Jan. 21, 1848)).

2. *See* Dowd, *supra* note 1, at 70; *see also id.* at 120 (fall villages).

3. *See* Dowd, *supra* note 1, at 89.

4. Rev. Frederick Baraga, Chippewa Indians 25 (Studia Slovenica/League of Slovenian Americans 1976), *quoted in* Dowd, *supra* note 1, at 90.

5. *See* Dowd, *supra* note 1, at 89.

6. *Cf.* Dowd, *supra* note 1, at 89–90 (describing the complaints of one Sault Ste. Marie *ogema* in regard to hunting trespasses by Grand Island Indians).

7. For example, the Little Traverse Bay Bands of Odawa Indians retains its individually named bands: North Shore, Beaver Islands, Cross Village, Burt Lake, Good Heart, Harbor Springs, Petoskey, Bay Shore, and Charlevoix. *See* Const. of the Little Traverse Bay Bands of Odawa Indians, preamble (2006).

8. *See* Dowd, *supra* note 1, at 92 (*quoting* Henry Rowe Schoolcraft, Personal Memoirs of a Residence of Thirty Years with the Indian Tribes of the American Frontiers 695 (1851) (AMS 1978)).

9. *See* Dowd, *supra* note 1, at 92.

10. Henry Schoolcraft, The Indian in His Wigwam, or Characteristics of the Red Race in America 142 (1948), *quoted in* Janet E. Chute, The Legacy of Shingwaukonse: A Century of Native Leadership 259 n. 13 (1998).

11. Dowd, *supra* note 1, at 90 (quoting Peter Dougherty to War Department, Office of Indian Affairs, Grand Traverse Bay (Jan. 21, 1848)).

12. Francis Assikinack, *Legends and Traditions of the Odawah Indians,* 3 Canadian Journal of Industry, Science, and Art 115, 117 (1858), *quoted in* Dowd, *supra* note 1, at 90–91.

13. *See* Dowd, *supra* note 1, at 93.

14. *See* Dowd, *supra* note 1, at 89.

15. *See* Dowd, *supra* note 1, at 95.

16. *See* Dowd, *supra* note 1, at 96.

17. *See* Dowd, *supra* note 1, at 98–99 (*citing* Charles E. Cleland, *From Ethnohistory to Archaeology: Ottawa and Ojibwa Band Territories of the Northern Great Lakes, in* Text-Aided Archaeology 97, 99 (Barbara J. Little, ed. 1992)).

18. *See generally* James M. McClurken, Gah-Baeh-Jhagwah-Buk: The Way It Happened, A Visual Culture History of the Little Traverse Bay Bands of Odawa Indians 75 (1991).

19. *See* Helen Hornback Tanner, *Mapping the Grand Traverse Indian Country: The Contributions of Peter Dougherty,* 31 Michigan Historical Review 45, 62 (2005).

20. *See* RUTH CRAKER, THE FIRST PROTESTANT MISSION IN THE GRAND TRAVERSE REGION 53–54 (1932) (Rivercrest House 1979).

21. *See* Richard White, *Ethnohistorical Report on the Grand Traverse Ottawas*, unpublished manuscript, at 101 (1979) ("[The *ogemuk*] accepted American assurances of the security of their titles, and most chiefs seem to have believed that the treaty gave them a perpetual right to their land.") (*citing* the 1855 Treaty journal).

22. *See* White, *Ethnohistorical Report on the Grand Traverse Ottawas, supra* note 21, at 102 ("Grave threats to the security of their lands were implicit in the treaty, although the American treaty negotiators did not see fit to explain this to the Indians.").

23. *See* Treaty of Detroit, art. I, 11 Stat. 621, 622–23 (July 31, 1855).

24. *See* White, *Ethnohistorical Report on the Grand Traverse Ottawas, supra* note 21, at 80–81.

25. *See* White, *Ethnohistorical Report on the Grand Traverse Ottawas, supra* note 21, at 102–03.

26. *See* White, *Ethnohistorical Report on the Grand Traverse Ottawas, supra* note 21, at 103.

27. *See* James M. McClurken, *The Ottawa, in* PEOPLE OF THE THREE FIRES: THE OTTAWA, POTAWATOMI, AND OJIBWAY OF MICHIGAN 1, 34 (1986).

28. White, *Ethnohistorical Report on the Grand Traverse Ottawas, supra* note 21, at 103.

29. *Miigwetch* to Jim McClurken for this information.

30. *See* Treaty of Detroit, amendment, 11 Stat. at 626 (April 15, 1856).

31. *See* Treaty of Detroit, 11 Stat. at 629.

32. *See* White, *Ethnohistorical Report on the Grand Traverse Ottawas, supra* note 21, at 103.

33. *See* White, *Ethnohistorical Report on the Grand Traverse Ottawas, supra* note 21, at 103–04.

34. *See* White, *Ethnohistorical Report on the Grand Traverse Ottawas, supra* note 21, at 104.

35. *See* White, *Ethnohistorical Report on the Grand Traverse Ottawas, supra* note 21, at 104.

36. *See* McClurken, *The Ottawa, supra* note 27, at 27.

37. *See* White, *Ethnohistorical Report on the Grand Traverse Ottawas, supra* note 21, at 104.

38. *See* White, *Ethnohistorical Report on the Grand Traverse Ottawas, supra* note 21, at 105 (*quoting* Michigan Indian Agent Smith to Commissioner of Indian Affairs (January 31, 1867)).

39. White, *Ethnohistorical Report on the Grand Traverse Ottawas, supra* note 21, at 105.

40. White, *Ethnohistorical Report on the Grand Traverse Ottawas, supra* note 21, at 105.

41. *See* White, *Ethnohistorical Report on the Grand Traverse Ottawas, supra* note 21, at 105–06. *See also* Sanders v. Lyon, 2 MacArth. 452, 1876 WL 19461 (D.C. Sup. 1876) (referencing the Blackman-Aghosa frauds and the suspension of new entries at Grand Traverse).

42. *See* White, *Ethnohistorical Report on the Grand Traverse Ottawas, supra* note 21, at 107.

43. *See* White, *Ethnohistorical Report on the Grand Traverse Ottawas, supra* note 21, at 107.

44. *See* White, *Ethnohistorical Report on the Grand Traverse Ottawas, supra* note 21, at 109.

45. White, *Ethnohistorical Report on the Grand Traverse Ottawas, supra* note 21, at 84–85. Other Ottawa communities suffered from discriminatory tax rates, as in Mason County, where the property tax rate for Indians was double that of non-Indians. *See* McClurken, *The Ottawa, supra* note 27, at 34.

46. *See* Treaty of Detroit, art. I, 11 Stat. at 623.

47. *See* White, *Ethnohistorical Report on the Grand Traverse Ottawas, supra* note 21, at 82–83.

48. *See* White, *Ethnohistorical Report on the Grand Traverse Ottawas, supra* note 21, at 83.

49. *See* White, *Ethnohistorical Report on the Grand Traverse Ottawas, supra* note 21, at 83.

50. *See* White, *Ethnohistorical Report on the Grand Traverse Ottawas, supra* note 21, at 106.

51. *See* White, *Ethnohistorical Report on the Grand Traverse Ottawas, supra* note 21, at 107.

52. *See* White, *Ethnohistorical Report on the Grand Traverse Ottawas, supra* note 21, at 108.

53. *See* White, *Ethnohistorical Report on the Grand Traverse Ottawas, supra* note 21, at 108.

54. White, *Ethnohistorical Report on the Grand Traverse Ottawas, supra* note 21, at 108–09 (*quoting* the Petition of the Grand Traverse Indians, April 17, 1871).

55. *See* White, *Ethnohistorical Report on the Grand Traverse Ottawas, supra* note 21, at 109.

56. *See* White, *Ethnohistorical Report on the Grand Traverse Ottawas, supra* note 21, at 109.

57. *See* White, *Ethnohistorical Report on the Grand Traverse Ottawas, supra* note 21, at 109.

58. *See* White, *Ethnohistorical Report on the Grand Traverse Ottawas, supra* note 21, at 110.

59. *See* White, *Ethnohistorical Report on the Grand Traverse Ottawas, supra* note 21, at 110.

60. *See* White, *Ethnohistorical Report on the Grand Traverse Ottawas, supra* note 21, at 72.

61. 17 Stat. 381 (June 10, 1872) ("1872 Act").

62. *See* 1872 Act § 2.

63. *See* 1872 Act § 3.

64. *See* 1872 Act § 4, cl. 1.

65. *See* 1872 Act § 4, cl. 2.

66. *See* 1872 Act § 5.

67. *See* White, *Ethnohistorical Report on the Grand Traverse Ottawas, supra* note 21, at 111–12.

68. Letter from the Secretary of the Interior to the Speaker of the House of Representatives (Feb. 10, 1873), *reprinted in* Restoration to Market of Certain Lands in Michigan, H.R. Exec. Doc. No. 208, 42nd Cong., 2nd Sess., at 1 (Feb. 13, 1873).

69. *See* White, *Ethnohistorical Report on the Grand Traverse Ottawas, supra* note 21, at 112–13.

70. *See* White, *Ethnohistorical Report on the Grand Traverse Ottawas, supra* note 21, at 113.

71. White, *Ethnohistorical Report on the Grand Traverse Ottawas, supra* note 21, at 113.

72. *See* White, *Ethnohistorical Report on the Grand Traverse Ottawas, supra* note 21, at 114.

73. *See* White, *Ethnohistorical Report on the Grand Traverse Ottawas, supra* note 21, at 113.

74. *See* White, *Ethnohistorical Report on the Grand Traverse Ottawas, supra* note 21, at 114.

75. *See* Ottawa and Chippewa Lands in Michigan, House Rep. No. 186, 43rd Cong., 1st Sess., at 1 (Feb. 25, 1974).

    The House Report also included a letter from a concerned citizen living in Cross Village, Michigan, who recommended that Congress allow poor non-Indians to homestead the land as well. *See* Letter from A. T. Burnett (Feb. 13, 1874), *reprinted in* Ottawa and Chippewa Lands in Michigan, House Rep. No. 186, 43rd Cong., 1st Sess., at 2 (Feb. 25, 1874).

76. *See* 18 Stat. 516 (Mar. 3, 1875) ("1875 Act").

77. *See* White, *Ethnohistorical Report on the Grand Traverse Ottawas, supra* note 21, at 116.

78. *See* 19 Stat. 55 (May 23, 1876) ("1876 Act").

79. *See* White, *Ethnohistorical Report on the Grand Traverse Ottawas, supra* note 21, at 116–17.

80. Report of George Lee (Feb. 1877), *reprinted in* White, *Ethnohistorical Report on the Grand Traverse Ottawas, supra* note 21, at 116.

81. White, *Ethnohistorical Report on the Grand Traverse Ottawas, supra* note 21, at 117 (*quoting* Letter from E. J. Brooks to the Commissioner of Indian Affairs (Jan. 12, 1878)).

82. Letter of E. J. Brooks to Commissioner of General Land Office (Dec. 27, 1877), *reprinted in* White, *Ethnohistorical Report on the Grand Traverse Ottawas, supra* note 21, at 121.

83. *See* White, *Ethnohistorical Report on the Grand Traverse Ottawas, supra* note 21, at 121.

84. *See* White, *Ethnohistorical Report on the Grand Traverse Ottawas, supra* note 21, at 118.

85. *See* White, *Ethnohistorical Report on the Grand Traverse Ottawas, supra* note 21, at 118.

86. *See* White, *Ethnohistorical Report on the Grand Traverse Ottawas, supra* note 21, at 118–19 (*citing* Letter from Agent Lee to the Commissioner of Indian Affairs (Jan. 4, 1880).

87. Letter from E. J. Brooks to the Commissioner of Indian Affairs (Jan. 12, 1878), *reprinted in* White, *Ethnohistorical Report on the Grand Traverse Ottawas, supra* note 21, at 119.

88. *See* White, *Ethnohistorical Report on the Grand Traverse Ottawas, supra* note 21, at 119 (*citing* "Notice of Sale of Real Estate," THE ENTERPRISE, Oct. 14, 1886; and John Redbird and William Redbird v. William Gill and Wilbur Gill, Leelanau County Circuit Court, Docket No. 103, cited in *Leelanau Indians Comprehensive Plan* (1977)).

89. *See* White, *Ethnohistorical Report on the Grand Traverse Ottawas, supra* note 21, at 119.

90. *See* White, *Ethnohistorical Report on the Grand Traverse Ottawas, supra* note 21, at 119.

91. *See* James McClurken, *South Fox Island: Its Historical Importance to the Grand Traverse Band of Ottawa and Chippewa Indians* at 1–9, Expert Report prepared for the Grand Traverse Band of Ottawa and Chippewa Indians *in* Grand Traverse Band of Ottawa and Chippewa Indians v. Michigan Department of Natural Resources, No. 01-5784 (13th Judicial Circuit Court, Aug. 21, 2001) ("McClurken, South Fox Expert Report").

92. *See* McClurken, *South Fox Expert Report, supra* note 91, at 22–28.

93. *See* McClurken, *South Fox Expert Report, supra* note 91, at 35–36.

94. *See* McClurken, *South Fox Expert Report, supra* note 91, at 32.

95. *See* McClurken, *South Fox Expert Report, supra* note 91, at 32.

96. *See* McClurken, *South Fox Expert Report, supra* note 91, at 32–33.

97. McClurken, *South Fox Expert Report, supra* note 91, at 37.

98. *See* McClurken, *South Fox Expert Report, supra* note 91, at 37.

99. *See* McClurken, *South Fox Expert Report, supra* note 91, at 38–41.

100. *See* McClurken, *South Fox Expert Report, supra* note 91 , at 42–43.

101. *See* McClurken, *South Fox Expert Report, supra* note 91 , at 53–54.

102. *See* McClurken, *South Fox Expert Report, supra* note 91, at 54–55.

103. *See* McClurken, *South Fox Expert Report, supra* note 91 , at 60–62.

104. *See* McClurken, *South Fox Expert Report, supra* note 91, at 60.

105. *See* McClurken, *South Fox Expert Report, supra* note 91, at 62–63.

106. *See* McClurken, *South Fox Expert Report, supra* note 91, at 64–65.

107. *See* McClurken, *South Fox Expert Report, supra* note 91, at 66–67.

108. *See* McClurken, *South Fox Expert Report, supra* note 91 , at 68–70.

109. *See* McClurken, *South Fox Expert Report, supra* note 91, at 70.

110. *See* McClurken, *South Fox Expert Report, supra* note 91, at 71–72.

111. *See* McClurken, *South Fox Expert Report, supra* note 91, at 72–73.

112. *See* Wenona T. Singel & Matthew L. M. Fletcher, *Power, Authority, and Tribal Property*, 41 TULSA LAW REVIEW 21, 28 & n. 59 (2005). *Cf.* Covelo Indian Community v. Watt, 1982 U.S. App. LEXIS 23138, at 8 n. 9 (D.C. Cir., Dec. 21, 1982) (per curiam) (defining "Secretarial transfers" and "forced fee patents").

113. McClurken, *South Fox Expert Report, supra* note 91, at 73–76 (footnotes omitted).

114. *See* McClurken, *South Fox Expert Report, supra* note 91, at 85.

115. *See* McClurken, *South Fox Expert Report, supra* note 91, at 85.

116. McClurken, *South Fox Expert Report, supra* note 91, at 85–89 (footnotes omitted).

117. *See* Grand Traverse Band of Ottawa and Chippewa Indians v. Michigan Department of Natural Resources, No. 01-5784 (13th Judicial Circuit Court 2002).

118. News coverage of the dispute: Associated Press, *Developer Gives Job to Former DNR Chief: K.L. Cool will work as a consultant for a company he helped with a land swap while with the state*, GRAND RAPIDS (MICH.) PRESS, Oct. 17, 2004, at B3, *available at* 2004 WLNR 17846635; *Treasure Island:*

Wrong Direction: South Fox Island should belong to all of Michigan, editorial, GRAND RAPIDS (MICH.) PRESS, Mar. 17, 2003, at A8, *available at* 2003 WLNR 13849291; John Flesher, *Tribe Sues to Block South Fox Swap*, GRAND RAPIDS (MICH.) PRESS, Jan. 5, 2002, at A5, *available at* 2002 WLNR 11902601; Associated Press, *Owner Denies Plans for an Island Golf Course*, GRAND RAPIDS (MICH.) PRESS, Nov. 23, 2001, at A20, *available at* 2001 WLNR 10061508; Cari Noga, *American Indian Tribe Frustrated over Lake Michigan Island Proposed Land Swap*, INDIAN COUNTRY TODAY (RAPID CITY, S.D.), July 16, 2001, *available at* 2001 WLNR 7666683.

119. *See* Singel & Fletcher, *supra* note 112, at 32–33.

120. *See* Nancy Oestreich Lurie, *The Indian Claims Commission Act*, 311 ANNALS 56, 56 (1957); Public Law 79-726, 60 Stat. 1049 (Aug. 13, 1946).

121. *See* Lurie, *supra* note 120, at 66–68.

122. *See* Lurie, *supra* note 120, at 68 ("The question of tribal replacements in given territories during historic times is exceedingly complex in such areas as the Ohio Valley–Great Lakes region. A shift in locations was set in motion by the Iroquois wars of the seventeenth century.").

123. Dominic v. United States, Opinion of the Commission, 2 Indian Claims Commission 469, 470 (Aug. 6, 1953) (Docket Nos. 40-B et seq.).

124. *See Dominic*, Opinion of the Commission, 2 Indian Claims Commission at 473; Dominic v. United States, Findings of Fact, 2 Indian Claims Commission 461, 462–63 (Aug. 6, 1953) (Docket Nos. 40-B et seq.).

125. *See Dominic*, Opinion of the Commission, 2 Indian Claims Commission at 478–80.

126. *See* Ottawa and Chippewa Indians of Michigan v. United States, Opinion of the Commission, 7 Indian Claims Commission 576, 607–08 (May 20, 1959) (Docket No. 58).

127. *See* Ottawa and Chippewa Indians of Michigan v. United States, Opinion of the Commission, 20 Indian Claims Commission 137, 176 (Dec. 23, 1968) (Docket No. 58).

128. *See* Bay Mills Indian Community v. United States, Amended Final Award, 27 Indian Claims Commission 94 (March 15, 1972) (Docket No. 58).

129. *See* Division, Use, and Distribution of Judgment Funds of the Ottawa and Chippewa Indians of Michigan, Public Law 105-143, 111 Stat. 2562 (Dec. 15, 1997).

130. *See* Affidavit of Barry L. Levine ¶ 2, Covelo Indian Community v. Watt, 551 F. Supp. 366 (D. D.C. 1982).

131. Levine Affidavit, *supra* note 130, at ¶¶ 7–9, 11.

132. *See* Grand Traverse Band of Ottawa and Chippewa Indians, Resolution No. 82-101 (Sept. 17, 1982).

133. *See* Covelo Indian Community v. Watt, 551 F. Supp. 366, 369 (D. D.C. 1982).

134. *See Covelo Indian Community*, 551 F. Supp. at 383–84. The government filed an appeal in the case, but the appellate court affirmed. *See* Covelo Indian Community v. Watt, No. 82-2377, 1982 U.S. App. LEXIS 23138 (D.C. Cir., Dec. 21, 1982). Then-Circuit Judge Scalia dissented, arguing that the tribes had no right to sue. *See Covelo Indian Community*, 1982 U.S. App. LEXIS 23138, at 38 (Scalia, C.J., dissenting).

135. 28 U.S.C. § 2415(a), Public Law 97-394, 96 Stat. 1976.

136. These claims are listed in 48 FEDERAL REGISTER 13,876 (March 31, 1983).

137. *See* Grand Traverse Band of Ottawa and Chippewa Indians, Resolution No. 07-25.1836 (Aug. 8, 2007).

CHAPTER FOUR. THE STORY OF THE FEDERAL RECOGNITION
OF THE GRAND TRAVERSE BAND

Some of the material in this chapter appeared in slightly different form in Matthew L. M. Fletcher, *Politics, History, and Semantics: The Federal Recognition of Indian Tribes*, 82 NORTH DAKOTA LAW REVIEW 487 (2006).

1. *See* Richard White, *Ethnohistorical Report on the Grand Traverse Ottawas*, unpublished manuscript, at 58 (1979).
2. MICHIGAN CONSTITUTION (1850), art. 7. *See generally* DEBORAH A. ROSEN, AMERICAN INDIANS AND STATE LAW: SOVEREIGNTY, RACE, AND CITIZENSHIP, 1790–1880, at 131–33 (2007).
3. White, *Ethnohistorical Report on the Grand Traverse Ottawas*, *supra* note 1, at 61.
4. *See* White, *Ethnohistorical Report on the Grand Traverse Ottawas*, *supra* note 1, at 62–64.
5. *See* White, *Ethnohistorical Report on the Grand Traverse Ottawas*, *supra* note 1, at 65.
6. *See* White, *Ethnohistorical Report on the Grand Traverse Ottawas*, *supra* note 1, at 74.
7. *See* White, *Ethnohistorical Report on the Grand Traverse Ottawas*, *supra* note 1, at 65. The Civil War–era ruling led a large number of Michigan Odawak to enlist in the American army during the Civil War as a means of acquiring American citizenship and therefore qualifying for homestead rights. *See generally* LAURENCE M. HAUPTMAN, BETWEEN TWO FIRES: AMERICAN INDIANS IN THE CIVIL WAR 125–44 (1995). *See also* RAYMOND J. HEREK, THESE MEN HAVE SEEN HARD SERVICE: THE FIRST MICHIGAN SHARPSHOOTERS IN THE CIVIL WAR 24–25 (1998) (discussing the citizenship issue in relation to the Ottawa and Chippewa recruits).
8. *See* White, *Ethnohistorical Report on the Grand Traverse Ottawas*, *supra* note 1, at 74.
9. Michigan Indian Agent James Long had declared in 1871 that the last treaty annuity payment meant that the Indians were "citizens and los[t] their tribal character—the tenure under which the U.S. has been their trustee is vitiated and rendered a nullity"; James Long to the Commissioner of Indian Affairs (April 3, 1871), *quoted in* White, *Ethnohistorical Report on the Grand Traverse Ottawas*, *supra* note 1, at 73. But even Long admitted that his argument made no sense given that other tribes who were treaty signatories remained under federal supervision. *See id.* at 74.
10. *See* White, *Ethnohistorical Report on the Grand Traverse Ottawas*, *supra* note 1, at 75.
11. White, *Ethnohistorical Report on the Grand Traverse Ottawas*, *supra* note 1, at 75–76.
12. Treaty of Detroit, art. 4, 11 Stat. 621, 624 (July 31, 1855).
13. Letter from Columbus Delano, Secretary of Interior, to F. A. Walker, Commissioner of Indian Affairs, at 1–2 (March 27, 1872) (emphasis added).
14. *Id.* at 3–7 (emphasis in original).
15. Dominic v. United States, Findings of Fact, 6 Indian Claims Commission 414, 415 (June 30, 1958) (Docket No. 40-K).
16. Letter from the Commission on Indian Affairs (January 27, 1869), *quoted in* Petition of the Grand Traverse Band of Ottawa and Chippewa Indians to the Secretary of the Interior for Acknowledgment of Recognition as an Indian Tribe, at 9 (1979) (hereinafter "Acknowledgment Petition of the Grand Traverse Band").
17. *See* White, *Ethnohistorical Report on the Grand Traverse Ottawas*, *supra* note 1, at 82.
18. E. J. Brooks, Special Agent, to Commissioner of Indian Affairs (January 4, 1878), *quoted in* White, *Ethnohistorical Report on the Grand Traverse Ottawas*, *supra* note 1, at 76.
19. *See* White, *Ethnohistorical Report on the Grand Traverse Ottawas*, *supra* note 1, at 76–77.
20. *See* White, *Ethnohistorical Report on the Grand Traverse Ottawas*, *supra* note 1, at 77.

21. *See* JAMES M. McCLURKEN, GAH-BAEH-JHAGWAH-BUK: THE WAY IT HAPPENED, A VISUAL CULTURE HISTORY OF THE LITTLE TRAVERSE BAY BANDS OF ODAWA INDIANS 81 (1991).

22. *See* McCLURKEN, GAH-BAEH-JHAGWAH-BUK, *supra* note 21, at 82 (discussing Petoskey et al. v. United States, No. 27,978). Under the law of the time, the Anishinaabek had to convince Congress of the validity of their case before bringing suit, after which Congress passed a statute allowing the Indians to sue the government. *See* Ottawa and Chippewa Indians of the State of Michigan v. United States, 42 Ct. Cl. 240, 1097 WL 888 (March 4, 1907); Act of March 3, 1905, § 13, 33 Stat. 1048, 1081–82 (authorizing the "Ottawa and Chippewa Indians of the State of Michigan" to sue).

23. *See* McCLURKEN, GAH-BAEH-JHAGWAH-BUK, *supra* note 21, at 82. The tribes had won a $62,496.40 judgment, with interest. *See* Ottawa and Chippewa Tribes, 42 Ct. Cl. 240.

24. *See* McCLURKEN, GAH-BAEH-JHAGWAH-BUK, *supra* note 21, at 82.

25. *See* McCLURKEN, GAH-BAEH-JHAGWAH-BUK, *supra* note 21, at 82; White, *Ethnohistorical Report on the Grand Traverse Ottawas, supra* note 1, at 77–78.

26. White, *Ethnohistorical Report on the Grand Traverse Ottawas, supra* note 1, at 77–78 (quoting the government's instruction letter).

27. White, *Ethnohistorical Report on the Grand Traverse Ottawas, supra* note 1, at 78.

28. *See* White, *Ethnohistorical Report on the Grand Traverse Ottawas, supra* note 1, at 78.

29. Commissioner of Indian Affairs to Secretary of Interior (January 25, 1910), *quoted in* White, *Ethnohistorical Report on the Grand Traverse Ottawas, supra* note 1, at 79.

30. *See* White, *Ethnohistorical Report on the Grand Traverse Ottawas, supra* note 1, at 79.

31. White, *Ethnohistorical Report on the Grand Traverse Ottawas, supra* note 1, at 137 (quoting TRAVERSE CITY EVENING RECORD, July 23, 1910).

32. *See* White, *Ethnohistorical Report on the Grand Traverse Ottawas, supra* note 1, at 137.

33. *See* White, *Ethnohistorical Report on the Grand Traverse Ottawas, supra* note 1, at 138. *See generally* William Barrillas, *Michigan's Pioneers and the Destruction of the Hardwood Forest,* 15 MICHIGAN HISTORICAL REVIEW, Fall 1989, at 1.

34. *See* White, *Ethnohistorical Report on the Grand Traverse Ottawas, supra* note 1, at 138.

35. *See* White, *Ethnohistorical Report on the Grand Traverse Ottawas, supra* note 1, at 147.

36. *See* White, *Ethnohistorical Report on the Grand Traverse Ottawas, supra* note 1, at 147.

37. *See* White, *Ethnohistorical Report on the Grand Traverse Ottawas, supra* note 1, at 148.

38. *See* White, *Ethnohistorical Report on the Grand Traverse Ottawas, supra* note 1, at 148.

39. *See* White, *Ethnohistorical Report on the Grand Traverse Ottawas, supra* note 1, at 148.

40. 48 Stat. 984–988 (1934), *codified at* 25 U.S.C. §§ 461 *et seq.*

41. *See* 25 U.S.C. §§ 16, 17. On tribal constitutions, see FELIX S. COHEN, ON THE DRAFTING OF TRIBAL CONSTITUTIONS (David E. Wilkins, ed. 2006).

42. Letter from Ben Peshawba and others to John Collier, Commissioner of Indian Affairs (Aug. 22, 1934), *reprinted in* Acknowledgment Petition of the Grand Traverse Band, *supra* note 16, Appendix 1(a) (1979).

43. *See* McCLURKEN, GAH-BAEH-JHAGWAH-BUK, *supra* note 21, at 83.

44. United States v. John, 437 U.S. 634, 653 (1978), *quoted in* Final Brief of Appellee Grand Traverse Band of Ottawa and Chippewa Indians, at 44, Grand Traverse Band of Ottawa and Chippewa Indians v. Office of the U.S. Attorney for the Western District of Michigan, 369 F.3d 960 (6th Cir. 2004) (No. 02-1679).

45. *See* White, *Ethnohistorical Report on the Grand Traverse Ottawas, supra* note 1, at 150.

46. Frank Christy to W. Carson Ryan (Dec. 6, 1934), *quoted in* White, *Ethnohistorical Report on the*

Grand Traverse Ottawas, supra note 1, at 150.

47. Letter from M. L. Burns and Frank Christy to Commissioner on Indian Affairs (March 4, 1935), *quoted in* White, *Ethnohistorical Report on the Grand Traverse Ottawas, supra* note 1, at 151.

48. Report by Peru Farver, Superintendent of the Tomah Indian Agency (July 30, 1938), *quoted in* Acknowledgment Petition of the Grand Traverse Band, *supra* note 16, at 15.

49. *See* White, *Ethnohistorical Report on the Grand Traverse Ottawas, supra* note 1, at 152.

50. *See* White, *Ethnohistorical Report on the Grand Traverse Ottawas, supra* note 1, at 152–53 (citing Letter from John Collier to Robert Dominic (Feb. 21, 1935); Letter from John Collier to Ben Shawanesse (April 23, 1935)). *See also* McClurken, Gah-Baeh-Jhagwah-Buk, *supra* note 21, at 83.

51. Letter from John Collier to Ben Shawanesse (April 23, 1935), *quoted in* White, *Ethnohistorical Report on the Grand Traverse Ottawas, supra* note 1, at 153.

52. Many Indian tribes, with federal participation, held major Indian congresses to debate the merits of the Indian Reorganization Act. The papers from these congresses are collected in The Indian Reorganization Act: Congresses and Bills (Vine Deloria Jr., ed. 2002).

53. *See* McClurken, Gah-Baeh-Jhagwah-Buk, *supra* note 21, at 84–85; White, *Ethnohistorical Report on the Grand Traverse Ottawas, supra* note 1, at 153.

54. *See* McClurken, Gah-Baeh-Jhagwah-Buk, *supra* note 21, at 83–84; White, *Ethnohistorical Report on the Grand Traverse Ottawas, supra* note 1, at 153.

55. White, *Ethnohistorical Report on the Grand Traverse Ottawas, supra* note 1, at 154.

56. *See* White, *Ethnohistorical Report on the Grand Traverse Ottawas, supra* note 1, at 155.

57. *See* White, *Ethnohistorical Report on the Grand Traverse Ottawas, supra* note 1, at 154–55.

58. *See* White, *Ethnohistorical Report on the Grand Traverse Ottawas, supra* note 1, at 156–57.

59. *See* White, *Ethnohistorical Report on the Grand Traverse Ottawas, supra* note 1, at 157.

60. *See* White, *Ethnohistorical Report on the Grand Traverse Ottawas, supra* note 1, at 157.

61. *See* White, *Ethnohistorical Report on the Grand Traverse Ottawas, supra* note 1, at 158–59.

62. Memorandum of Allan Harper, Field Administrator in Charge of Indian Organization, to Fred H. Daiker, Bureau of Indian Affairs (May 14, 1937), *quoted in* White, *Ethnohistorical Report on the Grand Traverse Ottawas, supra* note 1, at 159.

63. *See* White, *Ethnohistorical Report on the Grand Traverse Ottawas, supra* note 1, at 173–74.

64. *See* Letter from John Collier to Peru Farver and J. C. Cavill (May 29, 1940), *cited in* White, *Ethnohistorical Report on the Grand Traverse Ottawas, supra* note 1, at 174. *See also* McClurken, Gah-Baeh-Jhagwah-Buk, *supra* note 21, at 85.

65. *See Leelanau Lessons: Emelia Schaub*, Leelanau Enterprise Blog, http://www.leelanaunews.com/blog/2007/06/23/leelanau-lessons-emelia-schaub/.

66. Letter from Emilia Schaub to Eleanor Roosevelt (April 9, 1937), *quoted in* White, *Ethnohistorical Report on the Grand Traverse Ottawas, supra* note 1, at 160.

67. Letter from William Zimmerman to Emilia Schaub (June 4, 1937), *quoted in* White, *Ethnohistorical Report on the Grand Traverse Ottawas, supra* note 1, at 161. *See also* McClurken, Gah-Baeh-Jhagwah-Buk, *supra* note 21, at 85.

68. *See* White, *Ethnohistorical Report on the Grand Traverse Ottawas, supra* note 1, at 161.

69. *See* Letter from Frank Christy to Commissioner of Indian Affairs (June 16, 1937), *quoted in* White, *Ethnohistorical Report on the Grand Traverse Ottawas, supra* note 1, at 161–62.

70. *See* H. Scudder Meekel, *Report on the Michigan Indians*, Department of Interior (1937), *cited in* White, *Ethnohistorical Report on the Grand Traverse Ottawas, supra* note 1, at 163.

71. *See* White, *Ethnohistorical Report on the Grand Traverse Ottawas, supra* note 1, at 162.

72. *See* White, *Ethnohistorical Report on the Grand Traverse Ottawas, supra* note 1, at 165 (citing Letter from Peru Farver, Superintendent of the Tomah Indian Agency, to M. L. Burns (July 30, 1938)).

73. *See* White, *Ethnohistorical Report on the Grand Traverse Ottawas, supra* note 1, at 165.

74. *See* White, *Ethnohistorical Report on the Grand Traverse Ottawas, supra* note 1, at 166.

75. *See* White, *Ethnohistorical Report on the Grand Traverse Ottawas, supra* note 1, at 170.

76. John H. Holst, *A Survey of Indian Groups in the State of Michigan, 1939,* at 3 (1939); *see also* White, *Ethnohistorical Report on the Grand Traverse Ottawas, supra* note 1, at 170 (quoting Holst as asserting that there were no "community institutions" at Peshawbestown).

77. Holst, *supra* note, at 4.

78. Acknowledgment Petition of the Grand Traverse Band, *supra* note 16, at 16.

79. Text taken from a transcript of a slide-tape presentation compiled by Fr. James Gardiner and Sr. Marge Redmond, Gaylord Diocese Indian Ministry (1977), *reprinted in* Acknowledgment Petition of the Grand Traverse Band, *supra* note 16, at 16–17.

80. White, *Ethnohistorical Report on the Grand Traverse Ottawas, supra* note 1, at 170–71, 172–73.

81. *See* White, *Ethnohistorical Report on the Grand Traverse Ottawas, supra* note 1, at 178.

82. *See* Ann Miller, *Emilia Schaub: 100 Years of Leadership,* 79 MICHIGAN BAR JOURNAL, Jan. 2000, at 82, 82–83.

83. Minutes, Leelanau County Board of Supervisors, at 365 (April 15, 1943), *quoted in* Acknowledgment Petition of the Grand Traverse Band, *supra* note 16, at 19.

84. *See* White, *Ethnohistorical Report on the Grand Traverse Ottawas, supra* note 1, at 178.

85. *See* White, *Ethnohistorical Report on the Grand Traverse Ottawas, supra* note 1, at 178.

86. *See* White, *Ethnohistorical Report on the Grand Traverse Ottawas, supra* note 1, at 178.

87. *See* MCCLURKEN, GAH-BAEH-JHAGWAH-BUK, *supra* note 21, at 85–86; White, *Ethnohistorical Report on the Grand Traverse Ottawas, supra* note 1, at 179.

88. *See* White, *Ethnohistorical Report on the Grand Traverse Ottawas, supra* note 1, at 179.

89. *See* White, *Ethnohistorical Report on the Grand Traverse Ottawas, supra* note 1, at 179.

90. *See* 60 Stat. 1049 (1946); White, *Ethnohistorical Report on the Grand Traverse Ottawas, supra* note 1, at 179–80.

91. *See* Bay Mills Indian Community v. United States, Amended Final Award, 27 Indian Claims Commission 94 (March 15, 1972) (Docket No. 58). *See also* MCCLURKEN, GAH-BAEH-JHAGWAH-BUK, *supra* note 21, at 86; White, *Ethnohistorical Report on the Grand Traverse Ottawas, supra* note 1, at 180.

92. *See* White, *Ethnohistorical Report on the Grand Traverse Ottawas, supra* note 1, at 180 (citing Letter from Waunetta Dominic, Chair, Northern Michigan Ottawa Association, to Rogers Morton, Secretary of Interior (May 5, 1975)).

93. *See* MCCLURKEN, GAH-BAEH-JHAGWAH-BUK, *supra* note 21, at 86.

94. For a personal view of Waunetta Dominic, see RON PAQUIN AND ROBERT DOHERTY, NOT FIRST IN NOBODY'S HEART: THE LIFE STORY OF A CONTEMPORARY CHIPPEWA 178–80 (1992).

95. *See* White, *Ethnohistorical Report on the Grand Traverse Ottawas, supra* note 1, at 181.

96. *See generally* COHEN'S HANDBOOK OF FEDERAL INDIAN LAW § 1.06, at 89–97 (Nell Jessup Newton et al., eds. 2005).

97. *See* THEODORE W. TAYLOR, THE STATES AND THEIR INDIAN CITIZENS 58 (1972) (citing House Report No. 2680, 83rd Cong., 2d Sess. (Sept. 20, 1954)).

98. *See* White, *Ethnohistorical Report on the Grand Traverse Ottawas, supra* note 1, at 181.

99. *See* White, *Ethnohistorical Report on the Grand Traverse Ottawas, supra* note 1, at 181–82.

100. George Weeks, Mem-Ka-Weh: Dawning of the Grand Traverse Band of Ottawa and Chippewa Indians 67 (1992).
101. *See* White, *Ethnohistorical Report on the Grand Traverse Ottawas, supra* note 1, at 182.
102. *See* White, *Ethnohistorical Report on the Grand Traverse Ottawas, supra* note 1, at 182.
103. *See* Michael J. Chiarappa And Kristin M. Szylvian, Fish for All: An Oral History of Multiple Claims and Divided Sentiment on Lake Michigan 21 (2003) (quoting Skip Duhamel).
104. Chiarappa and Szylvian, *supra* note 104, at 21.
105. Chiarappa and Szylvian, *supra* note104, at 74.
106. *See* White, *Ethnohistorical Report on the Grand Traverse Ottawas, supra* note 1, at 182–83.
107. *See* White, *Ethnohistorical Report on the Grand Traverse Ottawas, supra* note 1, at 183 (citing Letter from L. John Lufkins to Superintendent, Michigan Agency (Feb. 27, 1978)).
108. Public Law 93-580 (Jan. 2, 1975).
109. American Indian Policy Review Commission, Final Report, at 470 (May 17, 1977).
110. 25 CFR Part 54. The current regulations are codified at 25 CFR Part 83.
111. Chiarappa and Szylvian, *supra* note104, at 88–89. Arthur noted also that the Northern Michigan Ottawa Association opposed the Grand Traverse Band petition:

> People from Northern Michigan Ottawa Association (NMOA) opposed our efforts too. The group had formed around claims and money due from an Indian Claims Commission judgment. They had come to feel that they spoke for the Indian people of that area. To be honest, NMOA had performed well in the past, but they had become ineffective. They could not protect our rights. They did not have the sort of clout we could get from recognition. I guess they saw us as usurpers.

Id. at 89.

112. Chiarappa and Szylvian, *supra* note104, at 89.
113. Weeks, Mem-Ka-Weh, *supra* note 101, at 44.
114. Transcript, Vol. 1, at 80–81, Grand Traverse Band of Ottawa and Chippewa Indians v. United States Attorney for the Western District of Michigan, 198 F. Supp. 2d 920 (W.D. Mich. 2002) (testimony of Ardith "Dodie" Chambers) (hereinafter Chambers Testimony).
115. Proposed Finding for Federal Acknowledgment of Grand Traverse Band of Ottawa and Chippewa Indians, 44 Federal Register 60171 (Oct. 18, 1979).
116. Determination for Federal Acknowledgment of the Grand Traverse Band of Ottawa and Chippewa Indians as an Indian Tribe, 45 Federal Register 18322 (March 25, 1980); *see also* Chambers Testimony, *supra* note 115, at 82.
117. Michigan Indian Recognition, Hearing before the Subcommittee on Natural Resources, House of Representatives, 103rd Cong., at 424 (Sept. 17, 1993) (Written Statement of Vine Deloria Jr., Professor of Law, Political Science, History, and Religious Studies, University of Colorado).
118. *See* Snyder Act, 25 U.S.C. § 13, 42 Stat. 208 (1921).
119. Chambers Testimony, *supra* note 115, at 70–71; *see also* Matthew L. M. Fletcher, *Stick Houses in Peshawbestown*, 2 Cardozo Public Law, Policy & Ethics Journal 189, 195 n. 12 (2004).
120. Chambers Testimony, *supra* note115, at 97; *see also* Fletcher, *Stick Houses in Peshawbestown, supra* note 120, at 235 n. 110.
121. Chambers Testimony, *supra* note115, at 77–78; *see also* Fletcher, *Stick Houses in Peshawbestown, supra* note 120, at 236 n. 113.
122. Deloria, *supra* note 118, at 425.

CHAPTER FIVE. THE STORY OF THE GRAND TRAVERSE
BAND'S TREATY RIGHTS FIGHT

1. United States v. Winans, 198 U.S. 371, 381 (1905).
2. 471 F. Supp. 192 (W.D. Mich. 1979), *aff'd in relevant part*, 653 F.2d 277 (6th Cir. 1981), *cert. denied*, 454 U.S. 1124 (1981).
3. *See generally* Gregory E. Dowd, *The Meaning of Article 13 of the Treaty of Washington, March 28, 1836*, Expert Report prepared for the Chippewa Ottawa Resource Authority *in* United States v. Michigan, No. 2:73 CV 26 (W.D. Mich., Oct. 11, 2004).
4. *See* ROBERT DOHERTY, DISPUTED WATERS: NATIVE AMERICANS AND THE GREAT LAKES FISHERY 8–9 (1990).
5. *See generally* MICHAEL J. CHIARAPPA AND KRISTIN M. SZYLVIAN, FISH FOR ALL: AN ORAL HISTORY OF MULTIPLE CLAIMS AND DIVIDED SENTIMENT ON LAKE MICHIGAN 3–4 (2003); GEORGE WEEKS, MEM-KA-WEH: DAWNING OF THE GRAND TRAVERSE BAND OF OTTAWA AND CHIPPEWA INDIANS 41 (1992).
6. 7 Stat. 491, 495.
7. *E.g.*, Minnesota v. Mille Lacs Band of Chippewa Indians, 526 U.S. 172 (1999); Washington v. Washington State Commercial Passenger Fishing Vessel Association, 443 U.S. 658 (1979); Menominee Tribe v. United States, 391 U.S. 404 (1968); Winters v. United States, 207 U.S. 564 (1908); United States v. Winans, 198 U.S. 371 (1905). *Cf.* Montana v. Blackfeet Tribe, 471 U.S. 759 (1985) (interpreting ambiguous federal statutes for the benefit of tribal interests).
8. For more detail, see chapter 2 on the 1836 Treaty of Detroit, and see Dowd, *supra* note 3, at 232–34 (noting Henry Schoolcraft's understanding), 266–65 (same), 274–75 (same), 290–93 (comparing settlers to miners), 293–99 (comparing settlers to lumbermen), 302–03 (comparing other Indian treaties using the word "settlement").
9. ERHARD ROSTLUND, FRESHWATER FISH AND FISHING IN NATIVE NORTH AMERICA 29–30 (University of California Publications in Geography 1952), *quoted in* Charles E. Cleland, *The Inland Shore Fishery of the Northern Great Lakes: Its Development and Importance in Prehistory*, 47 AMERICAN ANTIQUITY 761 (1982).
10. *See* DOHERTY, DISPUTED WATERS, *supra* note 4, at 23–24.
11. *See* Cleland, *The Inland Shore Fishery of the Upper Great Lakes, supra* 9, at 762 (quoting W. VERNON KINIETZ, THE INDIANS OF THE WESTERN GREAT LAKES, 1615–1760 24 (1965)).
12. *See* DOHERTY, DISPUTED WATERS, *supra* note 4, at 24.
13. *See* DOHERTY, DISPUTED WATERS, *supra* note 4, at 23.
14. *See* DOHERTY, DISPUTED WATERS, *supra* note 4, at 24–25.
15. *See* DOHERTY, DISPUTED WATERS, *supra* note 4, at 24–25; Grace Lee Nute, *The American Fur Company's Fishing Enterprises on Lake Superior*, 12 MISSISSIPPI VALLEY HISTORICAL REVIEW 483 (1926).
16. *See* DOHERTY, DISPUTED WATERS, *supra* note 4, at 25–28; CHIARAPPA & SZYLVIAN, *supra* note 5, at 2–4.
17. *See* DOHERTY, DISPUTED WATERS, *supra* note 4, at 38–39.
18. *See* DOHERTY, DISPUTED WATERS, *supra* note 4, at 40–41.
19. *See* DOHERTY, DISPUTED WATERS, *supra* note 4, at 53.
20. *See* DOHERTY, DISPUTED WATERS, *supra* note 4, at 53–54.
21. *See* DOHERTY, DISPUTED WATERS, *supra* note 4, at 48–49.
22. *See* Etta S. Wilson, *Personal Recollections of the Passenger Pigeon*, 51 THE AUK 157 (1934).
23. Robert H. Keller, *An Economic History of Indian Treaties in the Great Lakes Region*, AMERICAN

INDIAN JOURNAL, Feb. 1978, at 2, 13.

24. *See, e.g.,* Dowd, *supra* note 3, at 355–56 (reliance on hunting and fishing in 1847), 361 (killing wolves and ducks for breakfast), 360–61 (shining deer at night), 364 (harvesting berries).

25. *See* Dowd, *supra* note 3, at 360; RUTH CRAKER, THE FIRST PROTESTANT MISSION IN THE GRAND TRAVERSE REGION 7 (1932) (Rivercrest House 1979).

26. *See* Dowd, *supra* note 3, at 367–71.

27. *See* Dowd, *supra* note 3, at 372–79.

28. *See* DOHERTY, DISPUTED WATERS, *supra* note 4, at 56–57.

29. *See* JAMES M. MCCLURKEN, GAH-BAEH-JHAGWAH-BUK: THE WAY IT HAPPENED, A VISUAL CULTURE HISTORY OF THE LITTLE TRAVERSE BAY BANDS OF ODAWA INDIANS 50, 54 (1991).

30. *See* JAMES M. MCCLURKEN, GAH-BAEH-JHAGWAH-BUK, *supra* note 29, at 58.

31. *See* JAMES M. MCCLURKEN, GAH-BAEH-JHAGWAH-BUK, *supra* note 29, at 58, 66.

32. *See* DOHERTY, DISPUTED WATERS, *supra* note 4, at 66.

33. *See* JAMES M. MCCLURKEN, GAH-BAEH-JHAGWAH-BUK, *supra* note 29, at 58, 66; Dowd, *supra* note 3, at 379–80.

34. *See* Keller, *supra* note 23, at 13.

35. *See* DOHERTY, DISPUTED WATERS, *supra* note 4, at 49.

36. *See* DOHERTY, DISPUTED WATERS, *supra* note 4, at 49–50.

37. Dowd, *supra* note 3, at 353 (quoting A. B. Page to R. M. Smith (Aug. 1, 1866)) (emphasis added).

38. *See* DEBORAH A. ROSEN, AMERICAN INDIANS AND STATE LAW: SOVEREIGNTY, RACE, AND CITIZENSHIP, 1790–1880, at 146–47 (2007). Ironically, the Michigan constitution proposed in 1866 struck out any reference to Indians, with the expectation that the legislation that would become the Fourteenth Amendment to the United States Constitution would extend citizenship to all Indians—an expectation that turned out not to be true. *See id.* at 148; George Beck, *The Fourteenth Amendment as Related to Tribal Indians: Section I, "Subject to the Jurisdiction Thereof" and Section II, "Excluding Indians Not Taxed,"* 28 AMERICAN INDIAN CULTURE & RESEARCH JOURNAL 37 (2004).

39. *See* ROSEN, *supra* note 38, at 148.

40. CHARLES E. CLELAND, RITES OF CONQUEST: THE HISTORY AND CULTURE OF MICHIGAN'S NATIVE AMERICANS 280 (1992).

41. *See* Dowd, *supra* note 3, at 354; OJIBWA NARRATIVES OF CHARLES AND CHARLOTTE KAWBAWGAM AND JACQUES LEPIQUE, 1893–1895, at 16 (Arthur P. Bourgeois, ed. 1994).

42. *See* JAMES M. MCCLURKEN, GAH-BAEH-JHAGWAH-BUK, *supra* note 29, at 83 (*citing* Louis Micksauby to Commissioner of Indian Affairs (Feb. 21, 1896)).

43. *See id.* (*citing* D. W. Browning, Bureau of Indian Affairs, to Louis Micksauby (March 13, 1896)).

44. 233 N.W. 205, 207 (Mich. 1930).

45. CHIARAPPA & SZYLVIAN, *supra* note 5, at 18.

46. *See* DOHERTY, DISPUTED WATERS, *supra* note 4, at 58–61.

47. *See* DOHERTY, DISPUTED WATERS, *supra* note 4, at 58.

48. *See* DOHERTY, DISPUTED WATERS, *supra* note 4, at 58–60.

49. *See* DOHERTY, DISPUTED WATERS, *supra* note 4, at 61–64.

50. *See* CHIARAPPA & SZYLVIAN, *supra* note 5, at 5.

51. *See* CHIARAPPA & SZYLVIAN, *supra* note 5, at 5.

52. People v. Jondreau, 185 N.W.2d 375 (Mich. 1971). *See generally* Kathleen Brandimore, *Indian Law—Tribal Fishing Rights—The Michigan Position,* 24 WAYNE LAW REVIEW 1187, 1195–1204 (1978).

53. 10 Stat. 1109.

54. *See* People v. Jondreau, 166 N.W.2d 293 (Mich. App. 1968) (*citing* People v. Chosa, 233 N.W. 205 (Mich. 1930)).

55. *Jondreau*, 185 N.W.2d at 379 ("The People cite *Chosa* as determinative of the decision in this case. If *Chosa* is good law, then undoubtedly the People are correct. We believe that *Chosa* no longer states the applicable law. When *Chosa* was decided in 1930, our Court properly relied on the governing authorities as of that date. However, through the passage of time, the foundations upon which *Chosa* rested are no longer sustained as valid.").

56. *See* People v. LeBlanc, 248 N.W.2d 199 (Mich. 1976). *See generally* Diane H. Delekta, *State Regulation of Treaty Indians' Hunting and Fishing Rights in Michigan*, 1980 DETROIT COLLEGE OF LAW REVIEW 1097, 1116–20.

57. *See* DOHERTY, DISPUTED WATERS, *supra* note 4, at 70–71; Francis E. McGovern, *Toward a Functional Approach for Managing Complex Litigation*, 53 UNIVERSITY OF CHICAGO LAW REVIEW 440, 457 n. 92 (1986).

58. *See* 25 U.S.C. § 256 (1968).

59. *See* CHIARAPPA & SZYLVIAN, *supra* note 5, at 6.

60. CHIARAPPA & SZYLVIAN, *supra* note 5, at 77.

61. CHIARAPPA & SZYLVIAN, *supra* note 5, at 79 (*citing* People v. LeBlanc, 223 N.W. 205 (Mich. App. 1974)).

62. John Alexander, Interview, August 1983, *quoted in* DOHERTY, DISPUTED WATERS, *supra* note 4, at 80–81.

63. *See* DOHERTY, DISPUTED WATERS, *supra* note 4, at 72–73.

64. *See* DOHERTY, DISPUTED WATERS, *supra* note 4, at 81–84.

65. *See* DOHERTY, DISPUTED WATERS, *supra* note 4, at 82 (*quoting* TRAVERSE CITY RECORD-EAGLE, April 21, 1979).

66. RON PAQUIN AND ROBERT DOHERTY, NOT FIRST IN NOBODY'S HEART: THE LIFE STORY OF A CONTEMPORARY CHIPPEWA 190 (1992).

67. PAQUIN AND DOHERTY, *supra* note 66, at 190.

68. CHIARAPPA & SZYLVIAN, *supra* note 5, at 50.

69. *See generally* CHIARAPPA & SZYLVIAN, *supra* note 5, at 72–91 (reprinting interview transcripts with Arthur Duhamel and Babette Duhamel Patton by Robert Doherty (1980)); WEEKS, *supra* note 5, at 42, 61–64.

70. *See* WEEKS, *supra* note 5, at 62.

71. *See* DOHERTY, DISPUTED WATERS, *supra* note 4, at 68.

72. CHIARAPPA & SZYLVIAN, *supra* note 5, at 19–20.

73. CHIARAPPA & SZYLVIAN, *supra* note 5, at 21.

74. CHIARAPPA & SZYLVIAN, *supra* note 5, at 90.

75. CHIARAPPA & SZYLVIAN, *supra* note 5, at 30.

76. CHIARAPPA & SZYLVIAN, *supra* note 5, at 78.

77. CHIARAPPA & SZYLVIAN, *supra* note 5, at 21.

78. CHIARAPPA & SZYLVIAN, *supra* note 5, at 65.

79. CHIARAPPA & SZYLVIAN, *supra* note 5, at 65–66.

80. *See* WEEKS, *supra* note 5, at 62.

81. WEEKS, *supra* note 5, at 62 (quoting John Petoskey, Interview by George Weeks (Aug. 9, 1990)).

82. WEEKS, *supra* note 5, at 62 (quoting John Petoskey, Interview by George Weeks (Aug. 9, 1990)).

83. *Fish and Wildlife Miscellaneous—Part 3*, Hearings before the Subcommittee on Fisheries and

Wildlife Conservation and the Environment of the Committee on Merchant Marine and Fisheries, House of Representatives, 95th Cong., 2d Sess., at 157 (July 12, 1978) (Statement of Arthur Duhamel for the Leelanau Indians) ("Duhamel, 1978 Testimony").

84. Duhamel, 1978 Testimony, *supra* 83, at 158.
85. CHIARAPPA & SZYLVIAN, *supra* note 5, at 52.
86. CHIARAPPA & SZYLVIAN, *supra* note 5, at 82.
87. CHIARAPPA & SZYLVIAN, *supra* note 5, at 82.
88. Helen Hornbeck Tanner, *History vs. The Law: Processing Indians in the American Legal System*, 76 UNIVERSITY OF DETROIT MERCY LAW REVIEW 693, 700–01 (1999).
89. CHIARAPPA & SZYLVIAN, *supra* note 5, at 83.
90. CHIARAPPA & SZYLVIAN, *supra* note 5, at 85–86.
91. CHIARAPPA & SZYLVIAN, *supra* note 5, at 83.
92. *See* CHIARAPPA & SZYLVIAN, *supra* note 5, at 77.
93. WEEKS, *supra* note 5, at 61.
94. CHIARAPPA & SZYLVIAN, *supra* note 5, at 16.
95. CHIARAPPA & SZYLVIAN, *supra* note 5, at 16, 18.
96. *See* Duhamel v. Dept. of Natural Resources, State of Michigan, No. M84-1186, 1987 U.S. Dist. LEXIS 15721 (W.D. Mich., Jan. 22, 1987).
97. *See* WEEKS, *supra* note 5, at 63.
98. *Duhamel*, 1987 U.S. Dist. LEXIS at *2–3.
99. *Duhamel*, 1987 U.S. Dist. LEXIS at *6.
100. *Duhamel*, 1987 U.S. Dist. LEXIS at *7.
101. *See* WEEKS, *supra* note 5, at 45, 61.
102. *See* CHIARAPPA & SZYLVIAN, *supra* note 5, at 73; WEEKS, *supra* note 5, at 61.
103. CHIARAPPA & SZYLVIAN, *supra* note 5, at 20.
104. *See United States v. Michigan*, 471 F. Supp. at 212.
105. *See* Karen Ferguson, *Indian Fishing Rights: Aftermath of the Fox Decision and the Year 2000*, 23 AMERICAN INDIAN LAW REVIEW 97, 99 (1998–1999).
106. *See* CLELAND, RITES OF CONQUEST, *supra* note 40, at 283.
107. *United States v. Michigan*, 471 F. Supp. at 203.
108. James Brady, Trial Transcript, Vol. 1, at 18–19, United States v. Michigan, No. M26-73 (W.D. Mich., Feb. 27, 1978), *quoted in* WEEKS, *supra* note 5, at 42.
109. *See* WEEKS, *supra* note 5, at 43 (quoting Gregory T. Taylor, Trial Transcript, Vol. 5, at 1207–09, United States v. Michigan, No. M26-73 (W.D. Mich., Feb. 27, 1978)).
110. *Id.*
111. *See generally* Ferguson, *supra* note 105, at 125–30.
112. *See United States v. Michigan*, 471 F. Supp. at 205; CLELAND, RITES OF CONQUEST, *supra* note 40, at 284–85.
113. *See United States v. Michigan*, 471 F. Supp. at 213.
114. *See United States v. Michigan*, 471 F. Supp. at 216.
115. *See* DOHERTY, DISPUTED WATERS, *supra* note 4, at 87–89.
116. *See* DOHERTY, DISPUTED WATERS, *supra* note 4, at 89–91.
117. *United States v. Michigan*, 471 F. Supp. at 216; *see also* DOHERTY, DISPUTED WATERS, *supra* note 4, at 91–94 (describing testimony of James Clifton).
118. *United States v. Michigan*, 471 F. Supp. at 216.
119. *See United States v. Michigan*, 471 F. Supp. at 216.

120. *See* DOHERTY, DISPUTED WATERS, *supra* note 4, at 103.

121. *See* DOHERTY, DISPUTED WATERS, *supra* note 4, at 78–79.

122. *See* DOHERTY, DISPUTED WATERS, *supra* note 4, at 105.

123. *See* DOHERTY, DISPUTED WATERS, *supra* note 4, at 105–06; PAQUIN AND DOHERTY, *supra* note 66, at 193.

124. PAQUIN AND DOHERTY, *supra* note 66, at 193.

125. CHIARAPPA & SZYLVIAN, *supra* note 5, at 32.

126. CHIARAPPA & SZYLVIAN, *supra* note 5, at 44.

127. *See* DOHERTY, DISPUTED WATERS, *supra* note 4, at 115.

128. *See* United States v. Michigan, 623 F.2d 448, 449 (6th Cir. 1980) (referencing the Sixth Circuit's September 1979 stay on Judge Fox's order). *Cf.* CHIARAPPA & SZYLVIAN, *supra* note 5, at 46 ("When the court put a 'stay' on us, I thought it meant stay fishing, so I kept fishing. They busted me, of course.") (quoting Ronald Paquin).

129. *See* DOHERTY, DISPUTED WATERS, *supra* note 4, at 111–12.

130. *See United States v. Michigan*, 623 F.2d at 450.

131. *See* DOHERTY, DISPUTED WATERS, *supra* note 4, at 111, 113.

132. *See* United States v. Michigan, 653 F.2d 277, 279 (6th Cir. 1981) (*citing* People v. LeBlanc, 248 N.W.2d 199 (Mich. 1976)).

133. *See* DOHERTY, DISPUTED WATERS, *supra* note 4, at 73.

134. *See United States v. Michigan*, 653 F.2d at 279; DOHERTY, DISPUTED WATERS, *supra* note 4, at 114–15.

135. *See* DOHERTY, DISPUTED WATERS, *supra* note 4, at 73.

136. *See* DOHERTY, DISPUTED WATERS, *supra* note 4, at 74 (*citing* GTASFA v. Maudrie, et al., No. 79-510-CE (Grand Traverse County Circuit Ct. 1979)).

137. *See* McGovern, *supra* note 57, at 457.

138. McGovern, *supra* note 57, at 457.

139. PAQUIN AND DOHERTY, *supra* note 66, at 192.

140. *See* DOHERTY, DISPUTED WATERS, *supra* note 4, at 121.

141. *Cf.* McGovern, *supra* note 57, at 460 n. 103 (referencing the breakdown in negotiations in 1982 over the division of rights in the Grand Traverse Bay).

142. *See* McGovern, *supra* note 57, at 458. For decisions in *United States v. Washington*, see 384 F. Supp. 312 (W.D. Wash. 1974), *aff'd*, 520 F.2d 676 (9th Cir. 1975), *cert. denied*, 423 U.S. 1086 (1976); and *Washington v. Washington State Commercial Passenger Fishing Vessel Ass'n*, 443 U.S. 658 (1979).

143. *See* DOHERTY, DISPUTED WATERS, *supra* note 4, at 124.

144. Order of Reference 2, United States v. Michigan, No. M26-73 (W.D. Mich., Sept. 28, 1984), *quoted in* McGovern, *supra* note 57, at 458 n. 96.

145. *See* United States v. Michigan, 12 INDIAN LAW REPORTER 3079, 3080 (W.D. Mich., May 31, 1985).

146. *See* DOHERTY, DISPUTED WATERS, *supra* note 4, at 128–29; CHIARAPPA & SZYLVIAN, *supra* note 5, at 7; WEEKS, *supra* note 5, at 46; Ferguson, *supra* note , at 133–42; McGovern, *supra* note 57, at 465. The Bay Mills Indian Community, voting twice, rejected the consent decree. *See* McGovern, *supra* note 57, at 466 n. 115. Judge Enslen held a trial, after which he applied the consent decree to Bay Mills anyway. *See* United States v. Michigan, 12 INDIAN LAW REPORTER 3079 (W.D. Mich., May 31, 1985).

147. *See* DOHERTY, DISPUTED WATERS, *supra* note 4, at 128–29; Ferguson, *supra* note 105, at 132.

148. *See* Ferguson, *supra* note 105, at 132.

149. *See* WEEKS, *supra* note 5, at 46.

150. *See* DOHERTY, DISPUTED WATERS, *supra* note 4, at 129–30.

151. Transcript of Opening Remarks and Concluding Findings, Rulings, Statements of the Court at 7, United States v. Michigan, M26-73 (W.D. Mich. Oct. 9, 1992), *quoted in* Ferguson, *supra* note105, at 133.

152. WEEKS, *supra* note 5, at 46.

153. *See* WEEKS, *supra* note 5, at 46.

154. *See* WEEKS, *supra* note 5, at 46.

155. *See* Ferguson, *supra* note 105, at 134.

156. *See* Ferguson, *supra* note 105, at 135. Even the president of the Grand Traverse Sport Fishing Association admitted that the state had broken its promises to the Grand Traverse Band. *See* WEEKS, *supra* note 5, at 46–47 (quoting Bill Hicks, president of the Grand Traverse Sport Fishing Association).

157. *See* Ferguson, *supra* note 105, at 135.

158. *See* Ferguson, *supra* note 105, at 135–37, 140.

159. *See* DOHERTY, DISPUTED WATERS, *supra* note 4, at 132.

160. CHIARAPPA & SZYLVIAN, *supra* note 5, at 50.

161. *See* CHIARAPPA & SZYLVIAN, *supra* note 5, at 36 (quoting Skip Duhamel). *See also id.* at 69 ("They made it real clear that when I go below the 45th parallel in the year 2000 they are going to shoot me.") (quoting Skip Duhamel).

162. CHIARAPPA & SZYLVIAN, *supra* note 5, at 57. *See also id.* at 62–63 (quoting James Raphael arguing that the Grand Traverse Band started with 35 grids, and later was left with three).

163. CHIARAPPA & SZYLVIAN, *supra* note 5, at 61.

164. CHIARAPPA & SZYLVIAN, *supra* note 5, at 53.

165. CHIARAPPA & SZYLVIAN, *supra* note 5, at 58.

166. *See* CHIARAPPA & SZYLVIAN, *supra* note 5, at 38 (quoting Skip Duhamel).

167. CHIARAPPA & SZYLVIAN, *supra* note 5, at 42–43.

168. *See* CHIARAPPA & SZYLVIAN, *supra* note 5, at 9.

169. CHIARAPPA & SZYLVIAN, *supra* note 5, at 38. For more details on the problems with the conversion from gill nets to trap nets, see WEEKS, *supra* note 5, at 49–52.

170. CHIARAPPA & SZYLVIAN, *supra* note 5, at 41.

171. CHIARAPPA & SZYLVIAN, *supra* note 5, at 61.

172. CHIARAPPA & SZYLVIAN, *supra* note 5, at 70.

173. CHIARAPPA & SZYLVIAN, *supra* note 5, at 71.

174. CHIARAPPA & SZYLVIAN, *supra* note 5, at 49–50.

175. *See* CHIARAPPA & SZYLVIAN, *supra* note 5, at 59.

176. Grand Traverse Band of Ottawa and Chippewa Indians v. Director, Michigan Department of Natural Resources, 971 F. Supp. 282, 290 (W.D. Mich. 1995) ("Grand Traverse Band v. DNR").

177. *Grand Traverse Band v. DNR*, 971 F. Supp. at 290.

178. *Grand Traverse Band v. DNR*, 971 F. Supp. at 291.

179. Grand Traverse Band of Ottawa and Chippewa Indians v. Director, Michigan Department of Natural Resources, 141 F.3d 635 (6th Cir. 1998); CHIARAPPA & SZYLVIAN, *supra* note 5, at 59–60 (quoting Skip Duhamel on the case).

180. *See* Bob Gwizdz, *Indian Fishing Deal Reported Set for Signing: The key is the purchase and transfer of commercial fishing operations in northern Lake Michigan to the tribes,* GRAND RAPIDS PRESS,

Aug. 3, 2000, at A1.

181. Department of Interior, Office of the Secretary, Press Release, *Tribal Nations, State of Michigan and Interior Department Sign Agreement to Settle Indian Fishing Rights Dispute* (Aug. 7, 2000).

182. Keith Bradsher, *Michigan Pact Resolves Battle over Limits on Indian Fishing*, N.Y. TIMES, Aug. 8, 2000, at A16.

183. *Id.*

184. *See* Bob Gwizdz, *Indians Sign New Fishing Rights Pact: The deal includes $24 million for Indian fishermen to change from gill nets to trap nets*, GRAND RAPIDS PRESS, Aug. 8, 2000, at B4.

185. United States' Supplemental Complaint, United States v. Michigan, No. 2: 73 CV 26 (W.D. Mich., April 27, 2004), http://turtletalk.files.wordpress.com/2008/10/inland-complaint.pdf.

186. *See* Jennifer Dale-Burton, *Tribes Sign Gathering MOU with US Forest Service*, 9:6 PRESERVING THE RESOURCE: BIMONTHLY JOURNAL OF THE CHIPPEWA-OTTAWA RESOURCE AUTHORITY, Nov. 2006, at 1.

187. Consent Decree, United States v. Michigan, No. 2: 73 CV 26 (W.D. Mich., Nov. 2007), *available at* http://www.gtb.nsn.us/consent2007.html.

188. For other details on the 2007 consent decree, see Tina Lam and Eric Sharp, *Special Indian Hunting Rules OK'd: Proposal would end suit on use of 1836 Treaty*, DETROIT FREE PRESS, Sept. 26, 2007; Associated Press, *Treaty Rights*, GRAND RAPIDS PRESS, Sept. 28, 2007, at B5.

189. Bob Gwizdz, *Tribal Treaty Works: Settlement with state a winner for both sides*, GRAND RAPIDS PRESS, Oct. 19, 2007, at D10. *See also* Editorial, *Fair Game: Good deal between tribes, State over hunting and fishing*, GRAND RAPIDS PRESS, Sept. 20, 2008, at A24.

190. *Agreement Reached in Inland Treaty Rights Case*, US STATE NEWS, Sept. 27, 2007.

CHAPTER SIX. THE STORY OF THE DEVELOPMENT
OF MODERN TRIBAL LAW AND JUSTICE SYSTEMS

1. *See* Gregory E. Dowd, *The Meaning of Article 13 of the Treaty of Washington, March 28, 1836*, at 113, Expert Report prepared for the Chippewa Ottawa Resource Authority *in* United States v. Michigan, No. 2:73 CV 26 (W.D. Mich., Oct. 11, 2004).

2. *See* Dowd, *supra* note 1, at 113–14 (quoting and citing OJIBWA NARRATIVES OF CHARLES AND CHARLOTTE KAWBAWGAM AND JAQUES LEPIQUE, 1893–1895, at 71–72, 168 (Arthur P. Bourgeois, ed. 1994), and BASIL JOHNSTON, OJIBWAY HERITAGE (1976)).

3. *Cf.* KEITH H. BASSO, WISDOM SITS IN PLACES: LANDSCAPE AND LANGUAGE AMONG THE WESTERN APACHE 40 (1996) (making the same observation about another tribe).

4. *See* Dowd, *supra* note 1, at 95–96.

5. *See* Dowd, *supra* note 1, at 89–92. *See generally* Charles A. Bishop, *The Emergence of Hunting Territories among the Northern Ojibwa*, 9 ETHNOLOGY 1 (1971); John M. Cooper, *Is the Algonquian Family Hunting Ground System Pre-Columbian?*, 41 AMERICAN ANTHROPOLOGIST 66 (1939); Frank G. Speck, *The Family Hunting Band as the Basis of Algonkian Social Organization*, 17 AMERICAN ANTHROPOLOGIST 289 (1915).

6. *See* ROBERT DOHERTY, DISPUTED WATERS: NATIVE AMERICANS AND THE GREAT LAKES FISHERY 9–10 (1990); Dowd, *supra* note 1, at 93.

7. *See* DOHERTY, DISPUTED WATERS, *supra* note 6, at 19 (citing Letter from George Johnston to Henry Schoolcraft (June 20, 1833); Dowd, *supra* note 1, at 14–16.

8. ALEXANDER HENRY, TRAVELS AND ADVENTURES 149 (University of Michigan 1968), *quoted in* DOHERTY, DISPUTED WATERS, *supra* note 6, at 13.

9. JOHANN KOHL, KITCHI GAMI: LIFE AMONG THE LAKE SUPERIOR OJIBWAY 421 (Minnesota

Historical Society Press 1985), *quoted in* DOHERTY, DISPUTED WATERS, *supra* note 6, at 14.

10. *See* DOHERTY, DISPUTED WATERS, *supra* note 6, at 15 (citing Ruth Landes, *Ojibwa of Canada, in* COOPERATION AND COMPETITION AMONG PRIMITIVE PEOPLES, at 87 (Margaret Mead, ed. 1937).

11. *See* DOHERTY, DISPUTED WATERS, *supra* note 6, at 21–22.

12. James M. McClurken, *The Ottawa, in* PEOPLE OF THE THREE FIRES: THE OTTAWA, POTAWATOMI, AND OJIBWAY OF MICHIGAN 1, 11 (1986).

13. *See* McClurken, *The Ottawa, supra* note 12, at 11.

14. *See* McClurken, *The Ottawa, supra* note 12, at 12.

15. MICHAEL J. CHIARAPPA AND KRISTIN M. SZYLVIAN, FISH FOR ALL: AN ORAL HISTORY OF MULTIPLE CLAIMS AND DIVIDED SENTIMENT ON LAKE MICHIGAN 45 (2003).

16. *See* McClurken, *The Ottawa, supra* note 12, at 2.

17. *See* Dowd, *supra* note 1, at 11–12.

18. McClurken, *The Ottawa, supra* note 12, at 5.

19. *See* McClurken, *The Ottawa, supra* note 12, at 5.

20. McClurken, *The Ottawa, supra* note 12, at 5.

21. *See* McClurken, *The Ottawa, supra* note 12, at 6.

22. Dowd, *supra* note 1, at 359–60 (quoting Peter Dougherty to William A. Richmond (Sept. 26, 1846)).

23. *See* JAMES M. JAMES M. MCCLURKEN, GAH-BAEH-JHAGWAH-BUK: THE WAY IT HAPPENED, A VISUAL CULTURE HISTORY OF THE LITTLE TRAVERSE BAY BANDS OF ODAWA INDIANS 46 (1991).

24. JAMES M. MCCLURKEN, GAH-BAEH-JHAGWAH-BUK, *supra* note 23, at 46.

25. *See* JAMES M. MCCLURKEN, GAH-BAEH-JHAGWAH-BUK, *supra* note 23, at 73 (citing Paul Radin, *Ottawa-Ojibwe No. 5b*, notebook at 105 (American Philosophical Society) (noting information obtained from Joe Shomin of Cross Village in 1926 or 1927)).

26. JAMES M. MCCLURKEN, GAH-BAEH-JHAGWAH-BUK, *supra* note 23, at 73 (citing Paul Radin, *Ottawa-Ojibwe No. 5b*, notebook at 105 (American Philosophical Society) (noting information obtained from Joe Shomin of Cross Village in 1926 or 1927)).

27. *See generally* JAMES M. MCCLURKEN, GAH-BAEH-JHAGWAH-BUK, *supra* note 23, at 58.

28. *See* McClurken, *The Ottawa, supra* note 12, at 27.

29. *See* Dowd, *supra* note 1, at 100 (citing Robert Doherty, *We Don't Want Them to Hold Their Hands over Our Heads: Economic Strategies of the L'Anse Chippewas, 1830–1860*, 20 MICHIGAN HISTORICAL REVIEW 47, 58 (1994)).

30. *See* McClurken, *The Ottawa, supra* note 12, at 27.

31. *See* Determination for Federal Acknowledgment of the Grand Traverse Band of Ottawa and Chippewa Indians as an Indian Tribe, 45 FEDERAL REGISTER 18322 (March 25, 1980); Public Law 103-324, 108 Stat. 2156 (Sept. 21, 1994), *codified at* 25 U.S.C. § 1300k (recognizing the Little Traverse Bay Bands of Odawa Indians and the Little River Band of Ottawa Indians).

32. 25 U.S.C. § 476(a)(2).

33. For more detail about "model IRA constitutions," see David E. Wilkins, *Introduction, in* FELIX S. COHEN, ON THE DRAFTING OF TRIBAL CONSTITUTIONS xi, xxvii–xxviii (David E. Wilkins, ed. 2006).

34. *See* VINE DELORIA JR. & CLIFFORD M. LYTLE, AMERICAN INDIANS, AMERICAN JUSTICE 99–103 (1983).

35. *See* Snowden v. Saginaw Chippewa Indian Tribe of Michigan, 32 Indian L. Rep. 6047, 6048–49 (Saginaw Chippewa Indian Tribe Appellate Court 2005) (describing the history of the ratification

of the tribal constitution).

36. *See* Matthew L. M. Fletcher, *The Insidious Colonialism of the Conqueror: The Federal Government in Modern Tribal Affairs*, 19 WASHINGTON UNIVERSITY JOURNAL OF LAW AND POLICY 273, 279–80 (2005).

37. GEORGE WEEKS, MEM-KA-WEH: DAWNING OF THE GRAND TRAVERSE BAND OF OTTAWA AND CHIPPEWA INDIANS 68 (1992).

38. *See* Letter from Deputy Assistant Secretary, Indian Affairs (Operations) to Joseph C. Raphael, Chairman, Grand Traverse Band of Ottawa and Chippewa Indians (Nov. 4, 1983).

39. *See* Complaint, Grand Traverse Band of Ottawa and Chippewa Indians v. Bureau of Indian Affairs, No. 85-382 (W.D. Mich., April 25, 1985).

40. *See* Letter from Scott Keep, Assistant Solicitor, Tribal Government & Alaska Branch, to William Rastetter (July 2, 1985).

41. *See* CONST. OF THE GRAND TRAVERSE BAND OF OTTAWA AND CHIPPEWA INDIANS art. II, § 1(b)(2)(b)(ii) (Mar. 29, 1988).

42. *See* CONST. OF THE GRAND TRAVERSE BAND OF OTTAWA AND CHIPPEWA INDIANSart. II, § 1(b)(3) (Mar. 29, 1988).

43. WEEKS, MEM-KA-WEH, *supra* note 37, at 68–69 (quoting Open Letter from Chairman Joseph C. (Buddy) Raphael to the Tribal Membership (May 22, 1987)).

44. WEEKS, MEM-KA-WEH, *supra* note 37, at 69 (quoting Open Letter from Chairman Joseph C. (Buddy) Raphael to the Tribal Membership (May 22, 1987)).

45. *See* CONST. OF THE GRAND TRAVERSE BAND OF OTTAWA AND CHIPPEWA INDIANS art. V (Mar. 29, 1988).

46. *See* Michael D. Petoskey, *Tribal Courts*, 66 MICHIGAN BAR JOURNAL 366, 367–69 (1988).

47. *See* Petoskey, *supra* note 46, at 368.

48. *See generally* Timothy W. Joranko & Mark C. Van Norman, *Indian Self-Determination at Bay: Secretarial Authority to Disapprove Tribal Constitutional Amendments*, 29 GONZ. L. REV. 81, 92 (1993–1994).

49. *See* CCONST. OF THE GRAND TRAVERSE BAND OF OTTAWA AND CHIPPEWA INDIANS art. IV, § 1(k) (Mar. 29, 1988).

50. *See* Vine Deloria Jr., *A Walk on the Inside*, 71 UNIVERSITY OF COLORADO LAW REVIEW 397, 403–05 (2000).

51. *See* WEEKS, MEM-KA-WEH, *supra* note 37, at 77.

52. *See* WEEKS, MEM-KA-WEH, *supra* note 37, at 77–78.

53. WEEKS, MEM-KA-WEH, *supra* note 37, at 78.

54. *See* WEEKS, MEM-KA-WEH, *supra* note 37, at 78.

55. *See* Leelanau Indians, Inc. v. United States Dept. of Housing and Urban Development, 502 F. Supp. 741, 741–45 (W.D. Mich. 1980).

56. *Leelanau Indians, Inc.*, 502 F. Supp. at 745.

57. *See* Memorandum in Support of Plaintiff's Motion for Declaratory Judgment at 2, Grand Traverse Band of Ottawa and Chippewa Indians v. Leelanau Indians, Inc. and Leelanau County, No. 83-834 (W.D. Mich., April 15, 1987). *See also* Transcript, Vol. I, at 104, Grand Traverse Band of Ottawa and Chippewa Indians v. United States Attorney for the Western District of Michigan, 198 F. Supp. 2d 920 (W.D. Mich. 2002) (Testimony of Barry Burtt) (describing the difficult leadership transition from Leelanau Indians, Inc. to the Grand Traverse Band).

58. *See id.* at 2 (citing Opinion and Order, Grand Traverse Band of Ottawa and Chippewa Indians v. Leelanau Indians, Inc. and Leelanau County, No. 83-834 (W.D. Mich., Jan. 30, 1985)).

59. *See* Memorandum in Support of Plaintiff's Motion for Declaratory Judgment at 2, Grand Traverse Band of Ottawa and Chippewa Indians v. Leelanau Indians, Inc. and Leelanau County, No. 83-834 (W.D. Mich., April 15, 1987).

60. *See* Memorandum in Support of Plaintiff's Motion for Declaratory Judgment at 2, Grand Traverse Band of Ottawa and Chippewa Indians v. Leelanau Indians, Inc. and Leelanau County, No. 83-834 (W.D. Mich., April 15, 1987).

61. Leelanau County v. Grand Traverse Band of Ottawa and Chippewa Indians, No. 87-321 (W.D. Mich., April 7, 1987).

62. *See* Memorandum in Support of Plaintiff's Motion for Declaratory Judgment at 2–3, Grand Traverse Band of Ottawa and Chippewa Indians v. Leelanau Indians, Inc. and Leelanau County, No. 83-834 (W.D. Mich., April 15, 1987).

63. *See* WEEKS, MEM-KA-WEH, *supra* note 37, at 100–01.

64. *See* Deputization Agreement between the Grand Traverse Band of Ottawa and Chippewa Indians and the Sheriff of Leelanau County (March 19, 1997); Letter from Michael Oltersdorf, Sheriff, Leelanau County, to George Bennett, Chairman, Grand Traverse Band (Sept. 1, 1998).

65. *See* Brief for Amicus Curiae National Congress of American Indians et al. at 15, 25, Inyo County, Cal. v. Paiute-Shoshone Indians of the Bishop Community of the Bishop Colony, 538 U.S. 701 (2003) (No. 02-281).

66. *See* WEEKS, MEM-KA-WEH, *supra* note 37, at 95.

67. *See* Petoskey, *supra* note 46, at 368.

68. *See* Indian Tribal Good Governance Practices as They Relate to Economic Development, Hearing before the Senate Committee on Indian Affairs, 107th Cong., 1st Sess. at 23–25, 55–95 (July 18, 2001) (Testimony and Prepared Statement of Ardith (Dodie) Chambers, Councilwoman, Grand Traverse Band of Ottawa and Chippewa Indians).

69. *See* In re McSauby, No. 97-02-001 (Grand Traverse Band Tribal Court, July 29, 1997) (en banc), *reprinted in* Indian Tribal Good Governance Practices as They Relate to Economic Development, Hearing before the Senate Committee on Indian Affairs, 107th Cong., 1st Sess. at 67–78 (July 18, 2001) (Prepared Statement of Ardith (Dodie) Chambers, Councilwoman, Grand Traverse Band of Ottawa and Chippewa Indians).

70. *See McSauby*, No. 97-02-001, at 1–5.

71. *See McSauby*, No. 97-02-001, at 5–10.

72. *See* DeVerney v. Grand Traverse Band of Ottawa and Chippewa Indians, No. 96-10-201 (Grand Traverse Band Court of Appeals, Nov. 22, 1997), *reprinted in* Indian Tribal Good Governance Practices as They Relate to Economic Development, Hearing before the Senate Committee on Indian Affairs, 107th Cong., 1st Sess. at 79–82 (July 18, 2001) (Prepared Statement of Ardith (Dodie) Chambers, Councilwoman, Grand Traverse Band of Ottawa and Chippewa Indians).

73. *See DeVerney*, No. 96-10-201, at 1.

74. CONST. OF THE GRAND TRAVERSE BAND OF OTTAWA AND CHIPPEWA INDIANS art. II, § 2 (Mar. 29, 1988).

75. *See DeVerney*, No. 96-10-201, at 2–4.

76. *See* Indian Tribal Good Governance Practices as They Relate to Economic Development, Hearing before the Senate Committee on Indian Affairs, 107th Cong., 1st Sess. at 24 (July 18, 2001) (Testimony of Ardith (Dodie) Chambers, Councilwoman, Grand Traverse Band of Ottawa and Chippewa Indians).

77. *See generally* Nancy A. Costello, *Walking Together in a Good Way: Indian Peacemaker Courts in Michigan*, 76 UNIVERSITY OF DETROIT MERCY LAW REVIEW 875, 877 (1999).

78. Costello, *supra* note 77, at 876, 878.
79. *See* JoAnne Gasco, Address before the Michigan State University College of Law Indigenous Law and Policy Center, East Lansing, Michigan (February 17, 2009).
80. *See* Transcript, Vol. I, at 104, Grand Traverse Band of Ottawa and Chippewa Indians v. United States Attorney for the Western District of Michigan, 198 F. Supp. 2d 920 (W.D. Mich. 2002) (Testimony of Ardith Chambers) (hereinafter Chambers Testimony).
81. *See* Chambers Testimony, *supra* note 80, at 71.
82. *See* Chambers Testimony, *supra* note 80, at 70–71.
83. *See* Transcript, Vol. I, at 91, Grand Traverse Band of Ottawa and Chippewa Indians v. United States Attorney for the Western District of Michigan, 198 F. Supp. 2d 920 (W.D. Mich. 2002) (Testimony of Barry Burtt) (hereinafter Burtt Testimony).
84. Chambers Testimony, *supra* note 80, at 84 (emphasis added).
85. Burtt Testimony, *supra* note 83, at 91.
86. Burtt Testimony, *supra* note 83, at 94.
87. *See* Burtt Testimony, *supra* note 83, at 96, 97.
88. *See* Burtt Testimony, *supra* note 83, at 97.
89. *See* Burtt Testimony, *supra* note 83, at 103.
90. *See* Grand Traverse Band of Chippewa and Ottawa Indians Establishment of Reservation, 49 Fed. Reg. 2025 (Jan. 17, 1984).
91. *See* Burtt Testimony, *supra* note 83, at 104.
92. *See* Grand Traverse Band of Ottawa and Chippewa Indians v. United States Attorney for the Western District of Michigan, 369 F.3d 960, 962 (6th Cir. 2004).
93. *See* Federal Charter of Incorporation—Grand Traverse Band Economic Development Corporation (Oct. 23, 1998).
94. Section 17 corporations derive their name from Indian Reorganization Act § 17, *codified at* 25 U.S.C. § 477.
95. *See* Respondent's Brief at 1, Wilson v. Grand Traverse Band of Ottawa and Chippewa Indians Economic Development Corp., No. 04-08-566 (Grand Traverse Band Court of Appeals, Dec. 14, 2004).
96. *See* IRS Private Letter Ruling, March 8, 2000; IRS Private Letter Ruling, November 17, 1998; Respondent's Brief at 1, Wilson v. Grand Traverse Band of Ottawa and Chippewa Indians Economic Development Corp., No. 04-08-566 (Grand Traverse Band Court of Appeals, Dec. 14, 2004) ("One of the legal purposes for chartering the EDC was to allow the EDC to fall under Internal Revenue Service Revenue Ruling 94-16, 1991-4 C.B. 4 (March 1994) that exempts Section 17 corporations from federal and state income taxes."). *See generally* 18 GRAND TRAVERSE BAND CODE §§ 1602(a), 1605(d).

CHAPTER SEVEN. THE STORY OF THE GRAND TRAVERSE BAND'S GAMING OPERATIONS

1. Grand Traverse Band Ordinance No. 84-001 (Sept. 4, 1984), *quoted in* GEORGE WEEKS, MEM-KA-WEH: DAWNING OF THE GRAND TRAVERSE BAND OF OTTAWA AND CHIPPEWA INDIANS 129 (1991).
2. President Ronald Reagan, Statement on Indian Policy (Jan. 24, 1983), *quoted in* WEEKS, *supra* note 1, at 129.
3. United States Department of Interior Statement (March 2, 1983), *quoted in* WEEKS, *supra* note 1, at 129.

4. Indian Tribal Governmental Tax Status Act of 1982, Public Law 97-473, 96 Stat. 2607 (1982).

5. There simply is no tax base. *See generally* Matthew L. M. Fletcher, *In Pursuit of Tribal Economic Development as a Substitute for Reservation Tax Revenue*, 80 NORTH DAKOTA LAW REVIEW 759, 771–74 (2004). First, there are few property owners to pay property taxes, in part because there is relatively little Indian land in places like the Grand Traverse Reservation, and also because the tribe owns much of the Indian land within Indian Country. And, as tribal land bases grow through land purchases, much of that land is placed in trust for the benefit of the tribe by the secretary of the Interior. Finally, often there is little in the way of business activity to tax, so a sales tax or other business taxes would claim insignificant revenue.

   However, the Grand Traverse Band once authorized the tribal government to collect income taxes from tribal members within its jurisdiction (mostly employed by the tribe or its enterprises), but at this time it has not done so. *See* 4 GRAND TRAVERSE BAND CODE § 401 et seq. Some Indian law scholars recommend that Indian tribes begin taxing tribal members who live *off* the reservation as well, but no tribe has done this yet. *See* Alex Tallchief Skibine, *Tribal Sovereign Interests beyond the Reservation Borders*, 12 LEWIS AND CLARK LAW REVIEW 1003 (2008).

6. Worcester v. Georgia, 31 U.S. 515, 561 (1832).

7. Public Law 83-280, 67 Stat. 588 (1953).

8. It should be noted, however, that the Bureau of Indian Affairs and Congress looked the other way for decades as the State of Michigan exercised criminal jurisdiction in Indian Country in Michigan. *See* THEODORE W. TAYLOR, THE STATES AND THEIR INDIAN CITIZENS 35, 37 (1972).

9. *See* Seminole Tribe of Florida v. Butterworth, 658 F.2d 310 (5th Cir. 1981), *cert. denied*, 455 U.S. 1020 (1982); Barona Group of Capitan Grand Band of Mission Indians v. Duffy, 694 F.2d 1185 (9th Cir. 1982), *cert. denied*, 461 U.S. 929 (1983); Mashantucket Pequot Tribe v. McGuigan, 626 F. Supp. 245 (D. Conn. 1986); Oneida Tribe of Indians of Wisconsin v. Wisconsin, 518 F. Supp. 712 (W.D. Wis. 1981).

10. *See* KATHLEEN STOCKING, LETTERS FROM THE LEELANAU 108–12 (1990) (describing a 1986 visit to the bingo hall).

11. STOCKING, *supra* note 10, at 110 (quotation marks omitted).

12. *See* STOCKING, *supra* note 10, at 110 (noting the casino was packed at 6:30 P.M. on a March Wednesday).

13. *See* STOCKING, *supra* note 10, at 109.

14. *See* United States v. Bay Mills Indian Community, 692 F. Supp. 777 (W.D. Mich. 1988), *remanded*, 880 F.2d 415 (6th Cir., July 28, 1989), *on remand*, 727 F. Supp. 1110 (W.D. Mich. 1989).

15. *See* STEVEN ANDREW LIGHT AND KATHRYN R. L. RAND, INDIAN GAMING AND TRIBAL SOVEREIGNTY: THE CASINO COMPROMISE 172 n. 30 (2005).

16. For a later tribal statement supporting the benefits of Indian gaming before the Michigan Supreme Court, see Brief of *Amicus Curiae* Grand Traverse Band of Ottawa and Chippewa Indians et al., Taxpayers of Michigan against Casinos v. State of Michigan, 685 N.W.2d 221 (Mich. 2004), *available at* http://courts.michigan.gov/supremecourt/Clerk/03-04/122830/122830-Amicus-GrTraverse.pdf.

17. *See* Johnson Act, 15 U.S.C. § 1171 et seq.

18. For a general overview of the legislation that eventually became the Indian Gaming Regulatory Act, see Franklin Ducheneaux & Peter S. Taylor, *Tribal Sovereignty and the Powers of the National Indian Gaming Commission* 6–32 (undated manuscript); G. WILLIAM RICE, TRIBAL GOVERNMENTAL GAMING LAW: CASES AND MATERIALS 96–127 (2006) (reprinting Senate

Report No. 100-446 (Aug. 3, 1988)).

19. UNITED STATES CONSTITUTION art. I, § 8, cl. 3.

20. *See* United States v. Dakota, 796 F.2d 196 (6th Cir. 1986).

21. "Las Vegas North: Buying chips from the Chippewas," U.S. NEWS AND WORLD REPORT, Feb. 9, 1987, at 31, *quoted in* WEEKS, *supra* note 1, at 132.

22. *See* Ducheneaux & Taylor, *supra* note 18, at 14 (quoting Victoria Toensing, deputy assistant attorney general, United States Department of Justice, from November 14, 1985: "If the Department of Justice had its druthers, it would not have any gambling whatsoever [on Indian reservations] and I think everyone knows that.") (brackets in original).

23. *See* Robert B. Porter, *Indian Gaming Regulation: A Case Study in Neo-Colonialism*, 5 GAMING LAW REVIEW 299, 306 (2001); Ducheneaux & Taylor, *supra* note 18, at 25–26.

24. *See* Sen. John McCain, Additional Views, Senate Report No. 100-446, *reprinted in* RICE, *supra* note 18, at 125 ("Unfortunately, tribes never banded together and offered their own gaming proposal. They also never found a consensus for supporting any particular legislative solution. Some would say that the tribes were united in calling for no gaming legislation.").

25. 480 U.S. 202 (1987).

26. *See* Cabazon Band of Mission Indians v. Riverside County, 783 F.2d 900 (9th Cir. 1986).

27. *See* Amici Curiae Brief of States of Florida, Alaska, Connecticut, Idaho, Iowa, Kansas, Louisiana, Mississippi, Nevada, North Carolina, North Dakota, Ohio, Oklahoma, Oregon, Rhode Island, South Dakota, Utah, Wisconsin, and Wyoming in Support of Appellants' Jurisdictional Statement, California v. Cabazon Band of Mission Indians, 480 U.S. 202 (1987) (No. 85-1708), 1985 WL 669483.

28. *See* Ducheneaux & Taylor, *supra* note 18, at 20–22.

29. *See* Amici Curiae Brief of Chehalis Indian Tribe, Keweenaw Bay Indian Community, Santa Ynez Band of Mission Indians and Other Federally Recognized Indian Tribes, California v. Cabazon Band of Mission Indians, 480 U.S. 202 (1987) (No. 85-1708), 1986 WL 728109.

30. California v. Cabazon Band of Mission Indians, 480 U.S. 202 (1987).

31. *See* United States v. Bay Mills Indian Community, 692 F. Supp. 777 (W.D. Mich. 1988).

32. 25 U.S.C. § 2701 et seq., Public Law 100-497, 102 Stat. 2467 (Oct. 17, 1988).

33. *See* 25 U.S.C. §§ 2703(6)–(8).

34. *See* 25 U.S.C. § 2710(d).

35. *See* 25 U.S.C. § 2703(7)(C).

36. *See* 25 U.S.C. § 2710(d)(7).

37. *See* Sault Ste. Marie Tribe of Chippewa Indians v. State of Michigan, 800 F. Supp. 1484 (W.D. Mich. 1992), *aff'd*, 5 F.3d 147 (6th Cir. 1993).

38. *See* WEEKS, *supra* note 1, at 178.

39. *See* UNITED STATES CONSTITUTION amend. 11.

40. *E.g.*, Santa Clara Pueblo v. Martinez, 436 U.S. 49, 59 (1978); Huron Potawatomi, Inc. v. Stinger, 574 N.W.2d 706, 708–09 (Mich. App. 1997); Adams v. Grand Traverse Band of Ottawa and Chippewa Indians Economic Development Authority, No. 89-03-001-CV (Grand Traverse Band Tribal Court, June 18, 1992), *aff'd*, No. 89-03-001-CV (Grand Traverse Band Court of Appeals, Aug. 19, 1993), *amended on petition for reh'g*, No. 92-07-002-CV-App (Grand Traverse Band Court of Appeals, March 28, 1994).

41. 490 U.S. 1 (1989).

42. Blatchford v. Native Village of Noatak, 501 U.S. 775 (1991).

43. Sault Ste. Marie Tribe of Chippewa Indians v. State of Michigan, 800 F. Supp. 1484 (W.D.

Mich. 1992).

44. Sault Ste. Marie Tribe of Chippewa Indians v. State of Michigan, 5 F.3d 147 (6th Cir. 1993).

45. Ex parte Young, 209 U.S. 123 (1908).

46. All these documents are available online on the State of Michigan's website, http://www.michigan.gov/.

47. *Cf.* Michigan v. Little River Band of Ottawa Indians, No. 05-95, 2007 WL 1238907 (April 27, 2007) (interpreting a similar provision in gaming compacts signed in 1997).

48. *See* 25 U.S.C. § 2710(d)(4).

49. *See* 25 U.S.C. § 2719.

50. *See* 25 U.S.C. § 2719(b)(1).

51. Michigan Compiled Laws Annotated §§ 432.201–432.216. The state legislature then created the Michigan Gaming Control Board. S. B. No. 569, 89th Leg. Reg. Sess. (1997).

52. Sault Ste. Marie Tribe of Chippewa Indians v. Engler, 146 F.3d 367 (6th Cir. 1998).

53. Sault Ste. Marie Tribe of Chippewa Indians v. Engler, 93 F. Supp. 2d 850 (W.D. Mich. 2000), *aff'd*, 271 F.3d 236 (6th Cir. 2001).

54. 25 U.S.C. § 2719(a).

55. 25 U.S.C. § 2719(b)(1)(B)(iii).

56. 914 F. Supp. 1496 (W.D. Mich. 1996).

57. *See* Grand Traverse Band of Ottawa and Chippewa Indians v. United States Attorney for the Western District of Michigan, 46 F. Supp. 2d 689, 708 (W.D. Mich. 1999).

58. Keweenaw Bay Indian Community v. United States, 136 F.3d 469 (6th Cir. 1998), *cert. denied*, 525 U.S. 929 (1998).

59. *See Grand Traverse Band I*, 46 F. Supp. 2d at 695–704.

60. The State of Michigan appealed Judge Hillman's order delaying the litigation pending the legal opinion of the National Indian Gaming Commission, but the appeal was rejected. Grand Traverse Band of Ottawa and Chippewa Indians v. United States Attorney for the Western District of Michigan, No. 99-1584 (6th Cir., May 1, 2001) (per curiam).

61. Washburn is now dean of the University of New Mexico Law School and sits on the editorial board of *Cohen's Handbook of Federal Indian Law*.

62. Memorandum from the Assistant Solicitor to the Deputy Commission for Indian Affairs, *Gaming on Trust Land Acquired in Emmet County, Michigan for the Little Traverse Bay Bands of Odawa Indians* (Nov. 12, 1997); Memorandum from the Associate Solicitor to Director, Indian Gaming Management Staff, Bureau of Indian Affairs, *Little Traverse Bay Bands of Odawa Indians of Michigan "Victories Tract"* (Aug. 5, 1999); Memorandum from the Solicitor to the Secretary of Interior, *Pokagon Band of Potawatomi Indians* (Sept. 19, 1997).

63. Letter from the National Indian Gaming Commission General Counsel Kevin K. Washburn to Judge Douglas W. Hillman (Aug. 31, 2001).

64. Grand Traverse Band of Ottawa and Chippewa Indians v. United States Attorney for the Western District of Michigan, 198 F. Supp. 920 (W.D. Mich. 2002).

65. *Grand Traverse Band II*, 198 F. Supp. 2d at 925–26 (citations to record omitted).

66. Grand Traverse Band of Ottawa and Chippewa Indians v. United States Attorney for the Western District of Michigan, 369 F.3d 960 (6th Cir. 2004).

67. National Indian Gaming Commission, Growth of Tribal Gaming Revenues: 1995 to 2005, http://indianz.com/docs/nigc/nigc071106.pdf (last visited July 19, 2006).

68. "Mackinaw City Casino Plan Gets OK," GRAND RAPIDS PRESS, July 20, 2003, at A4.

69. Baird v. Norton, 226 F.3d 408 (6th Cir. 2001).

70. Taxpayers of Michigan Against Casinos v. State, 685 N.W.2d 221 (Mich. 2004).
71. TOMAC v. Norton, 193 F. Supp. 2d 182 (D. D.C. 2002); 240 F. Supp. 2d 45 (D. D.C. 2003); 2005 WL 2375171 (D. D.C. 2005); 433 F.3d 852 (D.C. Cir. 2006); CETAC v. Kempthorne, 2004 WL 5238116 (D. D.C. 2004); 492 F.3d 460 (D.C. Cir. 2007); MichGO v. Kempthorne, 477 F. Supp. 2d 1 (D. D.C. 2007); 525 F.3d 23 (D.C. Cir. 2008).
72. *See* David Capriccioso, *Grand Traverse Band Goes Green*, INDIAN COUNTRY TODAY, July 23, 2008, http://www.indiancountry.com/content.cfm?id=1096417781.

AFTERWORD: *CARCIERI V. SALAZAR* AND THE BAND'S FUTURE LAND BASE

1. 129 S. Ct. 1058 (2009).
2. 25 U.S.C. § 465.
3. 25 U.S.C. § 479 (emphasis added).
4. 48 FEDERAL REGISTER 6177 (1983).
5. 25 U.S.C. § 1701 et seq.
6. 398 F.3d 22 (1st Cir. 2005).
7. 497 F.3d 15 (1st Cir. 2007).
8. *See Carcieri*, 497 F.3d at 26–34.
9. *See id.* at 48 (Selya, J., dissenting); *id.* at 51 (Howard, J., dissenting).
10. Carcieri v. Salazar, 129 S. Ct. 1058, 1070 (Breyer, J., concurring).
11. *See Carcieri*, 129 S. Ct. at 1075 (Stevens, J., dissenting).
12. *See* Brief of Law Professors Specializing in Federal Indian Law as Amicus Curiae Supporting Respondents at 33–36, Carcieri v. Salazar, 129 S. Ct. 1058 (2009) (No. 07-526).
13. *See Where's the Trustee? Department of Interior Backlogs Prevent Tribes from Using Their Lands before the Senate Committee on Indian Affairs*, 111th Cong. (1st Sess. 2009).
14. *See Where's the Trustee? Department of Interior Backlogs Prevent Tribes from Using Their Lands before the Senate Committee on Indian Affairs*, 111th Cong. 24–30 (1st Sess. 2009) (Written Testimony of Derek Bailey, Grand Traverse Band of Ottawa and Chippewa Indians, Peshawbestown, Michigan), *available at* http://indian.senate.gov/public/_files/DerekBaileytestimony.pdf.
15. *See id.* at 2–3.
16. *See id.* at 3.
17. *See* Letter to Kenneth Salazar, Secretary, Department of Interior from Riyaz A. Kanji (June 22, 2009).
18. *See* Alex Piazza, *GT Band Picks Up 78 Acres for Expansion*, TRAVERSE CITY RECORD-EAGLE, Dec. 15, 2009, *available at* http://record-eagle.com/local/x546327515/GT-Band-picks-up-78-acres-for-expansion.

Bibliography

PRIMARY SOURCES

Cases

Adams v. Grand Traverse Band of Ottawa and Chippewa Indians Economic Development Authority, No. 89-03-001-CV (Grand Traverse Band Tribal Court, June 18, 1992), *aff'd*, No. 89-03-001-CV (Grand Traverse Band Court of Appeals, Aug. 19, 1993), *amended on petition for reh'g*, No. 92-07-002-CV-App (Grand Traverse Band Court of Appeals, March 28, 1994)

Baird v. Norton, 226 F.3d 408 (6th Cir. 2001)

Barona Group of Capitan Grand Band of Mission Indians v. Duffy, 694 F.2d 1185 (9th Cir. 1982), *cert. denied*, 461 U.S. 929 (1983)

Bay Mills Indian Community v. United States, 27 Indian Claims Commission 94 (1972) (Docket No. 58)

Blatchford v. Native Village of Noatak, 501 U.S. 775 (1991)

Cabazon Band of Mission Indians v. Riverside County, 783 F.2d 900 (9th Cir. 1986)

California v. Cabazon Band of Mission Indians, 480 U.S. 202 (1987)

Carcieri v. Kempthorne, 398 F.3d 22 (1st Cir. 2005), *aff'd*, 497 F.3d 15 (1st Cir. 2007) (en banc)

Carcieri v. Salazar, 129 S. Ct. 1058 (2009), *rev'g*, 497 F.3d 15 (1st Cir. 2007) (en banc)

CETAC v. Kempthorne, 2004 WL 5238116 (D. D.C. 2004), *aff'd*, 492 F.3d 460 (D.C. Cir. 2007)

Covelo Indian Community v. Watt, 551 F. Supp. 366 (D. D.C. 1982)

Covelo Indian Community v. Watt, 1982 U.S. App. LEXIS 23138 (D.C. Cir., Dec. 21, 1982) (per curiam)

DeVerney v. Grand Traverse Band of Ottawa and Chippewa Indians, No. 96-10-201 (Grand Traverse Band Court of Appeals, Nov. 22, 1997)

Dominic v. United States, 2 Indian Claims Commission 469 (1953) (Docket Nos. 40-B et seq.)

Dominic v. United States, 2 Indian Claims Commission 461 (1953) (Docket Nos. 40-B et seq.)

Dominic v. United States, 6 Indian Claims Commission 414 (1958) (Docket No. 40-K)

Duhamel v. Mich. Dept. of Natural Resources, No. G84-1186, 1987 U.S. Dist. LEXIS 15721 (W.D. Mich., Jan. 21, 1987)

Grand Traverse Band of Ottawa and Chippewa Indians v. Director, Michigan Department of Natural Resources, 141 F.3d 635 (6th Cir. 1998)

Grand Traverse Band of Ottawa and Chippewa Indians v. Director, Michigan Department of Natural Resources, 971 F. Supp. 282 (W.D. Mich. 1995)

Grand Traverse Band of Ottawa and Chippewa Indians v. Leelanau Indians, Inc. and Leelanau County, No. 83-834 (W.D. Mich., Jan. 30, 1985)

Grand Traverse Band of Ottawa and Chippewa Indians v. Michigan Department of Natural Resources, No. 01-5784 (13th Judicial Circuit Court 2002)

Grand Traverse Band of Ottawa and Chippewa Indians v. United States Attorney for the Western District of Michigan, 369 F.3d 960 (6th Cir. 2004)

Grand Traverse Band of Ottawa and Chippewa Indians v. United States Attorney for the Western District of Michigan, 198 F. Supp. 2d 920 (W.D. Mich. 2002)

Grand Traverse Band of Ottawa and Chippewa Indians v. United States Attorney for the Western District of Michigan, No. 99-1584 (6th Cir., May 1, 2001) (per curiam)

Grand Traverse Band of Ottawa and Chippewa Indians v. United States Attorney for the Western District of Michigan, 46 F. Supp. 2d 689, 708 (W.D. Mich. 1999)

GTASFA v. Maudrie, et al., No. 79-510-C.E. (Grand Traverse County Circuit Ct. 1979)

Huron Potawatomi, Inc. v. Stinger, 574 N.W.2d 706 (Mich. App. 1997)

Inyo County, Cal. v. Paiute-Shoshone Indians of the Bishop Community of the Bishop Colony, 538 U.S. 701 (2003)

Keweenaw Bay Indian Community v. United States, 914 F. Supp. 1496 (W.D. Mich. 1996), rev'd, 136 F.3d 469 (6th Cir. 1998), cert. denied, 525 U.S. 929 (1998)

Leelanau County v. Grand Traverse Band of Ottawa and Chippewa Indians, No. 87-321 (W.D. Mich., April 7, 1987)

Leelanau Indians, Inc. v. U.S. Dept. of Housing & Urban Dev., 502 F. Supp. 741 (W.D. Mich. 1980)

Leelanau Transit Co. v. Grand Traverse Band of Ottawa and Chippewa Indians, No. 92-240, 1994 U.S. Dist. LEXIS 2220 (W.D. Mich., Feb. 1, 1994)

Mashantucket Pequot Tribe v. McGuigan, 626 F. Supp. 245 (D. Conn. 1986)

In re McSauby, No. 97-02-001, 1997 WL 34691849 (Grand Traverse Band Tribal Court, July 29, 1997) (en banc)

Menominee Tribe v. United States, 391 U.S. 404 (1968)

MichGO v. Kempthorne, 477 F. Supp. 2d 1 (D. D.C. 2007); aff'd, 525 F.3d 23 (D.C. Cir. 2008)

Michigan v. Little River Band of Ottawa Indians, No. 05-95, 2007 WL 1238907 (W.D. Mich., April 27, 2007)

Minnesota v. Mille Lacs Band of Chippewa Indians, 526 U.S. 172 (1999)

Montana v. Blackfeet Tribe, 471 U.S. 759 (1985)

Oneida Tribe of Indians of Wisconsin v. Wisconsin, 518 F. Supp. 712 (W.D. Wis. 1981)

Ottawa and Chippewa Indians of Michigan v. United States, 7 Indian Claims Commission 576 (1959) (Docket No. 58)

Ottawa and Chippewa Indians of Michigan v. United States, 20 Indian Claims Commission 137 (1968) (Docket No. 58)

Ottawa and Chippewa Indians of the State of Michigan v. United States, 42 Ct. Cl. 240, 1907 WL 888 (March 4, 1907)

Pennsylvania v. Union Gas Co., 490 U.S. 1 (1989)

People v. Chosa, 233 N.W. 205 (Mich. 1930)

People v. Jondreau, 185 N.W.2d 375 (Mich. 1971)

People v. LeBlanc, 248 N.W.2d 199 (Mich. 1976)

Petoskey v. United States, No. 27,978

Sanders v. Lyon, 2 MacArth. 452, 1876 WL 19461 (D.C. Sup. 1876)

Santa Clara Pueblo v. Martinez, 436 U.S. 49 (1978)

Sault Ste. Marie Tribe of Chippewa Indians v. Engler, 146 F.3d 367 (6th Cir. 1998)

Sault Ste. Marie Tribe of Chippewa Indians v. Engler, 93 F. Supp. 2d 850 (W.D. Mich. 2000), aff'd, 271 F.3d 236 (6th Cir. 2001)

Sault Ste. Marie Tribe of Chippewa Indians v. State of Michigan, 800 F. Supp. 1484 (W.D. Mich. 1992), aff'd, 5 F.3d 147 (6th Cir. 1993)

Seminole Tribe of Florida v. Butterworth, 658 F.2d 310 (5th Cir. 1981), cert. denied, 455 U.S. 1020 (1982)

Snowden v. Saginaw Chippewa Indian Tribe of Michigan, 32 Indian L. Rep. 6047 (Saginaw Chippewa Indian Tribe Appellate Court 2005)

Taxpayers of Michigan against Casinos v. State of Michigan, 685 N.W.2d 221 (Mich. 2004)

TOMAC v. Norton, 193 F. Supp. 2d 182 (D. D.C. 2002), *after remand*, 240 F. Supp. 2d 45 (D. D.C. 2003), *after remand*, 2005 WL 2375171 (D. D.C. 2005), *aff'd*, 433 F.3d 852 (D.C. Cir. 2006)

United States v. Bay Mills Indian Community, 692 F. Supp. 777 (W.D. Mich. 1988), *remanded*, 880 F.2d 415 (6th Cir., July 28, 1989), *on remand*, 727 F. Supp. 1110 (W.D. Mich. 1989)

United States v. Dakota, 796 F.2d 196 (6th Cir. 1986)

United States v. John, 437 U.S. 634 (1978)

United States v. Michigan, 471 F. Supp. 192 (W.D. Mich. 1979), *aff'd in relevant part*, 653 F.2d 277 (6th Cir. 1981), *cert. denied*, 454 U.S. 1124 (1981)

United States v. Michigan, 623 F.2d 448, 449 (6th Cir. 1980)

United States v. Michigan, No. M26-73 (W.D. Mich., Sept. 28, 1984)

United States v. Michigan, 12 Indian Law Reporter 3079 (W.D. Mich., May 31, 1985)

United States v. Washington, 384 F. Supp. 312 (W.D. Wash. 1974), *aff'd*, 520 F.2d 676 (9th Cir. 1975), *cert. denied*, 423 U.S. 1086 (1976)

United States v. Winans, 198 U.S. 371 (1905)

Washington v. Washington State Commercial Passenger Fishing Vessel Association, 443 U.S. 658 (1979)

Wilson v. Grand Traverse Band of Ottawa and Chippewa Indians Economic Development Corp., No. 04-08-566, 2006 WL 6295938 (Grand Traverse Band Court of Appeals, April 19, 2006)

Winters v. United States, 207 U.S. 564 (1908)

Worcester v. Georgia, 31 U.S. 515 (1832)

Ex parte Young, 209 U.S. 123 (1908)

Treaties

Treaty of Detroit, 11 Stat. 621 (July 31, 1855)

Treaty of La Pointe, 10 Stat. 1109 (Sept. 30, 1854)

Treaty of Washington, 7 Stat. 491 (March 28, 1836)

Constitutions and Statutes

An Act to Amend the Act Entitled "An Act for the Restoration to Homestead-Entry and to Market of Certain Lands in Michigan," 18 Stat. 516 (Mar. 3, 1875)

An Act Extending the Time within Which Homestead Entries upon Certain Lands in Michigan May Be Made, 19 Stat. 55 (May 23, 1876)

Act of March 3, 1905, § 13, 33 Stat. 1048

An Act to Provide for the Establishment of the American Indian Policy Review Commission, Public Law 93-580 (Jan. 2, 1975)

An Act to Reaffirm and Clarify the Federal Relationships of the Little Traverse Bay Bands of Odawa Indians and the Little River Band of Ottawa Indians as Distinct Federally Recognized Indian Tribes, and for Other Purposes, Public Law 103-324, 108 Stat. 2156 (Sept. 21, 1994), *codified at* 25 U.S.C. § 1300k

An Act for the Restoration to Market of Certain Land in Michigan, 17 Stat. 381 (June 10, 1872)

Division, Use, and Distribution of Judgment Funds of the Ottawa and Chippewa Indians of Michigan, Public Law 105-143, 111 Stat. 2562 (Dec. 15, 1997)

Grand Traverse Band of Ottawa and Chippewa Indians Constitution (1988)

4 Grand Traverse Band Code § 401 et seq.

18 Grand Traverse Band Code § 1602(a)

18 Grand Traverse Band Code § 1605(d)

Grand Traverse Band Ordinance No. 84-001 (Sept. 4, 1984)

Grand Traverse Band of Ottawa and Chippewa Indians, Resolution No. 82-101 (Sept. 17, 1982)

Grand Traverse Band of Ottawa and Chippewa Indians, Resolution No. 07-25.1836 (Aug. 8, 2007)

Indian Claims Commission Act, Public Law 79-726, 60 Stat. 1049 (Aug. 13, 1946)

Indian Gaming Regulatory Act, 25 U.S.C. § 2701 et seq., Public Law 100-497, 102 Stat. 2467 (Oct. 17, 1988)

Indian Reorganization Act, 48 Stat. 984-988 (1934), *codified at* 25 U.S.C. §§ 461 et seq.

Johnson Act, 15 U.S.C. § 1171 et seq.

Little Traverse Bay Bands of Odawa Indians Constitution (2006), preamble

Michigan Constitution (1850), art. 7

Michigan Gaming Control and Revenue Act, Michigan Compiled Laws Annotated §§ 432.201–432.216

Michigan S. B. No. 569, 89th Leg. Reg. Sess. (1997)

Public Law 83-280, 67 Stat. 588 (1953)

Restoration to Market of Certain Lands in Michigan, H.R. Exec. Doc. No. 208, 42nd Cong., 2nd Sess., at 1 (Feb. 13, 1873)

Rhode Island Indian Claims Settlement Act, 25 U.S.C. § 1701 et seq.

Snyder Act, 25 U.S.C. § 13, 42 Stat. 208 (1921)

25 U.S.C. § 465

25 U.S.C. § 476

25 U.S.C. § 477

25 U.S.C. § 479

28 U.S.C. § 2415(a), Public Law 97-394, 96 Stat. 1976

United States Constitution art. I, § 8, cl. 3

Legislative Materials

Derek Bailey, Grand Traverse Band of Ottawa and Chippewa Indians, Peshawbestown, Michigan, Written Testimony, *in Where's the Trustee? Department of Interior Backlogs Prevent Tribes from Using Their Lands before the Senate Committee on Indian Affairs*, 111th Cong., 1st Sess. (2009)

Ardith (Dodie) Chambers, Councilwoman, Grand Traverse Band of Ottawa and Chippewa Indians Testimony and Prepared Statement, *in* Indian Tribal Good Governance Practices as They Relate to Economic Development, Hearing before the Senate Committee on Indian Affairs, 107th Cong., 1st Sess. (2001)

Vine Deloria Jr., Professor of Law, Political Science, History, and Religious Studies, University of Colorado, Written Statement, Michigan Indian Recognition, Hearing before the Subcommittee on Natural Resources, House of Representatives, 103rd Cong. (1993)

Arthur Duhamel, Statement, *in* Fish and Wildlife Miscellaneous—Part 3, Hearings before the Subcommittee on Fisheries and Wildlife Conservation and the Environment of the Committee on Merchant Marine and Fisheries, House of Representatives, 95th Cong., 2d Sess. (1978)

House Report No. 2680, 83rd Cong., 2d Sess. (Sept. 20, 1954)

Sen. John McCain, Additional Views, Senate Report No. 100-446 (1988)

Ottawa and Chippewa Lands in Michigan, House Rep. No. 186, 43rd Cong., 1st Sess. (1874)

Senate Report No. 100-446 (Aug. 3, 1988)

Regulations and Administrative Materials

25 CFR Part 54

24 CFR Part 83

Assistant Solicitor to the Deputy Commission for Indian Affairs, Gaming on Trust Land Acquired in Emmet County, Michigan for the Little Traverse Bay Bands of Odawa Indians (Nov. 12, 1997)

Associate Solicitor to Director, Indian Gaming Management Staff, Bureau of Indian Affairs, Little Traverse Bay Bands of Odawa Indians of Michigan "Victories Tract" (Aug. 5, 1999)

Commissioner of Indian Affairs, Annual Report (1853)

Commissioner of Indian Affairs, Annual Report (1885)

Department of Interior, Office of the Secretary, Press Release, "Tribal Nations, State of Michigan and Interior Department Sign Agreement to Settle Indian Fishing Rights Dispute" (Aug. 7, 2000)

Department of Interior Statement (March 2, 1983)

Determination for Federal Acknowledgment of the Grand Traverse Band of Ottawa and Chippewa Indians as an Indian Tribe, 45 Fed. Reg. 18322 (March 25, 1980)

Federal Charter of Incorporation—Grand Traverse Band Economic Development Corporation (Oct. 23, 1998)

Final Determination for Federal Acknowledgment of Narragansett Indian Tribe of Rhode Island, 48 Fed. Reg. 6177 (Feb. 10, 1983)

Grand Traverse Band of Chippewa and Ottawa Indians Establishment of Reservation, 49 Fed. Reg. 2025 (Jan. 17, 1984)

Internal Revenue Service Private Letter Ruling, March 8, 2000

Internal Revenue Service Private Letter Ruling, November 17, 1998

Internal Revenue Service Revenue Ruling 94-16, 1991-4 C.B. 4 (March 1994)

National Indian Gaming Commission General Counsel Kevin K. Washburn to Judge Douglas W. Hillman (Aug. 31, 2001)

Proposed Finding for Federal Acknowledgment of Grand Traverse Band of Ottawa and Chippewa Indians, 44 Fed. Reg. 60171 (Oct. 18, 1979)

Statute of Limitations Claims List, 48 Fed. Reg. 13,876 (March 31, 1983)

Solicitor to the Secretary of Interior, Pokagon Band of Potawatomi Indians (Sept. 19, 1997)

Court Materials

James Brady, Testimony, Trial Transcript, Vol. 1, United States v. Michigan, No. M26-73 (W.D. Mich., Feb. 27, 1978)

Barry Burtt, Testimony, Transcript, Vol. I, Grand Traverse Band of Ottawa and Chippewa Indians v. United States Attorney for the Western District of Michigan, 198 F. Supp. 2d 920 (W.D. Mich. 2002)

Ardith "Dodie" Chambers, Testimony, Transcript, Vol. 1, Grand Traverse Band of Ottawa and Chippewa Indians v. United States Attorney for the Western District of Michigan, 198 F. Supp. 2d 920 (W.D. Mich. 2002)

Chehalis Indian Tribe, Keweenaw Bay Indian Community, Santa Ynez Band of Mission Indians and Other Federally Recognized Indian Tribes, Amicus Brief, California v. Cabazon Band of Mission Indians, 480 U.S. 202 (1987) (No. 85-1708)

Consent Decree, United States v. Michigan, No. 2: 73 CV 26 (W.D. Mich., Nov. 2007)

Gregory E. Dowd, The Meaning of Article 13 of the Treaty of Washington, March 28, 1836, Expert Report prepared for the Chippewa Ottawa Resource Authority, United States v. Michigan, No. 2:73 CV 26 (W.D. Mich., Oct. 11, 2004)

Arthur Duhamel, Memorandum in Support of Plaintiff's Motion for Summary Judgment, Duhamel
 v. Michigan Dept. of Natural Resources, No. G84-1186, 1987 U.S. Dist. LEXIS 15721 (W.D.
 Mich., Oct. 13, 1985)
Grand Traverse Band of Ottawa and Chippewa Indians et al., Amicus Brief, Taxpayers of Michigan
 against Casinos v. State of Michigan, 685 N.W.2d 221 (Mich. 2004)
Grand Traverse Band of Ottawa and Chippewa Indians, Final Brief, Grand Traverse Band of Ottawa
 and Chippewa Indians v. Office of the U.S. Attorney for the Western District of Michigan,
 369 F.3d 960 (6th Cir. 2004) (No. 02-1679)
Grand Traverse Band of Ottawa and Chippewa Indians, Memorandum in Support of Plaintiff's
 Motion for Declaratory Judgment, Grand Traverse Band of Ottawa and Chippewa Indians
 v. Leelanau Indians, Inc. and Leelanau County, No. 83-834 (W.D. Mich., April 15, 1987)
Grand Traverse Band of Ottawa and Chippewa Indians, Respondent's Brief, Wilson v. Grand Traverse
 Band of Ottawa and Chippewa Indians Economic Development Corp., No. 04-08-566 (Grand
 Traverse Band Court of Appeals, Dec. 14, 2004)
Susan E. Gray, Article 13 in the Treaty of Washington and Land Use in the Session, 1836 to the
 Present 9-10, Expert Report prepared for the Chippewa Ottawa Resource Authority in
 United States v. Michigan, No. 2:73 CV 26 (W.D. Mich., Oct. 19, 2004)
Law Professors Specializing in Federal Indian Law as Amicus Curiae, Amicus Brief, Carcieri v.
 Salazar, 129 S. Ct. 1058 (2009) (No. 07-526)
Barry L. Levine, Affidavit, Covelo Indian Community v. Watt, 551 F. Supp. 366 (D. D.C. 1982)
James McClurken, South Fox Island: Its Historical Importance to the Grand Traverse Band of Ottawa
 and Chippewa Indians, Expert Report prepared for the Grand Traverse Band of Ottawa and
 Chippewa Indians in Grand Traverse Band of Ottawa and Chippewa Indians v. Michigan
 Department of Natural Resources, No. 01-5784 (13th Judicial Circuit Court, Aug. 21, 2001)
National Congress of American Indians et al., Amicus Brief, Inyo County, Cal. v. Paiute-Shoshone
 Indians of the Bishop Community of the Bishop Colony, 538 U.S. 701 (2003) (No. 02-281)
States of Florida, Alaska, Connecticut, Idaho, Iowa, Kansas, Louisiana, Mississippi, Nevada, North
 Carolina, North Dakota, Ohio, Oklahoma, Oregon, Rhode Island, South Dakota, Utah,
 Wisconsin, and Wyoming in Support of Appellants' Jurisdictional Statement, Amicus
 Brief, California v. Cabazon Band of Mission Indians, 480 U.S. 202 (1987) (No. 85-1708)
Gregory T. Taylor, Testimony, Trial Transcript, Vol. 5, United States v. Michigan, No. M26-73 (W.D.
 Mich., Feb. 27, 1978)
Transcript of Opening Remarks and Concluding Findings, Rulings, Statements of the Court, United
 States v. Michigan, M26-73 (W.D. Mich. Oct. 9, 1992)
United States' Supplemental Complaint, United States v. Michigan, No. 2: 73 CV 26 (W.D. Mich.,
 April 27, 2004)

Miscellaneous

American Indian Policy Review Commission, Final Report (May 17, 1977)
2 American State Papers: Indian Affairs 136–39 (1815–1827)
Deputization Agreement between the Grand Traverse Band of Ottawa and Chippewa Indians and
 the Sheriff of Leelanau County (March 19, 1997)
JoAnne Gasco, Address before the Michigan State University College of Law Indigenous Law and
 Policy Center, East Lansing, Michigan (February 17, 2009)
John H. Holst, A Survey of Indian Groups in the State of Michigan (1939)
John Hulbert, "Records of a Treaty Concluded with the Ottawa and Chippewa Nations at Washington,

D.C., March 28, 1836"

Riyaz A. Kanji to Kenneth Salazar, Secretary, Department of Interior (June 22, 2009)

Leelanau Indians Comprehensive Plan (1977)

Michael Oltersdorf, Sheriff, Leelanau County, to George Bennett, Chairman, Grand Traverse Band (Sept. 1, 1998)

Petition of the Grand Traverse Band of Ottawa and Chippewa Indians to the Secretary of the Interior for Acknowledgment of Recognition as an Indian Tribe (1979)

President Ronald Reagan, Statement on Indian Policy (Jan. 24, 1983)

SECONDARY MATERIALS

Books and Articles

Assikinack, Francis. "Legends and Traditions of the Odawah Indians." *Canadian Journal of Industry, Science, and Art* 3 (1858): 115–25.

Baraga, Frederick. *Chippewa Indians as Recorded by Reverend Frederick Baraga in 1847.* New York: Studia Slovenica, League of Slovenian Americans, 1976.

Barrillas, William. "Michigan's Pioneers and the Destruction of the Hardwood Forest." *Michigan Historical Review* 15 (Fall 1989): 1–22.

Basso, Keith H. *Wisdom Sits in Places: Landscape and Language among the Western Apache.* Albuquerque: University of New Mexico Press, 1996.

Beck, George. "The Fourteenth Amendment as Related to Tribal Indians: Section I, 'Subject to the Jurisdiction Thereof' and Section II, 'Excluding Indians Not Taxed.'" *American Indian Culture & Research Journal* 28 (2004): 37–68.

Benton-Benai, Edward. *The Mishomis Book: The Voice of the Ojibway.* Saint Paul, Minn.: Red School House, 1975.

Bishop, Charles A. "The Emergence of Hunting Territories among the Northern Ojibwa." *Ethnology* 9 (1971): 1–15.

Blackbird, Andrew J. *History of the Ottawa and Chippewa Indians of Michigan.* Ypsilanti, Mich.: Ypsilantian Job Printing House, 1887.

Blackburn, George M. "Foredoomed to Failure: The Manistee Indian Station." *Michigan History* 53 (1969): 37–50.

Blackburn, George M. "George Johnston and the Sioux-Chippewa Boundary Survey." *Michigan History* 51 (1967): 313–22.

Blackburn, George M. "George Johnston: Indian Agent and Copper Hunter." *Michigan History* 54 (1970): 108–21.

Bourgeois, Arthur P., ed. *Ojibwa Narratives of Charles and Charlotte Kawbawgam and Jacques LePique, 1893–1895.* Marquette, Mich.: John M. Longyear Research Library, Marquette County Historical Society, 1994.

Brandimore, Kathleen. "Indian Law—Tribal Fishing Rights—The Michigan Position." *Wayne Law Review* 24 (1978): 1187–1204.

Calloway, Colin G. "The End of an Era: British-Indian Relations in the Great Lakes after the War of 1812." *Michigan Historical Review* 12 (Fall 1986): 1–20.

Cappel, Constance, ed. *Odawa Language and Legends: Andrew J. Blackbird and Raymond Kiogima.* Philadelphia: Xlibris, 2006.

Cave, Alfred. "Abuse of Power: Andrew Jackson and the Indian Removal Act of 1830." *The Historian* 65 (2003): 1330–53.

Chiarappa, Michael J., and Kristin M. Szylvian. *Fish for All: An Oral History of Multiple Claims and*

Divided Sentiment on Lake Michigan. East Lansing: Michigan State University Press, 2003.

Chute, Janet E. *The Legacy of Shingwaukonse: A Century of Native Leadership.* Toronto: University of Toronto Press, 1998.

Cleland, Charles E. "From Ethnohistory to Archaeology: Ottawa and Ojibwa Band Territories of the Northern Great Lakes." In *Text-Aided Archaeology*, ed. Barbara J. Little, 97–102. Boca Raton, Fla.: CRC Press, 1992.

Cleland, Charles E. "The Inland Shore Fishery of the Northern Great Lakes: Its Development and Importance in Prehistory." *American Antiquity* 47 (1982): 761–784.

Cleland, Charles E. *Rites of Conquest: The History and Culture of Michigan's Native Americans.* Ann Arbor: University of Michigan Press, 1992.

Cleveland, H.W.S. "The Grand Traverse Region of Michigan." *Atlantic Monthly* 26 (August 1870): 191–95.

Clifton, James A. "Michigan's Indians: Tribe, Nation, Estate, Racial, Ethnic or Special Interest Group?" *Michigan Historical Review* 20 (1994): 93–152.

Clifton, James A. *The Prairie People: Continuity and Change in Potawatomi Indian Culture, 1665–1965.* Lawrence: The Regents Press of Kansas, 1977.

Cocks III, J. Fraser. "George N. Smith: Reformer on the Frontier." *Michigan History* 52 (1968): 37–49.

Cohen, Felix S. *On the Drafting of Tribal Constitutions*, ed. David E. Wilkins. Norman: University of Oklahoma Press, 2006.

Cooper, John M. "Is the Algonquian Family Hunting Ground System Pre-Columbian?" *American Anthropologist* 41 (1939): 66–90.

Costello, Nancy A. "Walking Together in a Good Way: Indian Peacemaker Courts in Michigan." *University of Detroit Mercy Law Review* 76 (1999): 875–901.

Craker, Ruth. *The First Protestant Mission in the Grand Traverse Region.* Mt. Pleasant, Mich.: Rivercrest House, 1979. Originally published in 1932.

Dale-Burton, Jennifer. "Tribes Sign Gathering MOU with US Forest Service." *Preserving the Resource: Bimonthly Journal of the Chippewa-Ottawa Resource Authority* 9, no. 6 (2006): 1.

Delekta, Diane H. "State Regulation of Treaty Indians' Hunting and Fishing Rights in Michigan." *Detroit College of Law Review* 1980 (1980): 1097–122.

Deloria Jr., Vine. *Red Earth, White Lies: Native Americans and the Myth of Scientific Fact.* Golden, Colo.: Fulcrum Publishing, 1997.

Deloria Jr., Vine. "A Walk on the Inside." *University of Colorado Law Review* 71 (2000): 397–407.

Deloria Jr., Vine, ed. *The Indian Reorganization Act: Congresses and Bills.* Norman: University of Oklahoma Press, 2002.

Deloria Jr., Vine, and Clifford M. Lytle. *American Indians, American Justice.* Austin: University of Texas Press, 1983.

Dickinson, Julia Terry. *The Story of Leelanau.* Omena, Mich.: Solle's Bookshop, 1951.

Doherty, Robert. *Disputed Waters: Native Americans and the Great Lakes Fishery.* Lexington: University of Kentucky Press, 1990.

Doherty, Robert. "We Don't Want Them to Hold Their Hands over Our Heads: Economic Strategies of the L'Anse Chippewas, 1830–1860." *Michigan Historical Review* 20 (1994): 47–70.

Dougherty, Peter. "Diaries." *Journal of the Presbyterian Historical Society* 30 (1952): 95–114.

Ducheneaux, Franklin, and Peter S. Taylor. "Tribal Sovereignty and the Powers of the National Indian Gaming Commission." Unpublished and undated manuscript.

Dunham, Douglas. "Rix Robinson and the Indian Land Cession of 1836." *Michigan History* 36 (1952): 374–88.

Eid, Leroy V. "The Ojibwa-Iroquois War: The War the Five Nations Did Not Win." *Ethnohistory* 26 (1979): 297–324.

Erdrich, Louise, and Michael Dorris. "Manitoulin Island." *Antæus* 64/65 (1990): 381–89.

Ferguson, Karen. "Indian Fishing Rights: Aftermath of the Fox Decision and the Year 2000." *American Indian Law Review* 23 (1998–1999): 97–154.

Fletcher, Matthew L. M. "The Insidious Colonialism of the Conqueror: The Federal Government in Modern Tribal Affairs." *Washington University Journal of Law and Policy* 19 (2005): 273–311.

Fletcher, Matthew L. M. "In Pursuit of Tribal Economic Development as a Substitute for Reservation Tax Revenue." *North Dakota Law Review* 80 (2004): 759–807.

Fletcher, Matthew L. M. "Stick Houses in Peshawbestown." *Cardozo Public Law, Policy & Ethics Journal* 2 (2004): 189–287.

Fuller, George N. "The Settlement of Michigan." *Mississippi Valley Historical Review* 2 (1915): 25–55.

Garritt, J. B. *Historical Sketch of the Missions among the North American Indians.* Philadelphia: Presbyterian, 1881.

Gates, Paul W. *History of Public Land Law Development.* New York: Arno Press, 1979.

Gilpin, Alec R. *The Territory of Michigan, 1805–1837.* East Lansing: Michigan State University Press, 1970.

Goss, Dwight. "The Indians of the Grand River Valley." *Michigan Pioneer and Historical Collections* 30 (1900): 172–90.

Gray, Susan E. "Limits and Possibilities: White-Indian Relations in Western Michigan in the Era of Removal." *Michigan Historical Review* 20 (1994): 71–91.

Greenman, Emerson F. "Chieftainship among Michigan Indians." *Michigan History* 24 (1940): 361–79.

Hauptman, Laurence M. *Between Two Fires: American Indians in the Civil War.* New York: Free Press, 1995.

Hedrick, U. P. *The Land of the Crooked Tree.* Oxford: Oxford University Press, 1948.

Henry, Alexander. *Travels and Adventures.* Ann Arbor: University of Michigan Press, 1968.

Herek, Raymond J. *These Men Have Seen Hard Service: The First Michigan Sharpshooters in the Civil War.* Detroit: Wayne State University Press, 1998.

Hinsdale, Wilbert B. "Indian Corn Culture in Michigan." *Papers of the Michigan Academy of Science, Arts, and Letters* 8 (1928): 31–49.

Horsman, Reginald. "British Indian Policy in the Northwest, 1807–1812." *Mississippi Valley Historical Review* 45 (1958): 51–66.

Johnston, Basil. *Ojibway Heritage.* New York: Columbia University Press, 1976.

Joranko, Timothy W., and Mark C. Van Norman. "Indian Self-Determination at Bay: Secretarial Authority to Disapprove Tribal Constitutional Amendments." *Gonzaga Law Review* 29 (1993–1994): 81–104.

Keller, Robert H. "An Economic History of Indian Treaties in the Great Lakes Region." *American Indian Journal* (February 1978): 2–20.

Kinietz, W. Vernon. *The Indians of the Western Great Lakes, 1615–1760.* Ann Arbor: University of Michigan Press, 1965.

Kohl, Johann Georg. *Kitchi-Gami: Life among the Lake Superior Ojibway.* Translated by Ralf Neufang and Ulrike Böcker. Saint Paul: Minnesota Historical Society Press, 1985.

Landes, Ruth. "Ojibwa of Canada." In *Cooperation and Competition among Primitive Peoples,* ed. Margaret Mead, 87–127. New York: McGraw-Hill, 1937.

Leach, M. L. *Grand Traverse Region: A History.* Traverse City, Mich.: D.C. Leach, 1883.

LeBeau, Patrick Russell. *Rethinking Michigan Indian History.* East Lansing: Michigan State University

Press, 2005.

Light, Steven Andrew, and Kathryn R. L. Rand. *Indian Gaming and Tribal Sovereignty: The Casino Compromise*. Lawrence: University of Kansas Press, 2005.

Linkletter, Hon. C. S. "Township History of Almira in Benzie County." *Michigan Pioneer and Historical Collections* 31 (1902): 102–13.

Lurie, Nancy Oestreich. "The Indian Claims Commission Act." *Annals of the American Academy of Political and Social Science* 311 (1957): 56–70.

MacDonald, Graham. "Introduction." In *Frederic Baraga's Short History of the North American Indians*. East Lansing: Michigan State University Press, 2004.

McClurken, James M. "Augustin Hamlin, Jr.: Ottawa Identity and the Politics of Persistence." In *Being and Becoming Indian: Biographical Studies of North American Frontiers*, ed. James A. Clifton, 82–111. Chicago: University of Chicago Press, 1989.

McClurken, James M. *Gah-Baeh-Jhagwah-Buk: The Way It Happened, A Visual Culture History of the Little Traverse Bay Bands of Odawa Indians*. East Lansing: Michigan State University Museum, 1991.

McClurken, James M. "The Ottawa." In *People of the Three Fires: The Ottawa, Potawatomi, and Ojibway of Michigan*. Grand Rapids: Intertribal Council of Michigan, 1986.

McClurken, James M. "We Wish to Be Civilized: Ottawa-American Political Contests on the Michigan Frontier." Ph.D. dissertation, Michigan State University, 1988.

McGovern, Francis E. "Toward a Functional Approach for Managing Complex Litigation." *University of Chicago Law Review* 53 (1986): 440–93.

McKenney, Thomas L. *Sketches of a Tour to the Lakes, of the Character and Customs of the Chippeway Indians*. 1841; reprint, Minneapolis: Ross and Haines, 1994.

Miller, Ann. "Emilia Schaub: 100 Years of Leadership." *Michigan Bar Journal* 79 (2000): 82.

Muller, Werner. *America: The New World or the Old?* New York: Verlag Peter Lang, 1989.

Mumford, Jeremy. "Mixed-Race Identity in a Nineteenth-Century Family: The Schoolcrafts of Sault Ste. Marie, 1824–1827." *Michigan Historical Review* 25 (1999): 1–23.

Neumeyer, Elizabeth. "Michigan Indians Battle against Removal." *Michigan History* 55 (1971): 275–88.

Newton, Nell Jessup, et al., eds. *Cohen's Handbook of Federal Indian Law*. Newark, N.J.: LexisNexis, 2005.

Noori, Margaret. "The Complex World of Jane Johnston Schoolcraft." *Michigan Quarterly Review* 47 (2008): 141.

Norton, Clark F. "Michigan Statehood: 1835, 1836, or 1837." *Michigan History* 36 (1952): 321–50.

Nute, Grace Lee. "The American Fur Company's Fishing Enterprises on Lake Superior." *Mississippi Valley Historical Review* 12 (1926): 483–503.

Paquin, Ron, and Robert Doherty. *Not First in Nobody's Heart: The Life Story of a Contemporary Chippewa*. Ames: Iowa State University Press, 1992.

Parker, Robert Dale. *The Sound the Stars Make Rushing through the Sky: The Writings of Jane Johnston Schoolcraft*. Philadelphia: University of Pennsylvania Press, 2007.

Parkins, A. E. "The Indians of the Great Lakes Region and Their Environment." *Geographical Review* 6 (1918): 504–12.

Petersen, Eugene T. "Wildlife Conservation in Michigan." *Michigan History* 44 (1960): 129–46.

Petoskey, Michael D. "Tribal Courts." *Michigan Bar Journal* 66 (1988): 366–69.

Pflüg, Melissa A. "'Pimiadaziwin': Contemporary Rituals in Odawa Community." *American Indian Quarterly* 20 (1996): 489–513.

Porter, Robert B. "Indian Gaming Regulation: A Case Study in Neo-Colonialism." *Gaming Law Review* 5 (2001): 299–309.

Prucha, Francis Paul. *American Indian Treaties: The History of a Political Anomaly*. Berkeley: University of California Press, 1994.

Prucha, Francis Paul. *The Great Father: The United States Government and the American Indians.* Vol. 1. Lincoln: University of Nebraska Press, 1984.

Radin, Paul. *Ottawa-Ojibwe No. 5b.* Philadelphia: American Philosophical Society, undated.

Ramirez-shkwegnaabi, Benjamin. "The Dynamics of American Indian Diplomacy in the Great Lakes Region." *American Indian Culture and Research Journal* 27 (2003): 53–77.

Rice, G. William. *Tribal Governmental Gaming Law: Cases and Materials.* Durham, N.C.: Carolina Academic Press, 2006.

Robertson, Lindsay G. *Conquest by Law: How the Discovery of America Dispossessed Indigenous Peoples of Their Lands.* New York: Oxford University Press, 2005.

Rosen, Deborah A. *American Indians and State Law: Sovereignty, Race, and Citizenship, 1790–1880.* Lincoln: University of Nebraska Press, 2007.

Rostlund, Erhard. *Freshwater Fish and Fishing in Native North America.* Berkeley: University of California Publications in Geography, 1952.

Royce, Charles C. *Indian Land Cessions in the United States.* Washington, D.C.: Government Printing Office, 1899.

Rubenstein, Bruce. "To Destroy a Culture: Indian Education in Michigan, 1855–1900." *Michigan History* 60 (1976): 137–60.

Schoolcraft, Henry. *The Indian in His Wigwam, or Characteristics of the Red Race in America.* Buffalo, N.Y.: Derby, 1851.

Schoolcraft, Henry Rowe. *Personal Memoirs of a Residence of Thirty Years with the Indian Tribes of the American Frontiers.* New York: AMS Press, 1978.

Singel, Wenona T., and Matthew L. M. Fletcher. "Power, Authority, and Tribal Property." *Tulsa Law Review* 41 (2005): 21–50.

Skibine, Alex Tallchief. "Tribal Sovereign Interests beyond the Reservation Borders." *Lewis & Clark Law Review* 12 (2008): 1003–46.

Speck, Frank G. "The Family Hunting Band as the Basis of Algonkian Social Organization." *American Anthropologist* 17 (1915): 289–305.

Stocking, Kathleen. *Letters from the Leelanau.* Ann Arbor: University of Michigan Press, 1990.

Tanner, Helen Hornback. *Atlas of Great Lakes Indian History.* Norman: University of Oklahoma Press, 1987.

Tanner, Helen Hornback. "History vs. the Law: Processing Indians in the American Legal System." *University of Detroit Mercy Law Review* 76 (1999): 693–708.

Tanner, Helen Hornback. "Mapping the Grand Traverse Indian Country: The Contributions of Peter Dougherty." *Michigan Historical Review* 31 (2005): 45–91.

Taylor, Theodore W. *The States and Their Indian Citizens.* Washington, D.C.: United States Bureau of Indian Affairs, 1972.

Unrau, William E., and H. Craig Miner. *Tribal Dispossession and the Ottawa Indian University Fraud.* Norman: University of Oklahoma Press, 1985.

Vogel, Virgil J. *Indian Names in Michigan.* Ann Arbor: University of Michigan Press, 1986.

Vogel, Virgil J. "The Missionary as Acculturation Agent: Peter Dougherty and the Indians of Grand Traverse." *Michigan History* 51 (1967): 185–201.

Wallace, Anthony F. C. *The Long, Bitter Trail: Andrew Jackson and the Indians.* New York: Hill and Wang, 1993.

Warren, William W. *History of the Ojibway People.* Saint Paul: Minnesota Historical Society, 1984.

Weeks, George. *Mem-ka-weh: Dawning of the Grand Traverse Band of Ottawa and Chippewa Indians.* Peshawbestown, Mich.: Grand Traverse Band of Ottawa and Chippewa Indians, 1991.

White, Richard. "Ethnohistorical Report on the Grand Traverse Ottawas." Unpublished manuscript, 1991.

Wilkins, David E. " Introduction." In *Felix S. Cohen, On the Drafting of Tribal Constitutions*, ed. David E. Wilkins, xi–xxxii. Norman: University of Oklahoma Press, 2006.

Wilson, Etta S. "Personal Recollections of the Passenger Pigeon." *The Auk* 51 (1934): 157–68.

Wood, Elizabeth. *Council Trees of the Ottawas.* Birmingham, Mich.: Birmingham Eccentric, 1937.

Newspaper/Radio/TV

"Agreement Reached in Inland Treaty Rights Case." *US State News*, Sept. 27, 2007.

Associated Press. "Developer Gives Job to Former DNR Chief: K. L. Cool will work as a consultant for a company he helped with a land swap while with the state." *Grand Rapids (Mich.) Press*, Oct. 17, 2004.

Associated Press. "Owner Denies Plans for an Island Golf Course." *Grand Rapids (Mich.) Press*, Nov. 23, 2001.

Associated Press. "Treaty Rights." *Grand Rapids (Mich.) Press*, Sept. 28, 2007.

Bradsher, Keith. "Michigan Pact Resolves Battle over Limits on Indian Fishing." *New York Times*, Aug. 8, 2000.

Bush, Frank. "Keepers of the Fire." *WNIT Public Television*, 1993.

Capriccioso, David. "Grand Traverse Band Goes Green." *Indian Country Today*, July 23, 2008.

Flesher, John. "Tribe Sues to Block South Fox Swap." *Grand Rapids (Mich.) Press*, Jan. 5, 2002.

Gwizdz, Bob. "Indian Fishing Deal Reported Set for Signing: The key is the purchase and transfer of commercial fishing operations in northern Lake Michigan to the tribes." *Grand Rapids (Mich.) Press*, Aug. 3, 2000.

Gwizdz, Bob. "Indians Sign New Fishing Rights Pact: The deal includes $24 million for Indian fishermen to change from gill nets to trap nets." *Grand Rapids (Mich.) Press*, Aug. 8, 2000.

Gwizdz, Bob. "Tribal Treaty Works: Settlement with state a winner for both sides." *Grand Rapids (Mich.) Press*, Oct. 19, 2007.

"Humans May Have Hunted Mastadons." *National Public Radio*, Nov. 27, 2007.

Lam, Tina, and Eric Sharp. "Special Indian Hunting Rules OK'd: Proposal would end suit on use of 1836 Treaty." *Detroit Free Press*, Sept. 26, 2007.

"Las Vegas North: Buying Chips from the Chippewas." *U.S. News and World Report*, Feb. 9, 1987.

"Mackinaw City Casino Plan Gets OK." *Grand Rapids (Mich.) Press*, July 20, 2003.

Noga, Cari. "American Indian Tribe Frustrated over Lake Michigan Island Proposed Land Swap." *Indian Country Today*, July 16, 2001.

Piazza, Alex. "GT Band Picks Up 78 Acres for Expansion." *Traverse City Record-Eagle*, Dec. 15, 2009.

"Treasure Island: Wrong Direction: South Fox Island should belong to all of Michigan." Editorial. *Grand Rapids (Mich.) Press*, Mar. 17, 2003.

Websites

Leelanau Lessons: Emelia Schaub, Leelanau Enterprise Blog, http://www.leelanaunews.com/blog/2007/06/23/leelanau-lessons-emelia-schaub/

John Low, Keepers of the Fire: The Pokagon Potawatomi Nation, slides 14-15 (2006), http://www.pokagon.com/presentation/SMCppt_20080112.pdf

National Indian Gaming Commission, Growth of Tribal Gaming Revenues: 1995 to 2005, http://indianz.com/docs/nigc/nigc071106.pdf

Index